THE SEVENTH
CRISIS

THE SEVENTH

CRISIS

WHY MILLENNIALS MUST RE-ESTABLISH
—— ORDERED LIBERTY ——

BOB MACGUFFIE and ANTONY STARK

Seventh Crisis Books

Library of Congress Control Number: 2020918559

Cover design by Aaniyah Ahmed

ISBN: 978-1-7360542-1-5 (paperback)
ISBN: 978-1-7360542-0-8 (ebook)

Interior Design by FormattedBooks.com

For Andrew Breitbart—the first American political warrior of the 21st century

History is seasonal and winter is coming—the very survival of the nation is at stake. Sometime before the year 2025 America will pass through a great gate in history—one commensurate with the American Revolution, the Civil War and the twin emergencies of the Great Depression and World War II. The risk of catastrophe will be high. The nation could erupt into insurrection or civil war violence, crack up geographically, or enter authoritarian rule.

—Neil Howe, author of The Fourth Turning

CONTENTS

INTRODUCTION

Why is this the *seventh* crisis? Our title is taken from the central thesis of the book, "The Fourth Turning," written by William Strauss and Neil Howe in 1997. In their book, demographers Strauss and Howe view Anglo-American history through a generational lens. Their fascinating and compelling account organizes Anglo-American history into seven repeating cycles starting in the late Medieval, 15th Century period.

The historical cycles are each referred to as a saeculum, a Roman term for a long human life, say eighty to one hundred years. As the generations are born, mature, age and pass, they give each saeculum a seasonal and cyclical quality. Their study and organization of history along these recurring cycles have informed the names they have applied to identify each of the phases: the High, the Awakening, the Unraveling, the Crisis.

They have also distinguished four generations by the phase into which each was born:

Prophets born in a High, *Nomads* in an Awakening, *Heroes* in an Unraveling and *Artists* in a Crisis. The book's focus is on the dominant characteristics of each generation, which is formed by the forces at play specific to the saeculum phase within which it is born. By examining the seven saecula from 1435 onward, the authors make a compelling case that man's nature as forged by generations, drives history through amazingly similar cycles.

The book examines the twentieth century's conclusion of the sixth "Great Power" and seventh "Millennial" saecula and their generations in detail. They illuminate the "Unraveling" of the 1920s leading to the "Crisis" of the '30s, which climaxed with WWII.

They chronicle the new Millennial saeculum's High of the post-war era, symbolically ending on November 22, 1963, at which point the Awakening of the '60s and '70s commences. They peg the start of the Unraveling at about 1984, and at the time of the book's printing in 1997 they forecast the Unraveling sliding into Crisis in the mid 2000s.

In a 2020 interview, author Neil Howe observed that "the Fourth Turning began around 2009 after the Great Financial Crisis…and received its second blow with the COVID lockdown." He also foretells that the Crisis will last through the 2020s. As Howe describes it, as Fourth Turnings progress they accelerate through a period of "creative destruction." They invariably entail a clash of generations, i.e., the old vs. the young. In the current Turning that would pit the Boomers and Gen-Xers against the Millennials and the rising Gen-Z. In this work, we will illuminate how that clash is shaping up, and the lines of engagement along which it will be contended and resolved. We also prescribe a solution: an "animating spirit" for the Millennial generation to embrace in order to confront, navigate and successfully resolve the Crisis.

With current hindsight, it's not breakthrough thinking to realize that between the 9-11-01 terror attacks and the '08 financial meltdown, America shifted into Crisis in the first decade of the twenty-first century. Whatever one thinks of the author's generational analysis, and they had their critics in 1997, they were indeed prescient in seeing that the Unraveling of the '80s and '90s would lead to a Crisis early in the new century.

As events presently stand, there are many among us who still do not accept that America is currently in a consequential and potentially existential Crisis. However, we believe that Strauss and Howe were really on to something. History is not linear. In addition, whether you draw your cycles by eighty to one hundred-year saecula, or something of larger magnitude, we believe an inflection point was reached at the turn of the 21st century. America has indeed entered into a mighty Crisis, the resolution of which will point its way for the next saeculum or more. This current Crisis concludes the Millennial saeculum, the seventh such cycle examined by Strauss and Howe, hence our title, The Seventh Crisis.

Prophetically, this saeculum has been aptly named, as history is rapidly summoning the rising Millennial generation into leadership. As we will illustrate further on, the Millennials will make the consequential choices directing the fate of the American Republic in the twenty-first century.

We will examine the cultural, political and economic events and trends driven by the generations comprising the Millennial saeculum to better understand and illuminate our current crisis. Those generations are the Baby Boomers born in the High, lasting from 1946 to 1964; Gen-X born in the Awakening years of 1965 to 1983; Millennials born in the Unraveling from 1984 to 1996; and Gen-Z born from 1997 on.

Cyclical history is not a new idea and it has been used in the past to both analyze the situation currently faced by those living through it, but to do so by identifying common trends and themes in order to predict the future based on past cycles. Oswald Spengler and Arnold Toynbee represent two such historians who based their writings on a cyclical idea of History.

While it may seem strange to some to think that those who lived hundreds of years in the past could act in a similar manner when facing crisis situations, both historians posit that while the specific nature of crises differ, their overall nature, as is the overall nature of the human beings reacting to it, often maintain remarkable similarities.

As noted above, Strauss & Howe focus on how different generations deal with crisis over a 100-year period they identify as a "saeculum." Toynbee likewise focused on generational response to periodic crisis and, more importantly, how they are ultimately reconciled. He discusses a concept in his magnum opus "A Study of History," that he calls a "Parvenu Archaistic Syncretism," which rises up during times of crisis that the old order can no longer handle.

Regarding the rather technical jargon in which the phrase is constructed, here is a basic definition of it: "Parvenu" is essentially any group, belief, religion, philosophy or culture that is rising up because it convinces the people in crisis that it has a solution. "Archaistic" is a belief, usually a component rather than a central belief, which is part of the older "archaic" established group, belief, religion, philosophy or culture etc. "Syncretism" is the blending of both.

The idea of a "parvenu archaistic syncretism" is essentially a reaction against a decaying system. It represents an "animating spirit" which seeks to build a new system by raising what was formerly only a component element of the traditional culture into the central motivating idea of that which replaces it. That is, it reaches back and grabs hold of some bedrock concept from the previous system and elevates it to a position of central motivational importance in the new order that will resolve the crisis.

One such "animating spirit" may be present among us today: Ordered Liberty.

The concept of Ordered Liberty is certainly not new; born in the Enlightenment, advocated by thinkers such as John Locke, Adam Smith, Edmund Burke and Charles-Louis Montesquieu and later embraced and put into full practice by Thomas Jefferson, Patrick Henry, James Madison and Benjamin Franklin.

But what is Ordered Liberty?

Ordered Liberty is:

The primacy of the Individual over the collective and the embrace of Western Enlightenment Political Values, Capitalism, Judeo-Christian Morality, de-centralized as opposed to centralized power, and a democratic Republic under Constitutional law rather than a majoritarian Democracy at the mercy of Mob Rule. All these elements work together to create *a society constituted on a national rather than an international basis* that protects its own history, its own ethical and religious values, its own myths, its own heroes, its own holidays and its own national heritage. It does not seek to impose these values or views on others, but it refuses to deny and denigrate its own distinct contributions to mankind, or to immerse itself into a transnational, globalist construction governed by multinational corporate elites.

Ordered Liberty is that which protects and nurtures Freedom; it is what prevents freedom from becoming license and then decaying into anarchy, which often results in chaos that in turn, calls on *oppression* for relief from violent disorder and confusion through the diminishment of freedom.

As a divine engine of creation, freedom unleashes great individual potential through the encouragement of reason and critical thinking; the ideas produced by such creative thought make society prosperous in economy as well as protective of human rights. Such rational boundaries of Ordered Liberty… as are found in our own U.S. Constitution… must be strong enough to preserve Freedom so as to prevent it from decaying into anarchy and chaos and thus unleash the forces of Oppressive Control. Freedom must be defended against the fate of *suffocation* that the false savior of political oppression, in the form of a Leviathan Government, seeks to inflict upon it.

Only Ordered Liberty can Square the Circle between the vital need for as much freedom as possible to exist, and the equally vital need to prevent it from destroying itself in its own name.

All these things make up Ordered Liberty and everything that undermines them, *undermines it.*

The first thing one needs to understand regarding Ordered Liberty is the difference between freedom, *which is the absence of responsibility* and liberty, *which is the shouldering of it.*

Shouldering Liberty requires that one maintain some level of critical thinking so that when, for example, one is using tools - cars, guns, medicines - one cannot simply accept that any such tools can be employed in one's favor without knowing how to use them responsibly; moreover, as such tools carry potential danger if misused, rational laws are required to prevent or at least minimize such misuse.

Of all the tools mankind uses to order and stabilize society, Government is the most dangerous tool of all. Of course, as the Founders realized, for Government to operate properly, it must be required to operate in a negatively regulative sense; that is, to regulate negative aspects of life that impinge on the Liberty of its citizens. These include providing an army to prevent foreign attack and invasion, a police force to regulate crime and ensure citizen safety and a court system to regulate legal disputes between law-abiding citizens. However, government can be perverted into becoming a highly dangerous tool in the hands of those in control of it. The control of Government can allow corrupt individuals to act in the *public's* name to advance a *private* power agenda. As Washington said, "Like fire, government is a dangerous tool... and a fearful master." By creating an ever more powerful government, Americans jeopardize their ability to control its excesses and consequently endanger their ability to maintain Ordered Liberty.

Therefore, we are not simply advocating "Liberty" defined as unlimited license without responsibility, but as *Ordered* Liberty, which requires rational application to the use of potentially dangerous tools, including the most dangerous tool of all: government. In the hands of wealthy, powerful and influential individuals or corporate entities, government becomes an especially dangerous tool wielded by those who seek a symbiotic, neo-fascistic relationship with their partners in the Leviathan State at the expense of the average citizen. In such hands, Government can be improperly... *or even criminally...* used to assault private property rights, restrict civil rights, obliterate privacy rights and obviate the constitutional protections found in the Bill of Rights of the U.S. Constitution. All in the name of addressing some "emergency" or "crisis."

It is of the greatest importance that Americans be aware of the potential danger this presents to both their individual autonomy as well as the threat such neo-Fascist relationships present to the type of Ordered Liberty a democratic Republic under the law of the Constitution must possess in order to face the Seventh Crisis.

Thus, it serves the long-term goal of the Elites that seek to buy sole use of the "governmental tool" and to use its false ideology of benevolent power as a means to increase their actual power to undermine those pillars of Ordered Liberty that prevent the governmental tool from being misused against its own citizens

This country has been inexorably moving away from Ordered Liberty and toward a society where that concept, once central and essential, has become almost an historical curiosity. The post-Civil War Industrialization era in the United States raised Corporate entities to such power that they were able to create a Government powerful enough to enforce their desires but corrupt enough to become an instrument of their economic and political agenda. By the opening of the twentieth century, it provoked those groups… farmers, factory workers, small business owners… to band together NOT to demand more Liberty, *but more government*, albeit working for *them and their interests* rather than the interests of the Plutocracy that it actually served. As we shall see, both Republicans like Teddy Roosevelt and Democrats like Woodrow Wilson embraced Big Government "solutions" to economic and social problems. This trend continued and metastasized to the point where Government became neo-Fascistic in all but name during the New Deal and where Liberty was buried under an avalanche of Big Government programs put into place by the Great Society.

Ordered Liberty became an anachronism; abandoned, forgotten and for the most part ignored by those who advocated an ever more "Progressive" view of *positively regulative* government. That is, a Government that is large, intrusive, dominant, patronizing, hectoring and fearful in its power to coerce obedience to its directives all while excreting propaganda regarding its fealty to "democracy," "egalitarianism," and "social justice."

The reaction against this type of thinking was slow to develop and difficult to enact. The growing Conservative and Libertarian movements of the 1960s—1980s provided some hope for a return of smaller government, but any gains made were always conditional and, ultimately, undone by return to power of those Democrats and Republicans who advocated the Progressive view. The Tea Party Movement of the 2010s made similar progress, only to be subverted and abandoned by far too many in the Republican Party, which too many in the Tea Party Movement mistakenly thought it could use to bring its limited government ideology into power.

This betrayal by Progressive Establishment Republicans led to the current alliance of Constitutional Conservatives and the Nationalist Populist followers of Donald Trump who have become the type of external proletariat that Toynbee noted was created when the Old Order reached its point of senility and impotence and had to rely more and more on coercion and repression to maintain its control.

But victory over the Establishment requires an animating spirit to bring those parvenu forces who oppose it to power; Ordered Liberty is that spirit. Without such a spirit, opposition remains scattered, disunited, inchoate and prey to counterattack by the many instrumentalities the Established powers can bring to bear.

Together, the parvenu forces representing the Constitutional Conservative / Trumpist Nationalist Populist Alliance must adopt that which was formerly just one part, albeit an important one, of the American past, but is now simply an almost abandoned concept of the Old Order... *viz. Ordered Liberty*... and utilize its vast potential as its Animating Spirit.

Ordered Liberty *is* the "parvenu archaistic syncretism" that is required to end the decay and decadence of the Old Order and allow the Millennial / Gen-Z generations to overcome the Seventh Crisis.

It is Ordered Liberty that will take them and their children into a peaceful, prosperous and stable future.

- 1 -

The Seventh Crisis

I t is our contention that, as presciently foreseen by Strauss & Howe, the United States entered the Fourth Turning era with the financial crisis and the ascendency of progressive control of the federal government in late 2008. As Strauss & Howe describe it, "a Crisis era begins with a catalyst—a startling event that produces a sudden shift in mood." It could also be said that the terrorist attack of 9-11 was that event. At a minimum, 9-11 showed that the Unravelling of the prior twenty years was over and a distinctly more personally uncomfortable and nationally dangerous era was upon us. As the country faced the full spectrum of a banking, capital market, and general economic collapse, no one considered use of the word crisis as hyperbole.

According to Strauss & Howe: "What makes a Crisis special is the public's willingness to let leaders lead even when they falter and to let authorities be authoritative even when they make mistakes." This assumes leadership, regardless of specific competence, is endeavoring to ameliorate the crisis, as in the early stages of Lincoln's and FDR's presidencies. Lincoln and FDR are the presidents who led the nation through the last two Fourth Turning crises.

1

However, this *Seventh Crisis* immediately took on a different complexion when President Obama's chief of staff, Rahm Emanuel, was overheard saying "never let a good crisis go to waste." Conservatives knew exactly what he meant— exploit the crisis to enact what you otherwise would be unable to enact under normal conditions. This statement was the keyhole through which to view all federal government machinations during the Obama years.

In this Seventh Crisis the permanent government, aka the "Deep State," is more interested in self-preservation and ousting from power any president representing a mortal threat to its political, financial and personal succor, such as Donald Trump. There is now a complete disconnect between the goals of the decaying establishment and the interests of normal Americans. Moreover, as the days pass the gulf only widens while an increasing number of Americans take notice.

During the summer of 2020, the Nation had a front row seat as violent Leftwing elements rioted in the streets across the country, attacking police, burning down their precincts and committing acts of looting, arson and cultural vandalism. In some instances, parts of major cities like Seattle were carved out as "autonomous zones" where leftwing vigilantism ruled by day and anarchy ruled by night. Almost all this unrest happened in cities run by Progressive politicians who either looked on and did nothing by ordering the police to "stand down" while criminals burned and robbed small businesses, or even attempted to make common cause with the rioters and indicate sympathy with their actions, which were, against all logic and plain visual evidence, described as "peaceful protests."

Such points of friction now run through most aspects of American society, along fault lines running beneath the surface. These lines have been stressed and exacerbated with increasing tension over the past couple of decades, driven by relentless enactment of the progressive agenda. Let's illuminate a couple of the more critical battle grounds.

THE CULTURAL DIVIDE

It is impossible to understand the so-called cultural clash in the United States without understanding the paradigm within which it has been played out for half a century. That paradigm is a very clever construct that has been created and nurtured by the political Left since the mid-twentieth century. Following

World War II it became apparent that taking down the capitalist west through the old Marxist economic class struggle argument was not going to prevail. So, modern leftist theorists, such as Gramsci, Lukacs and Marcuse refocused their emphasis to "cultural oppression" including race, gender, ethnicity, feminism and environmentalism. Identity politics and victimization would be the new battle lines where society's "inequalities" would be confronted. Thus the New Left was born and its vanguard ideology of Political Correctness would be the wedge driven right through an otherwise increasingly tolerant and modernizing American society.

The fateful opportunity for the New Left in America came with the student rebellion in the mid-1960s. Herbert Marcuse's book, "Eros and Civilization," became a virtual bible for the SDS and the student rebels of the '60s. He gave the burgeoning movement a philosophical theory and its underpinning is repression. The essentials of Critical Theory from the Frankfurt School tailored Marxism to the dynamics driving burgeoning student protests against the War in Vietnam. The Left moved beyond the simple capitalist-proletariat struggle of classic Marxism and expanded the dynamic into areas including generational strife (pitting the young who resisted the military Draft of their own against the old who were in charge of the Draft), blacks as the victims of discrimination, women seeking "liberation," ethnic groups seeking cultural validation, homosexuals seeking an end to social ostracism and even planet earth, seeking relief from rapacious capitalism! These would be the friction points the cultural Marxists would, with great success, exacerbate over the following decades.

The umbrella concept under which these strains of cultural Marxism are enforced is known as Political Correctness. Its proponents believe that history is determined not by assimilation into the over-arching national culture, but by one group's power prevailing over another. When "melting pot" assimilation is rejected in favor of separate identities defined by race, ethnicity, gender and sexual orientation, Political Correctness requires a mental jujitsu formally known as deconstruction. This is what you experience when the definitional reality of a concept or statement, which you've believed all your life, is summarily removed and replaced in the name of Social Justice with the meaning desired by smug Elites who deem themselves to be the arbiters of cultural norms.

PC examples in all these areas abound: Seattle public school children are compelled to refer to Easter eggs as "spring spheres;" chaplains in Charlotte are banned from using the name of Jesus on government property; the term "brown bag" is now deemed offensive; 'transgender' men can now expose themselves in women's locker rooms because they unscientifically claim gender is socially constructed rather than genetically determined. There seems to be no end to the expanding litany of these affronts to cultural tradition and common sense. The initial result of this is a form of coerced self-censorship, which over time evolves to reflexive thinking and finally acceptance of changed behavior.

Largely as a result of judicial rulings, executive orders, and bureaucratic regulations, we now have "gay marriage", transgender bathrooms, thirty-seven different genders, Christian bakers bankrupted for refusing to bake politically correct cakes and the Little Sisters of the Poor being sued by California for having theological disagreements with the prevailing wisdom of birth control and abortion. In the past decade, this assault on common sense has stressed the American psyche, forcing a separation between people who buy-in to the PC viewpoint vs. those who do not. As the culture continues to be stressed, people have become increasingly combative, agitated, and animated with their friends and families along these cultural battle lines.

While this cultural discord has upset many average Americans not in the ruling cultural elite, who get to set the standards and from which they grant themselves exemption, it has all played into the hands of the progressive Left. As hard as it is for the average American to accept, the Left seeks nothing less than the destruction of Western culture. For an explanation, we return to Critical Theory, which calls for the continual criticism of virtually every aspect of American history and contemporary society. It is a central tenet of transnational progressivism that the current order must be taken down before a new order can be built. It is approaching a crisis stage in Europe, with open borders and rampant immigration. Lawless sectors of major European cities have revealed irreconcilable divisions on the continent.

While the Left continues to erode western culture along these battle lines, it adamantly refuses to lay out an alternative vision for society. They express the insidious belief that they cannot envisage the future while still living under the repression of the capitalist order. Therefore, western culture must be burned down to the core, which is very convenient for these nihilists who deign to rule over the ruins of what will follow. Nevertheless, let's not let them evade exposing the truth of what they hold hidden in the wings of the current Crisis.

They seek a culture based on the needs of the *collective,* rather than the rights of the *individual;* on group preferences rather than equality within the citizenry; power-sharing among racial, ethnic and gender groups, rather than the rule of law within the construct of a constitutional republic; *transnational* law rather than *constitutional* law.

When viewed through the lens of politics being downstream from culture, the purpose of the current agitation along these cultural fault lines comes into exceedingly clear focus. With an American public already maneuvered onto tenterhooks over a series of contrived cultural clashes, we can see the end game will indeed be an ugly affair. Once the cultural crisis moves through its inevitable crucible, can the Millennials thwart the designs of the cultural Marxists and rejuvenate American society along the lines that propelled it to global leadership? Only by regenerating Ordered Liberty, with its defense of those notions which assure social stability, can this nihilistic attack on traditional culture be prevented; only though Ordered Liberty, with its advocacy of individual human rights, can minorities of all types, racial, religious, sexual, etc., be protected from the Mob. Only by regenerating Ordered Liberty can this nihilistic attack on traditional culture be prevented; only through Ordered Liberty can that which is the best of the past be preserved; only upon Ordered Liberty can a viable future be built.

THE ECONOMIC DECEITS

During the Unraveling years of the 1990s the unrelenting increase in federal debt constituted a steady, dour and uneasy background drumbeat to a seemingly robust and expanding U.S. economy. In 1980 U.S. debt was just under one trillion dollars. By 1990, it had grown to $3 trillion. When George W. Bush took office in 2001 it was $5.7 trillion, almost doubling during the decade. It was clear the country was habitually living beyond its means. The Fourth Turning authors noted it in 1997 when the book was published, and foretold it to be a driver of the coming Crisis in the new century.

The debt almost doubled again to $10.6 trillion during George W. Bush's tenure, then almost doubling again to $19.6 trillion during the Obama years. It is both astounding and alarming that from the first administration of George Washington to Ronald Reagan the country accumulated less than one trillion dollars in debt, but then in just 40 years accumulated another $19 trillion.

5

The media never covered this with the seriousness it warranted and anyone watching with open eyes knew we had crossed a financial Rubicon. We could refer to this building debt bubble as economic deceit number one. And the Millennials, Gen-Xers and Gen-Zs will be saddled with its debilitating effects.

The seminal event ushering in the Seventh Crisis was the national and world-wide financial crisis which erupted during the presidential campaign in the fall of 2008. While the banks reduced interest rates and reduced mortgage qualifying criteria and down payment requirements, a massive housing debt bubble developed. The government compounded the financial risk through its Fannie Mae and Freddie Mac guaranteed mortgage programs, which simply encouraged riskier behavior on the part of both lenders and borrowers.

When the mortgage bubble burst, the impact so crippled the financial system that Federal Reserve and Treasury leadership determined that the banking system should be bailed out in total via the Troubled Asset Relief Program (TARP) rather than let the bad actors face the consequences of their poor decision making. Congress rubber-stamped the plan. Regardless of whether they wanted, or needed federal assistance, CEOs of eight of the largest U.S. banks were summoned by Treasury Secretary Paulson to the White House and compelled to sign a one-page letter of participation in TARP. By stepping in, the government established the corrosive concept of "too big to fail", thereby creating a perpetual moral hazard in the financial system.

Virtually all bank management in the country remained in place, and though charges of illegal practices were aired throughout investigative reports in the media, not a banker was prosecuted for any fraudulent activity during or after the entire crisis. Between 'too big to fail' and the lack of will to prosecute, the moral hazard in the U.S. financial system was amped up to a realm where there are no consequences and there is no turning back. This hazard has been a poison permeating the entire financial system going forward.

Next, the Federal Reserve immediately commenced its controversial program of Quantitative Easing (QE). Its ostensible purpose was to provide massive liquidity to the banks so lending could begin again, thereby stimulating the economy out of the recession and set GDP onto a sustainable growth path. All sounds great, until you understand its mechanics. The Fed bought the impaired mortgages and other securities from the banks, providing them the cash to restore their balance sheets and commence lending. In addition, the Fed also began purchasing U.S. Treasury securities directly from periodic Treasury auctions. To make an inconvenient truth of it, one arm of the government was issuing debt and another arm was purchasing it. We are a republic, but we are not supposed to be of the banana variety. The stated objective was to keep interest rates low while stimulating demand and growth.

But where did the Fed get the money or credit to purchase these assets? They simply created it out of thin air within the bowels of its secretive un-audited operations. They make the necessary entries and overnight the banks have new reserves, entered as *payables*, in their respective accounts with the Fed. This is what's commonly referred to as "printing money" and the Fed added to the money supply by printing some $2 trillion in four rounds of QE from 2008 to 2014, quadrupling its balance sheet to $4.5 trillion. This perfunctory absorption of bad debt and bad decisions from the shoulders of the bankers to the belly of the Federal Reserve could be referred to as deceit number two.

In the years following the conclusion of the QE program, it is alleged that the Fed, with the cooperation of other member banks and other central banks, has continued to surreptitiously buy bonds on the open market—all in a desperate effort to keep interest rates low enough so the interest carrying costs can continue to be 'afforded' in the federal budget. Although it is practically impossible to prove, those watching trading on a daily basis see massive bond buying within the hour whenever stock prices begin to rapidly decline. With rates in an historic trough, there is just no reason individual bond buyers would be rushing in, on the hour, to support the prices of bonds. Low interest rates in the bond market is the principle factor keeping the stock market afloat, and indeed the world economy since the '08 crisis. Deceit number two begets deceit number three.

The national debt and its financing mechanism are a tectonic plate supporting the U.S. economy including financial markets, inflation potential, dollar valuation, commercial and consumer credit and employment. Financial plates have shifted significantly along this fault line during the Pandemic, with the entire economy shaken to its core, revealing the crisis of '08 as merely the early warning tremor of an ultimate financial reckoning. Little discussed in the media in the decade following the '08 crisis, and never with the appropriate weight, the national debt is a ticking bomb with the potential to ignite an international financial and social calamity climaxing the Seventh Crisis. The Millennials will need to strengthen themselves with the will to see the Crisis through with an agenda of Ordered Liberty and limited government principles. A keystone in executing a successful strategy will be the devolution of power from the federal government to the states. Should the Millennials fail to rise and direct the course of the Crisis, they will suffer the fate of prior generations who found themselves helpless serfs in service to an all-powerful Administrative State.

The fourth, and certainly the most tragic deceit for the average American is the half-century and continuing *decline* in our standard of living. Asserting that Americans' standard of living is in decline may be surprising to many readers accustomed to the illusions of prosperity promulgated by our ruling financial elite. But when evaluated outside government-issued statistics, daily merchandising distractions and illusions in the social media world, the reality is Americans' fundamental standard of living has fallen markedly from that of the 1950s and '60s.

The quickest thumbnail measure of course is the inflation rate over the intervening decades. However, federal government methodology for developing cost of living, inflation, and the resultant standard of living comparisons has become so distorted over the years as to be rendered close to meaningless. The methodologies at the Bureau of Labor Statistics, Congressional Budget Office and Census Bureau develop a myriad of reports which inexplicably include and exclude items at whim, seemingly to produce measurements predetermined by Administration and Congressional leaders. Apparently, key household needs such as fuel, medical care, education, automobiles and housing itself are subject to modification, weighting, averaging and exclusion from inflation and cost of living calculations. A reading of the empirical justification for these calculations quickly becomes laughable.

Government statistical development is the black box from which we are propagandized that inflation remains well under two percent and in some years virtually nonexistent. All while different elected federal mouthpieces incessantly remind us of the prohibitive costs of higher education, healthcare and housing. Do they realize how ridiculous they sound? Evidently they think we have the memory span of tropical fish.

Reality is that inflation for items necessary for modern life, i.e., housing, education, healthcare, automobiles, has been raging for decades, causing a precipitous decline in our standard of living. However, the American public remains distracted with incredibly cheap consumer electronics and clothing from China and the far east. These distractions provide fertile ground for the propaganda to take hold. There is certainly more "disposable income" available today for electronic gadgets, dinner out and modest vacations, but the availability of these ephemeral experiences is a diversion which masks a fundamental decline. And it all *seems* manageable when it is financed through long-term payback credit cards and other consumer debt schemes.

Due to the incredible capitalist economic machine and the ingenuity and productivity of the American worker, the U.S. standard of living continually rose from the nation's birth right on into the 1950s and '60s where it topped out. Though a full chapter here or certainly a book could be warranted, we offer a couple of key benchmarks to consider.

Median household income in 1969 was $9,400, while four years' tuition at a private college was averaging $6,000. Median household income in 2018 was $63,200, while four years' tuition at a private college averaged $164,000. So four years of college in 1969 was just two thirds of annual household income compared with some 2.6 times annual household income in 2018. This represents a *real* fourfold increase in the bite of the household economic pie for just this one item, for just one child.

The average price of a 1969 car was $3,000, representing 33 percent of annual household income. The average 2018 car runs $37,500, some 60 percent of annual household income, a virtual *doubling* of the demand on household income. But of course, not many can afford to outright own a new car anymore—most people are now reduced to leasing them.

The average price of a private home in 1969 was $25,000, representing 2.7 times annual household income. The average home price in 2018 was $237,000, some 3.75 times annual household income—a 40 percent larger bite of the family's income. But Americans are told that it's "affordable" thanks to the palliative of inordinately suppressed interest rates.

And then there's healthcare. In 1969 some 80 percent of Americans with health insurance received it through an employer-sponsored plan which the main breadwinner of the household received as a benefit from his employer— and most employees didn't even have to contribute to its cost! But today, after ObamaCare, health insurance has become the biggest political football of the last decade as costs have increased massively, and individuals have had to bear an increasing share of the costs. Largely, as a result of government interference in the market, health insurance now takes a larger bite of the household budget than any item other than the mortgage…and for many—more than the mortgage. And in 1969 this vital service was hardly an item in the household budget!

In the 1950s and '60s, in a majority of households, there was only one breadwinner—the stay-at-home mom was the rule, not the exception.

Everything necessary was provided for on one salary, generated from likely a quite unremarkable occupation. A man could get a job repairing cars, selling shoes, construction work, driving a truck and in a few years, he could afford a home, a car and have a wife at home raising a couple of kids. They didn't have money to go out to dinner every week, but all the important items necessary for middle class life were indeed affordable. And with credit cards in their infancy, consumer credit was limited to cars and an occasional household appliance.

Today, that same family has both parents working, at least one in a professional position and the entire household is likely floating on a river of consumer debt. The following chart illustrates a decline in the American standard of living of some 57 percent since the late 1960s.

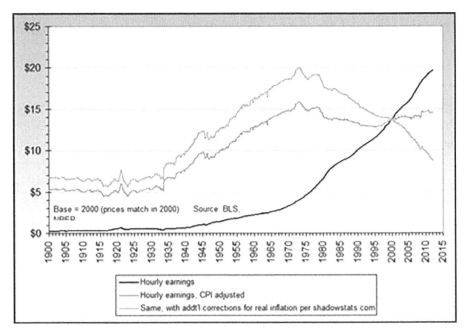

The Bureau of Labor Statistics provides the black static hourly earnings line, with two overlays. The middle line accounts for the Consumer Price Index and the green factors in inflation. Sadly, the top line illustrates the unvarnished reality. Look at any historical standard of living, real inflation or dollar purchasing power chart and you will see the same sharp inflection point in the early '70s as you can see above. There is a very definitive reason all such charts will inflect down, or up depending what is being measured, illustrating the change to a negative trend in the early '70s. On August 15th, 1971 President Nixon severed the last link between the U.S. dollar and the gold reserves of the United States. Without being tied to physical gold, the historic preserver of value over the centuries, the dollar's accelerating loss of purchasing power can be traced to this historic decoupling event.

The explanation for the decoupling given at the time was that foreign banks and governments were presenting dollars for conversion into physical gold at an increasing pace that was depleting the nation's gold reserves to unacceptable levels. Nixon's solution was to shut the gold exchange window and let the dollar's value *float* against the other currencies. The immediate result was an economic lost decade of high inflation and unemployment, stagnant wages and minimal opportunities for college graduates. Most all middle-income households became two-wage-earner families by necessity during the decade. Americans became used to running to keep up, and borrowing to make up the difference.

The Reagan Administration's free-market and tax cutting policies got the economic wheels turning again, but America's standard of living was still traveling on the downward slope of a great historic arc. And according to Strauss & Howe's *cyclical* historical analysis, America's "Awakening" had run its course, and it entered the third phase of the current saeculum, the "Unraveling" around 1984. Government had become far too big, intrusive, and expensive. But the body politic, rapidly being populated by Boomers, had no appetite to do what was necessary to cut it down to size and restore the arc to its upward slope. In fact, the Boomer-dominated electorate chose unbridled entitlement growth and accelerating deficit spending.

Instead of seriously attending to those challenges, the "culture wars" moved to center stage, and in the era of sluggish productivity Americans looked away and sealed their fate, continuing along the standard of living's downward slope. Should the Millennials turn away from the reality of their declining standard of living, the majority of the professional class of their generation will never be able to own their own homes or cars. They will become a permanent tenant class.

As the 1980s turned to the '90s, a new financial and social elite emerged, who would foist a fifth and most insidious deceit on America. Progressive Boomers, rid of Reagan and flush with new wealth, began to re-animate the utopian dreams that made their blood run fast in the 1960s. In addition to their growing hegemony of academia, they were now stepping up into senior leadership in the business and political world. How could they expand and accelerate the development of real wealth for the broader segment of their elite? Enter the big con of comprehensive international trade deals. And who better to sell it than the Boomers' first serious candidate for the presidency, Bill Clinton.

Computers became ubiquitous in the '80s, most visibly as they penetrated the consumer marketplace. But they were also impacting business, revolutionizing industrial processes, and shifting competitive advantage right beneath the feet of the new corporate titans. Before 1990 the only international threat faced by the American worker was the importation of competitive products. Though crafty importers could displace some U.S. workers on occasion with a hot new imported line, no import ever shook the underpinnings of the American worker. But computers were now enabling the remote assembling of component parts, and corporations were setting up assembly lines in undeveloped countries. The wage disparity was proving to be an enormous boost to corporations' bottom lines, and they wanted more of it.

What began with a trickle of "off-shoring" components quickly grew into complete operations, and ultimately entire factories. It seemed a disruption at first and was overshadowed by consumers' satisfaction with the importation of inexpensive, quality electronic gear of all types. Overnight, India seemed to become the go-to haven for software coding and data processing. Then suddenly it seemed every repetitive process job was pulled out from underneath the American workforce. By the time the auto makers were moving major operations to Mexico or East Asia, American workers knew they were in trouble.

While international competition was driving the exodus of so much of manufacturing, the corporate game plan seemed to be to restructure to keep the high value-add knowledge work in the United States. Youth was flooding into American colleges, and the economic theory was that the American workforce could move up the value chain of knowledge-work, thereby increasing its earning potential as it left the lower value-add assembly work for low-wage developing countries. But for a multitude of reasons, too many American workers were not training-up for the new knowledge economy which seemed to be shrinking opportunity in their eyes, not growing it.

Capitalizing on a brief S&L failure driven recession, globalist Bill Clinton marched in, seemingly with an economic plan for everyone. Promising a grand North American Free Trade Agreement, the slick-talking one had an answer for everything. Why those left behind displaced workers in Pennsylvania, Ohio, and Michigan would get spanking new federal worker re-training programs for every manner of new-fangled knowledge job! Vote for Bill Clinton and he would "focus like a laser" on revitalizing America in the new globalist economy. It didn't happen.

Instead, NAFTA was signed in Clinton's first year, 1993, and the prophesy of his independent rival for the presidency, Ross Perot was being realized. Yes, we all heard about that "giant sucking sound" Mr. Perot warned of during the campaign. Perot was ridiculed for saying that NAFTA would drive hordes of complete factories out of the country so fast we'd hear a sucking sound in the wake of their evacuation. The man was a bit of a flake, but he was dead-on bullseye on that score. Clinton opened the floodgate for a startling exodus of great American manufacturing plants that had formed the life-blood for countless families throughout the country….for generations.

As the domestic impact came into focus at the turn of the century, honest economic analysts were becoming troubled as the data began to take shape. Large corporations that offshored much of their production still seemed to create plenty of new design, engineering, marketing and finance jobs in the United States. But for the medium-size and small companies that focused on the domestic market, offshoring was simply exporting jobs to a foreign country. Many a small firm head who personally knew his workforce, was troubled by the practice, but did it simply to remain competitive and survive. A decade later the corporations were finding that product complexity was requiring they move more and more design and engineering jobs overseas to integrate with manufacturing.

The original theory of the case was that offshoring would be a win-win for the United States and its offshoring partners. The United States would be importing cheaper products, providing an economic benefit to domestic consumers, while the Chinese would have new-found income to spend on products from the United States. But not surprisingly to observers with a decent memory, the Chinese markets were proving as hard to penetrate as the Japanese twenty to thirty years before. The Chinese went to school on the Japanese fine art of making their markets impenetrable. This generated perennial trade deficits with China. Plus, it was no secret that China structured all joint ventures so it could regularly steal as many trade secrets and intellectual property from U.S. designers as possible.

The Chinese also mimicked the former Japanese practice of reverse-engineering and copying U.S.-designed products with the technology stolen via joint ventures with U.S. companies. They then marketed their own product lines, serving the domestic markets the joint ventures were supposed to serve, thereby crowding out U.S. opportunities, revenue and profit streams. The results of all this economic subterfuge are the $500 billion annual trade deficits often cited by President Trump. Economists differ on the magnitude of outsourcing's impact on the U.S. employment picture. But undoubtedly it has been a significant contributing factor to both U.S. structural unemployment, and the continuing decline in real wages.

Even in light of the ongoing significant trade deficits, an honest economic analysis must account for the tangible benefits to the U.S. economy. Profits generated by the firms flow to shareholders and investors, which are further invested or spent in the United States, thereby having a positive impact on employment. In addition, both the consumer and commercial customers of these companies have benefited from the lower prices.

But in a broad a sense, far too many average workers in outsourced industries have been left high and dry, or should we say "beached" over the past thirty years. These inequities must be addressed in any U.S. led prospective trade agreements with China. But these strict economic considerations are now being eclipsed by the national security issues illuminated by China's handling of the Pandemic. As the Wuhan Virus spread across the globe in the spring of 2020, the scales were lifted from the eyes of many leaders in the West. After all, the Chinese strategy for global dominance was written in plain sight—see programs "Belt and Road," "Made in China 2025," and "China 2049." The goals of the Chinese leadership, the CCP, are to dominate the globe both economically and militarily. The economic goals for the United States need to be brought into alignment with its imperative national security interests, i.e., on-shore back to the United States every national security-related economic operation currently on Chinese soil—ASAP! That includes a wide breadth of U.S. industries, particularly pharmaceuticals, military manufacturing, high-tech, engineering and any feeder industries to these.

Many corporations profiting mightily from offshoring in these industries will need to be patriots first and seekers of profit second. The loop has really closed on the off-shoring strategy. The economics of it all needn't be debated any longer: national security-related industries need to be on-shored; other off-shored operations would be wise to recognize it is in their best interests to shift their off-shoring to non-totalitarian developing countries. Millennials currently rising in corporate America need to face this patriotic reality and act upon it within their organizations.

The past two decades have seen a massive, and to many, alarming increase in government deficit spending and the resultant towering rise in Federal debt. As this century opened, the national debt stood at $5.6 trillion. As of the closing days of 2020 it exceeds $27 trillion, and driven by Pandemic-related stimulus is increasing by over $8 billion a day! This is truly unprecedented in the history of our country, for the national debt first breached just $1 trillion as recently as 1982. Today, it is widely acknowledged across both the political and economic spectrums that this debt is not going to be paid down. An honest accounting of the nation's books would indicate that because of this currency debasement there's a reckoning coming regarding the value of a dollar and its purchasing power. Some in public life realize this, many do not, and none will speak of it publicly.

Though the debt expansion has increased under both Democrat and Republican administrations, the main drivers of the debt are the out of control Federal "entitlement" programs of Social Security, Medicare and Medicaid. They represent more than 50 percent of the annual federal budget. Under pressure from the Tea Party Movement, some Republicans had called for reform of these programs, but the RINO Republican addiction to the bi-partisan "spend and elect" philosophy of Big Government, caused them to melt before the scoffing and demagoguery of the Democrats at the very mention of entitlement reform. But the bottomless Leftist think tanks and "Intelligentsia" have spawned a creature designed to permanently de-fang the issue of perpetual annual deficits and soaring national debt by rendering it moot—Modern Monetary Theory (MMT).

With a straight face we are conveniently told by academics and deep state "economists" that the deficits and debt don't matter any longer. MMT posits that government spending doesn't need to be "paid for" because governments, which issue fiat currency, can always pay back maturing debt by issuing more fiat currency. To ward off the problem of financing the debt, MMT advises keeping interest rates on federal bonds at near zero. Now isn't that an explanation that is tailor-made for carte-blanche spending for as far as the eye can see. The only problem MMT foresees is the potential for inflation, but it posits that problematic inflation can only occur when the economy pushes beyond full employment. At that point MMT proposes reducing spending and raising taxes. MMT proponents claim there is no inflation today but as we know housing, education, energy, and healthcare, where inflation rages on, are absent from the government's calculation. In MMT fantasy world, all wealth derives from the government; that is, the more the government spends *our own* money, *the richer we will all become*! You've heard of MMT from the likes of Bernie Sanders and AOC on the campaign trail, and economist Stephanie Kelton in academia and on cable TV.

As such, Modern Monetary Theory (MMT) is the most current snake oil economic theory that is increasingly being sprinkled into the Left's most audacious spending proposals in order to make them seem plausible. Those who push MMT believe that any government that issues fiat currency can do so without any fear of becoming insolvent because in their view currency has no objective value; therefore, the state can always print more money as it requires. From this it follows that budget deficits don't matter because, after all, the state can just create more fiat currency to pay for it. Further, since the printing of money out of thin air replaces the need to tax workers to get money to pay for government spending, the very role of taxation becomes the simple regulation of aggregate demand. In essence, MMT claims that money has worth *because the state says it does.* Hence, it is claimed that a country's National Debt is payable simply by creating fiat currency and thus obviating the threat of default. Therefore, if government spending has been set free from the constraints of having to raise tax revenue because it simply creates "money" as it is required, there is never any risk of insolvency. It is upon this utter absurdity that MMT is based and it is why it is so dangerous.

The Economy is a multilayered phenomenon; on the top layer is the consumer economy as it is lived through everyday transactions: work, wages, consumer spending, saving and investing in the future. The consumer economy functions symbiotically with a commercial economy consisting of manufacturing, services, business start-ups and expansion, business borrowing, investing, shareholder ownership and valuation as expressed on the various stock exchanges and equity markets. Yet at a far deeper and more fundamental level, there are elements that form what might be called "Economic Tectonic Plates", upon which all else above them rests and whose surface stability is at the mercy of their movements. Those Economic Tectonic Plates are the Credit Markets and the critical short-term liquidity they represent, longer-term Debt (both public and private), and the Stability of the Dollar. With government spending totally out of control due to political impotence in the face of greed, interest rates will inevitably erupt and spike *beyond control* due to the debt's stratospheric rise by tens of trillions of dollars, choking off the credit markets, and seizing up both banking and business operations. The economy experienced such warning tremors in August '07 and October '08. What could do more to aggravate the plates and cause them to shift than invoking MMT? What kind of money could be more fake? Of course, like all seismic tectonic plate movement, it is largely not thought about as it is too horrible to contemplate. However, as those living on seismic fault lines know, when a shift happens all that is above it is in peril because there is little shelter from the massive earthquake caused by the plate shift. By divorcing money from any relation to objective value, the MMT system will exacerbate the tension in the underlying Economic Tectonic Plates to an extreme degree. It will then force the Fiat Dollar plate to grind against the Debt and Liquidity plates by endlessly escalating government spending and thus creating the devastating economic earthquake that is inevitable if such irrational academic fantasies like MMT are adopted... and this is precisely the goal of the Left. By creating an economic catastrophe of unparalleled proportions, the Left will have the Economic Crisis it seeks to exploit in order to expand its power to control the chaos it has created.

Should a creature such as MMT be adopted as our economic system, we will have crossed the bridge into Emerald City and entered yet another false utopia! From Saint-Simon to Robert Owen to Edward Bellamy to Hugo Chavez to Alexandria Ocasio-Cortez, all such economic fantasies have never produced anything but failure, poverty and misery. MMT is an idea so dangerously stupid that it could only find fertile ground to grow in the Academic Dreamworlds that are, by their very nature, cut off from social reality. The drumbeat for adoption of this fraudulent and economically insane transformation of the financial system is underway, and if the Millennials are to return society to economic sanity, they'll have to slay this dragon as well. Any simple application of common sense to this Marxist fairy tale of creating wealth out of nothing renders this scheme worthless.

The simple fact is that no nation, not even a very rich country like the United States, would be able to withstand the devastating effects of a anything as economically suicidal as Modern Monetary Theory.

SUBVERSIVE ACADEMIA AND MEDIA

Today's American college campuses are a minefield of political correctness. In the land of victimology one is never quite sure what is *permitted* to be said. Further, despite all the purging and re-purging of speech, there is always another *victim-in-waiting* ready to take offense. Once offended, the process of leveling false charges and having the person who gave offence hauled before a Bias Review Board or some other Campus Kangaroo Court composed of hostile leftwing radical student leaders and the college administrators they have terrorized into submission, begins. Once convicted of having the temerity to dare to speak one's mind, one's predetermined fate... being denounced, being forced to "confess" your "wrong," being required to take Social Justice "training seminars," facing forced furlough or suffering outright termination or expulsion... is announced to the jeering mob outside the campus Journalism School, on whose wall one of Edward R. Murrow's paean's to freedom of thought are etched.

The entire totalitarian hypocrisy is a celebration of censorship and coercive groupthink that is the exact opposite of the free and open exchange of ideas that college is designed to create and encourage in order to broaden the vistas of perspective and open the mind to thinking critically about ideas to young people starting out in life.

Instead, it insists that one's mind be closed to any thought that is not oriented to prefer collective groupthink over individual judgement. That groupthink itself is multicultural and transnational in its orientation, is reflexively politically correct and perpetually pushes the boundaries of social revolution ever further away from traditional values of Faith and Family until students return home embittered and angry against all that has nurtured them to that point.

All confidence in the traditional values of the student's society are deliberately destroyed, all Faith ridiculed, all conservative politics and policy smeared and vilified, all History trashed and re-written in compliance with Transnational Progressive thought, all myths debased, all heroes torn down and all patriotism excoriated.

The goal of Academia is not education, it is indoctrination; it is not critical thinking, it is unthinking acceptance of Leftwing dogma on pain of being denounced as a political heretic who is guilty of the sins of racism, of sexism, of hate-speech, of harboring "phobias" against gay, trans and Muslim people and of seeking and trusting the Objective Truth over what Alexandria Ocasio-Cortez calls "the Moral Truth" - aka., the Dogmas of Progressive Liberalism. Anyone who dares to think outside or question any of these odious nostrums is condemned and ostracized for disagreeing with any of the doctrines or dogmas of the Left's perversely atheistic Catechism.

In fact, the Left very much resembles the Medieval Church in that it tolerates no deviation from its vision of "Moral Truth" which neither accepts nor allows any to dare to contradict it without severe censure, punishment and social banishment or "cancellation."

Academia has basically become a book burning without the fire; it is the horrible realization of the threat Alan Bloom once warned against: "the closing of the American mind."

Academia's role in the Seventh Crisis is to pervert and rape the minds of those who will most need to think critically and act forcefully in order to overcome it and will subsequently find themselves bereft of such tools as the Crisis runs its course . When those who have been made unable to think critically realize they cannot overcome the Crisis, they will call on those who provide a Big Government "solution" to do it for them.

Of course, Big Government intervention will, as it inevitably does, exacerbate the problem and then use that exacerbation of the problem to justify even more intervention! "The problem was worse than we thought!" they will cry! "We need more power…" purchased at the cost of the individual's Liberty… "to resolve it!"

Thus begins the cycle downward to the USSR, to Cuba, to Venezuela and to North Korea, with each government failure leading to its next subtraction from the freedom that Ordered Liberty tries to preserve, because the needs of crisis and war always encroach on the needs of freedom in the name of victory.

And that failure will represent everything you mis-learned in school.

America's founders understood the role of a free press as an essential bulwark against government for securing individual rights. Ideally, the mass press was to serve as a means through which to enforce accountability and responsibility in government. Benjamin Franklin gave much thought to the subject, making several penetrating observations. He noted that the press exercises power unchecked by the Constitution. He stated, "It may rule tyrannically because it is liberated from considerations of justice or precedent." He saw the press wielding power like a "court" with the power to "judge, sentence, and condemn to infamy" the country's both private and public citizens. In addition, in practice he cautioned, "The press is neither restrained by legal precedent nor by evidentiary standards that assure the maintenance of any claims to equity and justice."

Hence, the term "fourth estate", first ascribed to the press by British politician Edmund Burke, who viewed the galleries observing parliament as more powerful than the other three "Estates." Today, in evidence of its fall from prior lofty heights, the "press" is derisively referenced by one and all as simply "the media."

However, the sad fact is that something more insidious than what Franklin feared has occurred. The press is not currently "controlled" by the government in the manner Franklin was referring to; indeed, as we can see in its relationships with Presidents like Nixon and Trump, it vociferously opposes the government when it disagrees with its agenda. However, when a government (or the semi-permanent bureaucracy that constitutes what many call "the Deep State") is in power or in control of some government apparatus and pursues policies it agrees with, the press seeks to collaborate with it in order to get their mutual agenda passed, as was the case in the Clinton and Obama administrations.

Therefore, the Press, while independent, has become a willing tool of those whose political agendas with which it agrees. When those sharing their agenda have control of the government, the press uses its resources to help enact it. It is no longer an objective media; it is not even a legitimate opposition media, which holds the government's statements and policies to scrutiny. It has cast itself in the role of an ally, or public relations firm, for the type of Leftwing political, cultural and social policies promulgated by Progressive Liberals. In this, it has become the enemy of everything that represents the traditional social and moral order as well as the enemy of anything that would limit government's power to enact the Progressive agenda. It is that very political, economic, social and moral order that Ordered Liberty seeks to maintain, because it understands that order undergirds Freedom, including Freedom of the Press.

In fact, if one is an anti-Statist who opposes the ever-growing power of the central government and the militantly secular, anti-Traditional, Globalist agenda it pursues, the Press (as propagandist for the Globalist agenda) assumes the character of an opponent, a self-righteous propagandist and an enemy of Ordered Liberty.

For those seeking to establish Ordered Liberty, it has become *the Enemedia*!

During the Obama years, this incestuous relationship between itself and the Enemedia Press was clearly evidenced by the fawning press coverage it lavished on his regime with its egregious acts of omission, commission and blatant water-carrying of every Administration pronouncement and story angle. Since the election of Donald Trump, it is the permanent government, the bureaucratic "Deep State" that is working below public radar, which colludes with the progressive media. Trump's election has exposed legions of bureaucrats and "journalists" for the partisans they have always been.

As seen in the outright felonious leaks that have emanated from the FBI and Justice Department, the Deep State operatives have entrenched themselves within the bowels of the government as progressive activists who feed both classified facts and outright falsehoods to their allies in the complicit Enemedia. These false accounts and leaked state secrets are then reported in print and broadcast with the intent of shaping both the public narrative and the citizenry's core perception of events.

The entrenchment and growth of this symbiotic relationship between the Progressive political class and the Enemedia has produced a complex of opinion control that has led many sober observers to characterize our public media space as a 'propaganda state.' The progressive message is reinforced on TV, in print and on government-sponsored public radio. The classified leaks and false stories of just the first year of Trump's presidency could warrant a book just to summarize. So why has the national mainstream media become a virtual arm of progressive government and in an unholy alliance, abandoned its role as the voice of the people demanding accountability?

It all accelerated in the '90s, when the advantage for access shifted from the press to government mouthpieces. When there were minimal media outlets, politicians would vie to have access and they would endure most any gauntlet of tough questioning. But as media outlets exploded with cable TV and the Internet, reporters had to compete for access, and with a coercive nudge from the pols their stories became more compliant with the government or political agenda. Add to that the corrosive practice of political operatives leaving the political world for lucrative, high-profile media positions and the toxic nature of the relationship becomes evident.

Completing this corrupt brew is the fact that there are an amazing number of government officials married to influential media operatives.

We are now subjected to the fabrication and continual selection and repeating of news story narratives designed to advance the progressive agenda. Stories that conflict with it are ignored and simply not covered. The result has been the insinuation into the public consciousness of progressive values, opinions and judgements. Pictures are shown on TV news with voiceovers telling us what to think of what we see. Newscasters narrate their programs holding the progressive point of view as the presumed correct, normal or average viewpoint. It has all become a seamless and insidious affair across most of the broadcast and cable spectrum.

For those who still crack open a newspaper to follow events, if their paper is *The New York Times, Chicago Tribune, Boston Globe, LA Times, Miami Herald,* and so on, their daily news diet consists of only the progressive party line. While this is well known throughout the Liberty Movement and other awakened citizens, far too many Americans remain unaware, distracted and incredulous that these powerful, trusted institutions would lie to them. However, the Enemedia itself has now become so trapped in the web of its own lies, as it is forced to have its "reporters" issue absurd denials of what is clearly occurring in the video of their own reports. During the Leftwing anarchist riots in Kenosha, Wisconsin, on August 27, 2020, Joe Concha of *The Hill* wrote "CNN was ridiculed for a video caption Wednesday night that read "Fiery But Mostly Peaceful Protests After Police Shooting" during a report from national correspondent Omar Jimenez in front of a building engulfed in flames during protests over the shooting of Jacob Blake in Kenosha, Wis."

As evidence of Enemedia disinformation and lies spread, one is left to wonder what is the media's anticipated end-game, as a more and more angry public awakens to the Enemedia's subversive deceptions while the Crisis spirals to climax?

First and foremost, the media elite consider themselves an essential part of the ruling class. As such, they presume to be part of those who are "the protected" and fully expect to be inside the castle walls should things get chaotic or violent out among the commoners. They expect to be among the saved. They know that without their complicity the progressive politicos would never be able to so easily enact their agenda in plain sight.

Many of them, particularly the Gen-Xers, are the products of the progressive creed that has been persistently pounded into them by the Post-Modernists that dominate Academia. By the time they graduate into the "real world" many of them have embraced the collectivist model at an almost sub-consciousness level. They leave college arrogantly assured that they possess what Thomas Sowell accurately calls "the vision of the anointed" and therefore equipped to know what's right for the rest of us. They view the middle and working classes as incapable of successfully ordering our lives without government "experts" telling us what to do and worse, what to think. Given this, it is no surprise that they exhibited widespread support for Obamacare.

The subversive Enemedia may be viewed as the on-going propaganda arm of the Academia / Enemedia "complex" that targets the young after Academia has laid the foundation and built the framework. After 12 years of public school and 4 (or more) years of college and post-grad work, students come out blindly accepting a Progressive-Left view of society as that which is not only normal, but unassailable.

Once released from the grip of Post-Modernists in Academia, the Enemedia goes to work on its products to re-enforce all the moral conceptions of right and wrong, political conceptions of good and evil, economic conceptions of success and failure, and social conceptions of just and unjust that were taught to them in school and at university.

The Enemedia engages in an unrelenting, daily attack on the ability of young people just starting out and those just coming into maturity and gaining positions of power to think critically. Instead, Academia and the Enemedia seek to install a set of mental "circuit breakers," whose intent is to cut off any form of critical thinking that questions Progressive Orthodoxy or that would lead to an acceptance of the type of Ordered Liberty necessary to oppose that Orthodoxy's control, let alone be able to face the developing crisis.

These include concepts that are to be as blindly accepted and unquestioned as the doctrines of the medieval church, except that these dictate that the only moral way to face life is to be politically correct, multicultural, non-judgmental, globalist oriented, economically socialist and existentially pacifist.

For any Gen-Xer, Millennial or Gen-Z to oppose this doctrine is to risk scorn, bullying, shunning and social excommunication; to be put "beyond the pale" of "decent" progressive society and cast into the outer darkness populated by the "deplorable," the "ignorant," the "bigoted," the "mean-spirited," the "intolerant," the "xenophobic," the "greedy," the "unfair" and the "warmongering."

Opposition to Progressive doctrine is not simply considered to be *wrong*; it is to be considered *evil*.

To impose this doctrine on the Gen-X, Millennial and Gen-Z generations is to saddle them with everything that will prevent them from first, waking up to the immediacy of the danger facing them and second, to how dangerous and debilitating such doctrine is to their ability to fight the cyclical crisis that history indicates is about to engulf them.

The solution lies not in control of the Enemedia, but in the exposure of its lies; not in the curtailing of Progressive opinion, but in the right to be liberated from it.

For one cannot accept the concept of Ordered Liberty, which is essential to overcoming the Seventh Crisis, if one has been conditioned into rejecting everything that Ordered Liberty requires to be effective.

THE ROOTS OF NATIONALISM AND PATRIOTISM

Of course, this is not just an American issue; the Seventh Crisis confronting the Gen-X / Millennial cohort is international in scope, as befits a crisis faced not just by the United States but by the West itself. In fact, the Gen-X / Millennial demographic may be in even more danger in Europe, where the conceptual tools required to fight it with Ordered Liberty are even more lacking due to the longer exposure of Europe to Transnational Progressivism's attack on critical thinking.

Yet the unrest caused by the Transnational attack has already provoked a backlash that is coinciding with the Seventh Crisis.

All around the world people are gradually rising up and protesting against the incredibly dangerous power of Transnational Progressive "Globalism" and are seeking to fight it by embracing not Ordered Liberty, but a rather atavistic form of Nationalism. Despite the very real and far worse danger of Transnational Globalism, people should be very careful before embracing the idea that "Nationalism" should necessarily be a central aspect of their fight against it.

While Patriotism is an ennobling attribute, which entails loving all that is good about one's country and which therefore deserves to have its interests put first, Nationalism is its more perilous twin: a more brutal, more debased, less tolerant and more easily perverted version than its more enlightened fellow as well as one that presents its own threat to that which is most required to fight and win against the travails of the Seventh Crisis - Ordered Liberty.

Patriotism involves love for one's country in the service of one's family, one's Nacio (i.e., "kindred group" or "native land") and one's religion.

Nationalism indicates one must put one's country before *everything* else... including, God, Family and Nacio… and Freedom: Patriotism *merits* its devotion via its sublimation of the four to the achievement of some national purpose; Nationalism *demands the four submit* to the State via coercion and if need be, at bayonet point in order to achieve some corporatist purpose that it insists serves the "National Good."

Patriotism is God & Country; Nationalism is Blood & Soil.

Yet Nationalism is not necessarily evil; certainly, in times of extreme danger, such as from an invasion by a hostile foreign power or some other existentially dangerous situation, Nationalism may serve the purpose of enforcing extreme measures to coerce compliance and unity on the part of the people in order for the State and the people to be able to face the crisis as closely in union as possible.

Nor is Nationalism necessarily "right wing" as the term is currently, in our view, generally misunderstood.

Nationalist solutions not only tend to trample individual rights in the name of dealing with difficult problems, but they far more often than not demand welfare-state solutions in the name of the type of leveling required to make everyone an "equal" citizen serving the singular, Nationalist interest of the State.

The innate social Progressivism, forced egalitarianism, arrogant cultural imperialism and crusading, aggressive foreign policies Nationalism uses to "solve problems" can be found in almost every Statist policy this country has been burdened with, from Teddy Roosevelt's Square Deal, to Woodrow Wilson's Democracy Crusade, to Franklin Roosevelt's New Deal, to Harry Truman's Fair Deal to Lyndon Johnson's Great Society. George H.W. Bush went so far as to wrap his Big Idea (viz. "a New World Order") in America's "national security interest" to carry out a Globalis agenda, just as his son George W. committed the United States to militarized, Neo-Conservative, open-ended nation-building in Iraq and Afghanistan that did the same.

However, history has proven how easily such do-good Progressivism can be perverted toward evil purposes, precisely because it puts what *the State, not the people,* insists is best for the country first. All other concerns are squelched in favor of the State's definition and rationale of what constitutes "best" and the State substitutes the priorities of its leadership class above the priorities of the people it governs in pursuance of that goal.

In fact, we do not have to look very far or very long ago to find a place and a time when the world faced "Nationalist" states that did exactly that.

The toxic blending of Nationalist demands for complete unity with an utter submission to the goals of the State and the Socialist demand for fanatically ruthless egalitarianism created a political force of such evil power that it practically destroyed Western Civilization in the 1930s and 40s before it was overcome at a catastrophic cost.

Nor is Nationalism "White" Supremacy; this can be seen in our own country in Louis Farrakhan's group, the Nation of Islam, as well as the various

Latino "Aztlan" revanchist groups that are very open about being ethnically based Nationalist movements. Among other Non-White Nationalists that can be found among many, many others were those led by Toussaint L'Ouverture, Kemal Atatürk, Hideki Tojo, Muammar Gaddafi, Ho Chi Minh, Saddam Hussein, Idi Amin and the Kim Dynasty in North Korea.

Our own country is not immune to a form of Nationalism that can be perverted and twisted in order to justify an increase of power to the State at the expense of Ordered Liberty, and the Freedom it seeks to protect.

Since our Founding, the United States has experienced what might be called a series of "virtual republics," all of which justified spurts of massive government growth since the end of the Civil War.

During the Progressive Era, government power was expanded to counter-act the power of the Industrial Monopolies; during WWI, government was expanded in the name of the need for "emergency war measures"; during the Neo-fascistic New Deal, it was expanded to enact "emergency economic mea-sures" supposedly required to end the Great Depression; during the Great Society, it was expanded in the name of an "emergency need for social and economic justice" to even the playing field for all races and classes.

These increases in the size, centralization, reach and power of the State have always been justified as a response to some National emergency. This occurred whether the emergency existed (such as the Great Depression) or not (such as the "Red Scare" of the 1920s, which ultimately led to our *National Police Force, the FBI.*)

All "National Emergencies," we are told, require "National Remedies" and all "National Remedies" require more power ceded to the Central Government, which then demands we adopt a united "Nationalist Attitude" or be accused of being "disloyal."

Disloyal to whom? Why, the *Nation* of course!

Nationalism, when perverted to serve the designs of the powerful, con-siders anything less than total submission to be suspect, subversive or even treasonous.

Worse, whether the expansion of government power helps or, as is far more often the case, hurts the response to the emergency and hinders affecting a solution to it, it uses its own failure as a justification not for less government power *but for more*, since the State inevitably contends that the emergency was worse than suspected and requires even more power be granted to it to resolve.

All in the name of Nationalism.

In fact, this very rationale has, ironically, been picked up by the *Internationalists* themselves in the European Union who, while replacing the word "Nationalism" with "Transnationalism" similarly embrace the idea of self-created "emergency crises" as an excuse for the expansion of their power.

The Not-So-Cold Civil War that is now manifesting itself in Europe between "Nationalists" seeking power to stop "Transnationalists" from expanding their own power is alive in the Brexit Movements in Britain as well as in the anti-immigration parties in France, Poland, Hungary, Austria, Sweden and Germany.

This movement is directly opposed to the centralized, socialistic bureaucracy emanating out the E.U. Headquarters in Brussels, whose "progressive" mask has fully fallen off and whose brute *Statism* is openly championing the end of the Nation-State in favor of the homogenized political, economic and, most importantly, cultural tyranny espoused by the anti-Capitalist, multicultural Transnationalism that the European Left has been dreaming about, in one form or another, since Marx pseudo-intellectually excreted Das Kapital.

In our own country, a process similar to that of the E.U. has continued and grown stronger under both Establishment Republican and Progressive Democrat administrations. That Duopoly had drifted so far from any concept of a legitimate call for patriotic unity in the face of danger that is consistent with limited, Constitutional government, that the people rejected Establishment candidates wholesale in 2016 for a maverick non-politician, Donald Trump... who successfully, though sometimes erroneously, conflates Nationalism and Patriotism to great effect.

The problem is not so much that Trump uses the word "Nationalism" to distinguish it from "Globalism" and thus serve his political purposes. It is that he seems to ignore the fact that it is a politically loaded term, fraught with much negative historical baggage. Therefore, when he explains to reporters what the definition of "Nationalism" is to him (viz. "America First") it really doesn't matter insofar as what the reality behind the term is.

Politically, his use of it as an attack on powerful groups that have often sneered at the needs and problems of the Middle Classes that will be on the front lines when the Seventh Crisis peaks, indicates to those on the Right, in general (and in his base in particular), that he opposes arrogant transnational elites, and champions those who have been disdained and disparaged by them as "a basket of deplorables."

This is all well and good, since Trump's rhetorical imprecision is far less of a danger than the menace of Transnationalism that his words, imprecise or not, vividly expose as the arrogant, quasi-aristocratic philosophy that it is. Yet because Trump's tendency is to think that whatever is politically good for Trump is also good for the country, he rather blithely passes over the potentially dangerous misunderstanding his speech leaves behind.

It would be far better all-around if he would say that he supports "national sovereignty" which, while it is just as anti-Globalist as the term "Nationalism," is far more accurate as well as being far less provocative - which may be why Trump doesn't use it.

A counter-puncher by nature, Trump is always ready to double-down on any rhetorical excess he engages in, especially when playing such "reality show" games with "reporters" in the left-biased Enemedia.

He understands the over-riding need to maintain solidarity with his devoted Nationalist Populist "MAGA" supporters, as well as with Constitutional Conservatives who are against both those factions, which are quite rightly despised as scribbling propagandists in the service of the elites who hate both Trump and his voters.

Conservatives, while uneasy with the rhetorical red-meat he throws his Base regarding his "Nationalist" bona fides, may see such ploys as a politically self-serving but necessary response to the dishonest propaganda manufactured against him and his supporters by the left-wing Enemedia.

Therefore, Constitutional Conservatives tend to support Trump because while they realize he conflates the word "Nationalism" with the word "Patriotism," he is deploying these words to attack the Globalist policies that have done so much harm to everything both his Base and his Constitutional Conservative allies support.

However, the danger of Trump's rhetorical excess, or worse, of some far more malignant successor who better understands how appeals to Nationalism can be manipulated to serve the purposes of expanding the power of the State, remains.

If past is indeed prologue, the results of such appeals in terms of individual Liberty are all too depressingly predictable:

When the government expands, *the people shrink.*

Dr. Samuel Johnson famously said: "Patriotism is the last refuge of a scoundrel"; given that, we suppose that one can also say, "Nationalism is the *first* refuge of the would-be authoritarian or dictator."

Nationalism, the handmaiden of expansive government power at the expense of individual liberty, is not to be praised or trusted without great caution.

Far worse than even this is that by harping on what he calls "Nationalism" as a "cure" for Transnational Globalism", he neglects that which is by far the strongest weapon against the current Globalist Threat and the coming Seventh Crisis: Ordered Liberty.

For it is only Ordered Liberty, with its concepts of national sovereignty, decentralization of power away from the center and adherence to a strict interpretation of the Constitution that can offer a solution to our most pressing cultural issues.

BRIDGING THE CHASM ON ABORTION

We stand today in the United States agonizing over abortion, the most divisive social issue since slavery and one that also threatens to ignite a violent outcome. It seems to many on both sides that there can be no squaring of the circle on an issue that goes to the very heart of what it is to be or not be human; it is a truly existential debate as it either affects the expansion and maintenance of freedom as its advocates contend, or it is just another form of brutal genocide, albeit committed for different, though disturbingly familiar, rationales offered in the past to justify similar mass killings.

For the central question regarding Abortion comes down to one thing and one thing only and it is only in the answer to that single question that the issue can be resolved:

Either the being - the fetus, the baby, the collection of cells, the unborn - whose existence is being threatened is a *human* being or it is not.

Either answer effectively *ends* the debate for either side: if the unborn *are not* human beings, they can be killed, but not murdered; if the unborn *are* human beings, they cannot be killed (except under the most extreme of health circumstances regarding the mother and child) without resorting to murder.

If the being in question is human, then the tens of millions of deaths caused by legalized abortion is an act of violence on a genocidal scale and a crime against humanity; it's an atrocity that engenders, mandates and literally demands violence against innocent life. It is an act of violence so profound that it makes society itself complicit, corrupt and defined by its acceptance of it.

However, if the being is not human, then the issue becomes moot; after all, one can kill a single dog and only be guilty of cruelty to animals or a property crime, but one cannot be guilty of murder. Further, one can exterminate an entire hive of wasps, but one cannot be considered guilty of mass murder.

If those unborn are, by the very fact that they are unborn, not to be classified as human beings, then there is a right to terminate them, sell their body parts for profit and justify the act as a moral good and a social benefit.

Therefore, the Left's program for the unborn is that they are to be judged as lacking person-hood (i.e., they are to be judged as "*sub-humans*" who are alive and whose teleological result will be full humanity, but who have not yet achieved that classification because of some arbitrary condition - in this case, location outside the womb - and even this boundary is becoming blurred with the advance of rationales for "post-abortion" infanticide.)

From this they assert that the granting of rights to those classified as "tumors" "appendages" and "tissue masses" without the rights of person-hood *is an attack on the rights of "real" female human beings and a threat to their "freedom of choice."*

After all, if the being whose life is terminated is not a person, it can be killed *but it cannot be murdered.*

The "freedom" to kill that (the unborn) which is to be considered "sub-human" overrules a right to life that, according to the pro-Abortion argument, can only belong to those deemed "full" human beings. And any disagreement, let alone political attack, on that Elitist Leftwing view is hysterically deemed to be an "attack" on "women's freedom" and their "right to choose."

However, the cruel depravity of this false rationale is too historically evident to ignore. Any time that a being is to be judged, by some arbitrary standard—race, religion, class, gender, ethnicity, health, intelligence—to be "sub-human," oppression and murder follow. Be they Black people enslaved and mass murdered during the African Slave Trade, European Jews suffering genocide at the hands of the Nazis during the Holocaust, Capitalists and other "Class Enemies" exterminated by the various Communist regimes that polluted the 20th Century around the world or Rwandan Hutus committing genocide against Rwandan Tutsis, once the idea of "sub-humanity" is given legitimacy, it becomes open season on those described as such.

If one is deemed to be "sub-human" by virtue of its *location* (viz. inside the womb) then, according to the heartless rationales of the pro-abortion advocates, one may kill that being which is deemed to be "sub-human" and not be guilty of homicide… after all, according to this corrupted, grotesque "logic," if it is a "sub-human" that is being killed then it's supposedly not the same as committing murder against a "real" human being (i.e., a life *located outside* the mother's womb.)

Thus falsely framed, those seeking to expand and protect human rights for the unborn are represented as seeking to curtail the rights of "fully human" women; those seeking freedom and life for the most weak and innocent among us are castigated as seeking to destroy the rights of women and even kill them by endangering their "reproductive health" and returning them to the "barbarism" of restrictive abortion laws.

It is, in essence, a demand that only the Left's self-anointed moral vision of what constitutes "freedom" is to be considered morally and legally sanctioned and any disagreement with it is automatically exiled beyond the permissible parameters of public parlance.

So how can anything, including Ordered Liberty, solve an issue so intractable and so morally and philosophically difficult?

One answer, the answer we currently live under since the Roe v. Wade decision in the Supreme Court, is to nationalize it; in this manner, the decentralized, Federalist system is overruled by a decision to offer a final solution to the Abortion Question by legalizing the sub-human status of the Unborn in every state in the Union regardless of whether the people in those states agree or not.

The national solution we live under because of Roe is identical to the Dred Scott decision that led directly to the Civil War in the 19th Century; by legalizing the Fugitive Slave laws and by constitutionally mandating the supposed sub-humanity of Black slaves across the entire nation, the long held, fragile compromises that permitted the states to allow slavery or not were over-ruled from the Center and, due to the existential nature of the questions it raised regarding the morality of slavery, made the situation untenable.

Dred Scott arrogantly overrode the 10th Amendment, which granted great power to the individual states to run themselves as they saw fit; by sanctioning a central government solution, the issue exploded out of control with the anti-slavery states refusing to accept the decision because it sanctioned a concept of sub-humanity that was morally abhorrent. At the same time the pro-slavery states sought to secede from the Union because they viewed this refusal to accept the decision as a lawless attempt to foster acceptance of that which they saw not as humanity but as sub-human property.

Once nationalized, it was again a case of Either / Or; either the slaves *were* human beings, in which case they could not be held in bondage as the property of the slave-owner *or they were not* human beings and therefore could be held in such a manner.

As we are nearing a similar point of no return with the Abortion Question, we must realize that we have come to this not because of the decentralized federalism / strict interpretation view of the Constitution embraced by those who seek Ordered Liberty and believe in the need for limited government run by the common people; it comes from those who hold the "Progressive" view that a powerful, central government, run by "experts" and intellectual "elites," knows better...

...and the latter view, which currently holds sway, has delivered us into this already violent, cultural disaster, where the pro-Life side frustratingly watches the other murder babies while the other side expresses great fear regarding the subjugation and loss of women's rights to male dominance.

The only way out is to return to the far clearer, far more equitable view held by those seeking Ordered Liberty and its support for Freedom under a stable, Constitutional order. No new answer need be sought, and no new modification need by undertaken.

The answer lies in the 10th Amendment: *put the issue back to the individual states.*

There is no way that "progressive" states such as New York, California or Massachusetts will ever vote to overturn Roe; similarly, there is no way that a "conservative" state such as Texas, Alabama or Idaho is likely to ever accept it as moral or legal.

Of course, those in the minority on either side can try to change the minds of those who disagree with them, but if they cannot countenance the policy of their state, they should move to one more in keeping with their views and values. In this manner, pro-Life advocates are not paying their taxes to state governments that sanction what they see as murder and pro-Abortion advocates will not pay their taxes to a state government that they see as oppressing women.

In either case, the solution offered by Ordered Liberty - a solution that already exists in the U.S. Constitution in the 10th Amendment - would lower the heat generated by the conflicting sides by allowing for pro-Life sanctuaries in anti-Abortion states; meanwhile, those living in pro-Abortion states can feel safe in the knowledge that what they see as the rights of women are secure.

If any change is made in states on either side, it will be a contained, local decision; it will come over a longer period of time and be decided by the voters rather than be accomplished by the elitist diktat of nine lawyers sitting in splendid isolation in their judicial ivory towers on the bench of the Supreme Court.

When the Seventh Crisis peaks, we must be strong enough to realize that there is no solution to be found in the panaceas vomited out by the Leviathan, which is designed to induce us not to overcome the Crisis but to *succumb* to a State power falsely claiming to be able to do it for us.

We must face the fact that *everything* the Left proposes as a solution *is a façade for their statist, collectivist agenda.*

Ordered Liberty is the only answer to the false dichotomies and manufactured controversies created by the Leviathan State in order to engender crisis and then claim the need for ever greater State power to "resolve" it. Ordered Liberty is anchored in the Constitution and it is in the Ordered Liberty of the Constitution that society will find the bridge across the chasm that has opened up between the pro-Life and pro-Abortion forces. It is the only thing that will provide the strong traditional foundation, the conceptual tools and the type of free, critical thinking that will be absolutely necessary to not only overcome the Seventh Crisis, but to prevent those advocating for the State to use the Crisis as a means to further its power over us.

THE TYRANNY OF SOCIAL MEDIA

The advent of Social Media presents its own set of problems concerning its effect on the ability of the Gen-Xers, Millennials and Gen-Z to confront and survive the Seventh Crisis. Let us be clear: *depriving* these generational groups the conceptual tools required to deal with the Crisis is the whole point of the Left's anti-intellectual attack on their ability to think critically. Denuded of the resources that are essential to dealing with the coming Time of Troubles, that has been in fact, created by the Left in order to use the expansion of its power as a justification to deal with it, the generational groups on the front lines of the Crisis will be *forced* to accept the only solution available to them: the one provided by the Ruling Elite, *which is not at all a solution but a power grab.*

A cultural awakening is desperately needed by two generations mired in lives that are less lived than watched on TV, on I-phones and through an endless barrage of imagery designed to replace humans with humanoids. Such simulacra will increasingly experience existence as largely made up of conspicuous consumption and who may more and more tend to blindly accept, as both normal and inevitable, that their hopes and dreams are nothing more than the sterile impulse-buying whims one experiences in a suburban strip mall.

While they vacantly stare into their hand-held device, looking for the positive affirmations that social media programmers are counting on to stimulate a Dopamine High, the parasitic Establishment is free to batten off victims whose capacity for critical thinking has been crippled. The generations who will face the developing crisis will have little chance of overcoming it if they have been rendered, through scholastic training, Enemedia propaganda and social media addiction to remain not merely intellectually absent-minded, but conceptually impaired as well. They will have been robbed of any ability to think beyond that which is presented to them as socially acceptable doctrine, complete with a sweet, somatic reward.

Too many Gen-Xers, Millennials and Gen-Z seem mentally chained to their devices, where they sit, lost in the hyper-reality of its powerfully shaped, pre-digested and directly received images undiluted by any interaction with real life.

These "un-awakened" are absorbed by the Establishment technology's vacuous simulated "reality" and dominated by its directives, which indicate that truth is only represented by that which can be commodified and sold, and that there are no abstract ideals or principles worth fighting for in an ultra-cynical view of the world where all ideas are co-equal and all morality is relative. Life becomes a place where individual creativity, critical thinking and self-expression are viewed as no longer viable or even socially dangerous.

In this sense, the Decayed Establishment seeks to extend its rule by attacking the Gen-X, Millennial and Gen-Z generations by cutting them off from any competing worldview. Their attack is all the more insidious in that it encourages its victims to seduce themselves into accepting the virtual reality presented to them; connected to their devices, they self-manage and self-regulate their lives all within the context of the collective, where they become identical atoms trapped in a closed, electronic universe. Within that universe, their thoughts remain uncritical and unoriginal, their privacy is non-existent and their actions are monitored for intellectual heresy by a paranoid Establishment concerned only with maintaining their own fragile existence at the expense of those they seek to control.

To live in a virtual reality controlled by a decadent Post-Modern ruling class will render them defenseless against the developing Crisis in any of its forms: domestic, foreign or social.

One cannot fight the Seventh Crisis if he or she is convinced that they exist merely as atomized units, psychologically separated and physically apart, unable to form political associations that are independent of and contrary to those approved by the Ruling Class.

One cannot muster the spiritual reserves required to overcome the Seventh Crisis if one is trapped in the false, virtual reality quicksand that is created by the internet social media networks.

Those who are seduced by the psychological soma that is released into the brain whenever one is "liked" online (which is served up like a reward for those who "stay plugged in") will become the types of meek, inert, non-critical, non-judgmental, compliant drones that will dumbly submit to the Elite's demand for more power to "overcome" a Crisis that they themselves have brought about.

In November 2017 Sean Parker, who co-founded Napster and served as Facebook's first president, publicly stated, "God only knows what it's doing to our children's brains… I don't know if I really understood the consequences of what I was saying, because of the unintended consequences of a network when it grows to a billion or 2 billion people and it literally changes your relationship with society, with each other… It probably interferes with productivity in weird ways. God only knows what it's doing to our children's brains… The thought process that went into building these applications, Facebook being the first of them, … was all about: 'How do we consume as much of your time and conscious attention as possible?'… And that means that we need to sort of give you a little dopamine hit every once in a while, because someone liked or commented on a photo or a post or whatever. And that's going to get you to contribute more content, and that's going to get you … more likes and comments… It's a social-validation feedback loop … exactly the kind of thing that a hacker like myself would come up with, because you're exploiting a vulnerability in human psychology… The inventors, creators — it's me, it's Mark [Zuckerberg], it's Kevin Systrom on Instagram, it's all of these people — understood this consciously. And we did it anyway." https://www.axios.com/sean-parker-unloads-on-facebook-2508036343.html

A street corner drug dealer could not have been more contemptuous of his pathetic victims than Parker is of the social network addicts he continues to ensnare in his techno-drug net.

Everyone in Big Tech knows the truth Parker dared to speak; in fact, legendary Apple co-founder Steve Wozniak, also thinks the social media giants are becoming too powerful. In an interview he stated, "Some of the benefits of Facebook are worth the loss of privacy. But to many like myself, my recommendation to most people is—you should figure out a way to get off Facebook." https://www.businessinsider.com/apple-cofounder-steve-wozniak-urges-people-to-leave-facebook-2019-7

While his addicted victims have surrendered their Liberty, smug elitists like Parker manipulate the Crisis, as well as their self-serving responses to it - they double-lock the chains on the public's self-imposed exile from responsibility and their indulgence in the faux "freedom" of expression offered by Social Media.

This is the bargain drug addicts make with their suppliers. And the results - dependence at the least, slavery at the worst - arrive unseen. And, due to the insidious nature of Social Media's ability to create a reality that doesn't exist in actuality, arrive un-noticed by the victim until it is too late to be able to tell the difference between the false and the true.

Worse, by falsely posing as a non-biased platform operator without a political agenda, it allows itself to covertly aid those whose political agendas they *do* align with outside the simulacrum, or facsimile world, created by the social networks where they trap their victims. Inside the simulacrum, they provide information tailored to advance their political agenda, as well as the political agendas of the government Leviathan they seek to batten off of, to a captive audience that increasingly no longer recognizes truth from lies.

By creating search algorithms to produce results that give preference to and thus advance those political, economic and social nostrums they support and reject or minimize those they do not, they are able to shape the opinions of those trapped inside their bubble in order to affect their actions outside it. By creating "answers" and "information" found in "results lists" that support those of the Leviathan, the Social Media insures that they are part of its operation and not subject to its wrath.

That is, in creating news algorithms that pretend to give objective results but which, in fact, produce results biased in favor of one candidate's political, economic or social views over another, the social network has in effect given a kind of campaign contribution to the one candidate over another.

If this is the case, then any society that seeks to preserve Ordered Liberty must secure itself against a fraudulent process that seeks to subvert its election laws.

Of course, there is also the problem that Social Media may be in violation of the very provision that provided the legal basis for its existence, viz. Section 230 of the Communications Decency Act of 1996.

Section 230 states that "No provider or user of an interactive computer service shall be treated as the publisher or speaker of any information provided by another information content provider."

This basically means that websites are not legally responsible for the type of content posted by others on their platform. Section 230 applies to all internet sites from Social Media platforms such as Facebook, Google and Twitter to those which post customer reviews, such as Yelp and Amazon; it also covers any website that contains a comment section.

The need for Section 230 (with some exceptions, including the violation of federal criminal or intellectual property laws) is based on the requirement designed to prevent websites from being sued over a statement posted by one of their users or sued by anyone whose post was deleted by the website.

This has led to the charge that internet platforms, because they are editing content (that is, content that lies beyond that which is restricted by Federal Law, including that which is considered to be obscene, violent or promoting harassment) they have forfeited the "platform" status they claim under Section 230 and have instead become, in effect, a publisher of content (such as a newspaper or magazine) thereby opening them up to civil liability lawsuits.

If internet platforms are "editing" or "moderating" content based on their own political bias it would be a violation of Section 230. For example, if a platform decides to "moderate" a post that it deems to be "hate speech" or "offensive" or "untrue" it can do so based on its own interpretation. Since many of the biggest internet platforms, such as Google, Facebook and Twitter, tend to be socially and politically progressive, they are often accused of repressing, editing or deleting conservative opinion and content; this is an editorial decision that is legitimate for a publisher but not for an internet content platform operating under the rules of Section 230.

The banning of posts supporting Conservative groups and ideas has markedly accelerated in 2020 by the giant Social Media firms that run the most influential websites, as opposed to ones that agree with the Progressive agenda they promote. As private companies, they are well within their right to do this, but curating information that is clearly biased against conservative opinion while promoting that of progressive opinion makes the Social Media firms as responsible for its content as any other publisher. In fact, social media executives have freely commented that Conservative opinion is "dangerous."

Social Media tech giants like Google, Facebook and Twitter pose as social media platforms but have not-so-cryptically transformed themselves into publishers; as such, they don't simply present what users post but only what those who run the platform-cum-publishers want other users to see.

As usual, RINO Republican legislators have long cried and complained about such bias but have done nothing to revoke the "platform status" granted under Section 230 to Big Tech, even though they now act like any other publisher. They have also failed to update campaign finance laws that would prevent Social Media giants from providing in-kind campaign contributions to Liberal individuals, groups and causes in the form of censoring opposing conservative opinion while not applying the same standards to the Left.

Investigations into whether or not bias exists on the part of politically progressive Internet platform companies against conservative content and opinion should be convened to determine whether or not the Social Media is acting in good faith when it is censoring conservative content in favor of progressive viewpoints. Congress should remove the protections Section 230 provides for Social Media sites engaging in such censorship, opening them up to lawsuits like any other more traditional publisher, to be sued without such suits being dismissed as they are now under the aegis of Section 230.

Congress needs to remove the false cover Social Media enjoys under Section 230, where it is protected for being an internet platform open to all kinds of thought and opinion (as long as they are within Federal Law) while still being able to operate as a publisher that can censor content it doesn't like.

That is, Big Tech can't have its Section 230 protection cake for being simply an "open platform" and, via its editorial censorship, eat it too!

The power of Big Tech to ruthlessly exercise its immense power was seen in the 2020 election. It openly spiked any coverage of potentially game-changing information in favor of one candidate (former Vice President Joe Biden) over another (President Donald Trump). Big Tech oligarchs such as Twitter and Facebook purposely ignored all reporting by the NY Post, the country's number one newspaper by circulation (Agility P.R. Solutions, (2020, August) - https://www.agilitypr.com/resources/top-media-outlets/top-10-daily-american-newspapers/.) This reporting highlighted information that was later the subject of a federal investigation regarding potential illegal activity on the part of Joe Biden's son, Hunter Biden, as well as the candidate's own involvement in his son's shady foreign business deals with Communist China and the Ukraine.

"The majority of voters believe the media buried the story about Hunter Biden's foreign business dealings to help his father Joe Biden's 2020 presidential campaign, according to a survey. The poll found that 52 percent of likely voters think the absence of Hunter Biden coverage was intended to boost the campaign, while 32 percent considered it a partisan hit job and 17 percent are unsure, Rasmussen Reports said on Tuesday. An even higher margin — 56 percent — said it's "likely" the elder Biden was consulted about his son's business with Ukrainian energy company Burisma and ties to China, and perhaps profited." Moore, Mark (2020, December 16) *Majority believe media buried Hunter Biden story to aid dad's campaign: poll* - https://nypost.com/2020/12/16/most-voters-believe-media-hid-hunter-biden-coverage-to-help-his-dad-poll/

The spiking of this important news story comprised an in-kind campaign contribution to the Biden campaign. It was an egregious attack against one candidate, President Donald Trump, who was known to favor removing Section 230 protections from the Tech Cartel in favor of Joe Biden, who was far closer to Big Tech's transnational progressive political ideology. Like most Democrats who identify with the Party's corporate wing, he was far more sympathetic to their regulatory concerns and business needs. Also, since Trump was largely despised by many of the Leftwing, West Coast workers employed by Big Tech, their donations to his opponent, Biden, far outstripped the amount of money Big Tech donated to Trump.

"Employees at Big Tech giants, including Alphabet, Amazon, Facebook, Apple and Microsoft, donated millions to various Democrats' campaigns in the 2020 election cycle. Employees at the five companies shelled out a combined $12.3 million to Biden's campaign and millions more to Democrats in high-profile Senate contests, such as recently-elected Jon Ossoff (D-GA) and Raphael Warnock (D-GA). Employees of Big Tech firms ranked among the top donors to each of those Democrats.... Erik Gordon, a professor at the University of Michigan's Ross School of Business, said... he expects the Biden administration and Congress to settle antitrust lawsuits filed against companies like Google and Facebook — but with compromises to avoid upsetting big tech donors without looking "softer on big business than the Republicans." Legislation that's more difficult to compromise on will likely move more slowly, he said." Hur, Kyrstal (2021, *January 12) Big tech employ-*

ees rally behind Biden campaign - https://www.opensecrets.org/news/2021/01/big-tech-employees-rally-biden/

These combined actions had the desired result:

> "Even fewer Biden voters, 45.1 percent, knew about the Hunter Biden email scandal, which implicates Biden himself. Had those voters been aware of the scandal, 9.4 percent of them would have defected."—Jones, Kip (2020, November 24) *Poll: 17% of Biden Voters Would Have Abandoned Him if They Knew About Stories the Media Censored* - https://www.westernjournal.com/poll-17-biden-voters-abandoned-knew-stories-media-censored/

After the election, Big Tech, supposedly an "open platform" dedicated to free speech, unilaterally removed the President of the United States from communication on its platforms. It also took the opportunity to exploit the violence in the nation's capital on January 6, 2021 when Amazon, Google and Apple colluded in a classic Cartel manner to ruthlessly de-platformed a truly "open platform" website called "Parler," which was seen as "the alternative social media platform favored by conservatives." They temporarily put Parler out of business by removing it from their web-hosting services and "APP Stores." Such actions effectively destroyed Parler's ability to compete by banning... or rather, *cancelling*, its access to the online public. - Fung, Brian (2021, January 11) *Parler has now been booted by Amazon, Apple and Google* CNN Business - https://www.cnn.com/2021/01/09/tech/parler-suspended-apple-app-store/index.html).

Big Tech's increasing power to mine private information, censor critics, influence election outcomes and curtail commerce by crushing competition is a clear threat to personal privacy and free thought as well as to free markets.

WEAPONIZING THE ENVIRONMENT

When considering the issue of committing virtually unlimited resources (which is what any commitment of scores of trillions of dollars represents) one should at least consider if what one is committing it to actually exists as a problem that can be addressed with any hope of solution given the limits of modern technology.

For example, before committing scores of trillions of dollars to a project envisioned to design a ship that can exceed the speed of light - which physics tells us is scientifically impossible - one should at least consider if such a thing is at all possible with current technology, even were the money available.

The problem is that the *Green New Deal* faces similar difficulties.

The question is simple: Is Anthropogenic (i.e., man-made) Global Warming actually caused by Man and further, if it is, what if anything can be done about it?

Let us first dispense with the propaganda terms designed to curtail the debate.

The idea that Anthropogenic Global Warming is "settled science" is ridiculous; for one thing, numerous scientists disagree with the idea. For another, theories are not "settled science." Little in science is "settled" because as new discoveries advance scientific knowledge; what was once thought of as being "settled" is often revealed to be nothing of the sort.

The closest thing there is to "settled science" are scientific laws such as the Laws of Motion, the Laws of Thermodynamics and the Law of Conservation of Energy. Scientific Laws reflect a causality that is basic and fundamental to what is perceived to be reality. Such Laws are not "invented"; they are discovered over the course of long research into their nature.

Such Laws are based on the results of experiments within a certain field of inquiry and the accuracy of the Law is not affected when new theories regarding it are broached; however, the mathematics upon which the Law rests remains despite further observations that are made about it and, therefore, the Law itself remains valid.

One only has to look back at the Ptolemaic Universe as conceived by the ancients who, based on their intense observations of nature, theorized a flat Earth in the center of a non-Heliocentric solar system.

This view was "settled science" for centuries, accepted by all intelligent people and certainly by what passed for men of science in their day. The fact is that the ancient conception of the World and the Universe could account for all geographical and astronomical phenomenon in a manner that was logically consistent with its premise of a flat Earth existing in a non-Heliocentric solar system; both a flat Earth and a non- Heliocentric solar system appear completely internally logical and consistent with observations made by the people that advanced the idea.

Unfortunately, both views are completely wrong; of course, Progressive Liberalism does the same with politics, economics and social issues.

That is, it creates a false narrative (viz. that the world is warming due to Man's greedy and destructive exploitation of the environment) around a scientific claim that is highly problematic and roundly denied by as many scientists as there are that promote it.

Then it announces that this claim is a dire threat requiring vast amounts of power - and money - to be ceded to the central government for it to "solve." Any disagreement with this claim, no matter how well documented or logically consistent, is considered a dangerous heresy to the sanctity of what it demands be considered "settled science" and is, therefore, to not only be dismissed out of hand but is also to be considered a dangerous lie designed to promote the evil greed of those who profit from causing it, i.e., fossil fuel companies, car companies, the meat industry and industry in general, which promotes mass consumption and soulless materialism.

To ensure compliance with the Progressive dogma of Man-Made Global Warming, any attempt to disagree with it is met with the type of angry fanaticism one might expect from a medieval society shrinking back in horror from someone who denied an accepted dogma of the Church.

And it is this that is at the center of the whole controversy and the entire rationale for a "Green New Deal": what we are dealing with here is *not* science - it is *religion;* a secular or neo-pagan religion true, but a religion nonetheless.

Such rejection of dogma is therefore not treated as a scientific debate but as a morally reprehensible attack on what is, in essence, a pseudo-religious substitute for the types of traditional religions the secular Progressive Left has hated and opposed as a detriment to its plans since Marx wrote the Manifesto.

In the place of the traditional religion it despises, it offers a new secular substitute which not only manufactures a neo-pagan spiritualism to take the place of all other forms of spirituality but also serves the Left's anti-Capitalist socio-political purpose.

What it offers in traditional religion's stead is *Gaia Worship*.

Gaia Worship is a complete package, an anti-Capitalist, anti-Traditional religion that masquerades as a "science"; it is designed to be inculcated in people throughout their schooling until they believe that any opposition to Gaia Worship is a selfish and evil attack on the personification of the Environment: the Earth Goddess Gaia.

All the elements of religious compulsion and religious propaganda are present:

- A transcendent god: Nature.
- A personification of divinity: Gaia.
- A Devil: Capitalism.
- A mass of devotee cult followers immune to counter-argument.
- A large corpus of literature justifying doctrine.
- An unassailable set of dogmas that it is a sin to contradict.
- A "priesthood" to act as intermediaries, teachers, guides, gurus and prophets.
- A revelation: Environmentalism
- An End-Time eschatology: World catastrophe as a result of failure to heed the warnings of the goddess.
- A paradise: A "Green" world without industry, capitalism, pollution or carnivores existing in a perfect climactic balance.

To disagree with it is not a "debate" to be resolved through the Scientific Method; *it is heresy to be extirpated lest it spread.*

Thus it serves the long-term goal of the Left and the Elites that use its false ideology to increase their power to undermine one of the pillars of Ordered Liberty: Traditional Religion and Transcendent Spirituality - and replace it with the prefabricated, secular political religion of Gaia Worship.

From kindergarten to college, children are taught they must "save the Earth" from "greedy businessmen" who care more about profit than the environment or the health of the people that live in it.

Nothing is said regarding how Capitalism presides over the most environmentally clean countries or that the very industrialized, Capitalist societies that are demonized by Gaia Worship are the basis of a society that is the most prosperous and healthy in history.

These teachings, spread by giant Government bureaucracies such as the Department of Education, are re-enforced by ludicrously alarmist news reports and misleading "documentaries."

The same "scientists" who now tell us that a global warming "Climate Change" (an empty phrase falsely implying that such change is not a naturally ongoing process) will end the world in 12 years told us we were about to enter a New Ice Age back in the early 1970s; political hacks seeking to extend their careers publish books making all sorts of alarmist predictions - "The ice caps will melt, the polar bears will drown and NYC will be underwater in ___ years!" - are never called to account when their erroneous predictions fail to materialize. Instead, Hollywood pitches in and produces "disaster movies" using special effects to depict that which failed to happen in real life.

Ordered Liberty supports science; it supports reason and logic; it supports the idea that Traditional Religion is the key to social stability; it supports Capitalism and Free Markets because they lead to clean and healthy societies... and it supports legitimate debate on environmental issues, not faux-theological morality plays based on fake science that are not designed to create a healthy society, but one mutilated and impoverished in order to advance the political power of a secular, Transnational elite.

THE BABY BOOMERS' ORIGINAL SIN

If the generational analysis of historical cycles posed by Strauss and Howe hold, and we are indeed already descending into a "Seventh Crisis" all these factors and more will come into play. The corruption of the culture; the economic deceits designed to attack the prosperity of the many in order to place them at the mercy and dependency of the few; the subversion of Truth undertaken by Academia, the Social Media and the Enemedia; the debasement of Patriotism into the false alternative of brute Nationalism and border-less Transnationalism all encourage the needless exacerbation of social tensions surrounding hot-button issues such as abortion and the environment. These are just some of the tools the enemies of Ordered Liberty seek to use in order intensify the problem of the Seventh Crisis and, indeed, make it exponentially worse so as to increase the need for the false savior of a Leviathan Government.

Big Government will not resolve the Seventh Crisis; *Big Government is the engine of the Seventh Crisis.* Moreover, those who serve it have no interest in resolving it but rather *their interest lies in making it worse.*

To accomplish this, those who seek to increasingly grow the power of Big Government must denude those it seeks to rule of the very tools necessary to fight it. It must undermine the traditions that make for stability, the free markets that make for prosperity, the free critical thinking that makes Truth discernable from manufactured lies, and the indispensable sanctity of individualism against the predatory designs of the collective State that make it possible for Ordered Liberty to maintain and protect Freedom from devolving into chaos, anarchy and eventually, oppression and tyranny.

The Baby Boom generation has, tragically, laid the foundations for a society infected with a political virus born of its own arrogant solipsism and ruptured idealism. As it decays and passes into its final Prophet role that the generational cycle of History has ordained for it, it must… at long last… recognize the corruptingly devastating effect its rejection of everything that made the American society of its parents triumphant in the previous Crisis will have on the Gen-X, Millennial and Gen-Z generations that came after it.

If the Baby Boom generation is to avoid being anything other than an ugly stain on the history of this Nation, it must call out to those subsequent generations whom it has betrayed with its obsessive self-righteousness regarding politics, religion, tradition and culture *to avoid its example at all costs.*

It must alert those whose future it has traduced with the inane, psychedelic fueled, Socialist utopianism caused by its seemingly permanent state of arrested adolescence to the danger such mindlessness has produced. It must do so lest those betrayed suffer the continuing consequences born out of the Boomer's folly. For as the Baby Boom generation fades from view, it will not pass on the type of stable, secure and prosperous Nation that its parents in the WW II generation left them, but will instead saddle the Gen-X, Gen-Z and most importantly (since they will be the ones who will face the Seventh Crisis "in the trenches") the Millennials, who will suffer most from the nemesis the Baby Boom hubris has called forth.

The anti-values of the Baby Boom generation's ridiculous flower-power utopianism have been latched onto by the very plutocratic, Transnational Progressive forces the Baby Boomers ludicrously sought to overcome with their shallow pseudo-revolutionary play acting and silly, juvenile aspiration to create peace and love and egalitarian community of purpose through art, music and an unhealthy dose of recreational drugs. Incredibly, they seemed to think that a world that could not be saved by princes, prophets and presidents would be saved by drug addled, hedonistic guitar players. As fundamentally stupid as this viewpoint is and always was, it has nonetheless been seized upon by those who know very well how to use such utopian fantasies as weapons to falsely posit a peaceful "transnational" world ruled by an "expert class" of post-modern all knowing "progressive Elites" that in actuality represent the most cynical, insidious form of control imaginable: *that is, one in which people willingly enslave themselves to in the name of "social justice."* Such control will be seized by those Elites through the creation of a Crisis that will inexorably drive society into the clutches of a ruling group that seeks a permanent and unbreakable hold over their lives and, even more importantly, over their ability to think critically enough to fight back against it.

This is the purpose of this book: to alert the Gen-X, Gen-Z and Millennial generations to the poisonous danger that has been allowed to fester for decades within almost all the foundational institutions society depends upon to remain prosperous, heathy and free… and which, without a direct intervention by the Millennials, will burst forth in a social, political, economic and cultural plague that will decimate Liberty and destroy the Nation as we have known it, in the wake of the Seventh Crisis.

The 19th Century English poet and literary critic Matthew Arnold encapsulated the idea that each generation owes something to the next when, in his work "Essays In Criticism" he remarked:

"From the retrieval of the generations, order is born."

With this in mind, as a last act of expiation for their myriad sins before they shuffle off this mortal coil the Boomer generation should, at long last, adopt the role of mature adults and strive to alert the Millennials not to emulate the selfishly foolish disaster they made of their own historical experience… and instead encourage them to understand and embrace Ordered Liberty.

- Once some catalyst ignites the Seventh Crisis, it will be used by the Transnational Progressive Deep State as a pretext to further its control of society by exploiting various fault lines that lie just beneath the surface of American life.
- They will use the tools of Multiculturalism, Political Correctness, Critical Theory and radical Social Justice "warfare" to undermine and subvert all that has been considered the bedrock of successful American life since its inception: Liberty, Capitalism, Traditional Family Values and Judeo-Christian based morality.
- They have infected the Free Enterprise system that is vital to the prosperity of the Nation with a series of economic deceits, including super-massive Federal debt; neo-Fascist "bailouts" for favored corporate interests at the expense of the taxpayer; the creation of "fiat" money without objective value or worth that is, in reality, merely a manifestation of "monetized debt."

- Unless these deceits are exposed and addressed, the standard of living that the Millennials and their younger Gen-Z siblings think is their birthright, will vanish and they will find themselves facing an economic catastrophe unprecedented in this country's history, including the Great Depression of the 1930s.
- The Deep State will use its instrumentalities in the Enemedia and Academia to create a false "virtual reality" that they want to be impervious to honest reporting and truth as well as allow no opposition to their viewpoint that cannot be immediately smeared as cruel, intolerant, bigoted, greedy and, of course, racist.
- The Enemedia is no longer an objective media or even a legitimate opposition media, which holds the government's statements and policies to scrutiny. It has cast itself in the role of an ally, or public relations firm, for the type of Leftwing political, economic, cultural and social policies promulgated by Progressive Liberals.
- The Enemedia has created a situation where the quest for truth has been turned into a series of competing propaganda memes, which for most people replaces a search for the truth with a search for solace in "news sites" that promulgate and re-enforce their pre-conceived political preferences. This leaves the Millennials bereft of the reliable information they must have if they are to think critically and understand how to overcome the Seventh Crisis; moreover, they will find themselves shunned and shamed if they question the propaganda memes of the Enemedia and will find their reputations smeared and vilified for opposing it.
- To fight the deceits of the Deep State, the generations on the front lines of the Crisis must not blindly embrace forms of crude Nationalism with its potentially statist adulation of "Blood & Soil," but instead express support for their Nacio (viz. their "kindred group") in a Patriotic vision that stresses the more edifying concepts of GOD, Country & Ordered Liberty.

- Social issues are also used by the Deep State to accrue power to itself. Abortion, the ultimate social issue, would cause far less division in the country if the decision-making power on the issue was devolved back to the states, rather than being decided by the central government in Washington D.C. Decentralization of power back to the States is more in tune with Ordered Liberty than the centralization of power; it is in this decentralization of power that the generations fighting the Seventh Crisis will find their strength and the solutions they seek to difficult social issues through Ordered Liberty.

- If the front-line generations are to prevail over the Seventh Crisis, they must understand the insidious nature of Social Media and the digital addiction it pushes on them as viscously and relentlessly as the most degenerate drug dealer who destroys the lives of his customers for illegal profits. Liberty is not unlimited license without responsibility, but *Ordered* Liberty requires a rational application to the use of potentially dangerous tools, including Social Media, which can be used by wealthy, powerful and influential companies that are eager to work in a neo-fascistic relationship with their partners in the government to mold the minds of their users in ways the Deep State can use in its quest for dominance and control.

- Those who seek to exploit the Seventh Crisis seek to replace traditional religion with a faux-religion that serves to underscore their propaganda memes; the Green New Deal is one such faux-religion and its siren call, as with all the siren calls of the Deep State, requires the surrender of Ordered Liberty in the name of some transcendent goal, in this case, a form of pagan Gaia Worship that attacks not only traditional religion and traditional cultural expressions, but also undermines Capitalism with it false pseudo-religious "environmental" dogmas.

- The at-risk generations fighting the Seventh Crisis can find ways to fight against the Deep State by emulating the example of the earlier Tea Party Movement, which demonstrated how to organize a movement based on organic power. Such a movement is difficult for the Deep State to control and even disparage because such a movement welcomes its hatred as a badge of honor. The Deep State despises that which it cannot control, especially movements dedicated to the type of Ordered Liberty that are the most dangerous to their plans and ambitions. Millennials and Gen-Z fighters must form their own movement and use it to heroically dispute the Deep State operatives not just on the political level but on *all* levels: the cultural level, the economic level, the Enemedia level, the Social Media level, the crudely Nationalist level and the pseudo-religious environmental level.
- If the Seventh Crisis is fought to be won, it must be carried out as a *total* political war on *all levels.*

– 2 –

Our Current Decaying Establishment Duopoly

BEHIND THE SEVENTH CRISIS: HISTORY HIDDEN IN PLAIN SIGHT

One may be tempted to ask a very pertinent question regarding the Seventh Crisis; that is, "How could our democratically elected government let such a thing happen?"

After all, the primary function of government is to maintain law, order, stability and security, all of which would come under direct threat of such an all-encompassing, political, economic, social and cultural crisis. Surely, a government as big as ours is, with all its bureaucracies, political parties, information outlets, cultural institutions and economic power could not be caught by a crisis of such magnitude unawares... *could it?*

And if it is caught unaware, how is it possible that an entity as powerful as the U.S. Government will not be able to deal with the crisis, as it has with so many crises in the past?

The unfortunate answer to the question regarding the lack of response and/or seeming inability to respond at all, fails to consider another option: *that the Government doesn't respond because its interests lay not with overcoming the Crisis but with exploiting it.* It doesn't seek to expend its power *countering* the Crisis but to *expand* its power as an ongoing pretext for "dealing" with it.

The Seventh Crisis is suddenly taking shape before our eyes, but it did not develop overnight. Incremental developments toward it becoming a reality have been going on for over a century and it is imperative to understand the how and why behind this developmental history. By understanding the history behind the Seventh Crisis, we can come to understand why it is happening and, more importantly, whose interests such a Crisis serves.

It requires us to know the nature of the Republican and Democrat Parties, which as decaying and increasingly corrupt instrumentalities of a sclerotic Establishment, can still successfully work *together* as a highly dangerous Ruling Duopoly. For as the Duopoly pretends to be engaged in a political struggle based on a clash of conflicting ideologies, the hidden history of both parties indicates that they actually both serve, albeit in their own specific ways, the same master.

The history of this decaying yet still formidable Duopoly, falsely posing as rival political parties contending for votes in a democratic Constitutional Republic rather than serving as the instrumentalities of a Plutocratic Elite, is essential to understand the danger they present. The elitist power that pulls the strings of the Duopoly is antithetical to Liberty, which remains… as long as it exists… a direct threat to their goal of creating an ever more gigantic Leviathan Government capable of destroying our culture, our traditions, our national sovereignty, our prosperity and our constitutional rights.

To be able to fight and overcome the Seventh Crisis, we must understand the cloudy history behind who and what it is that caused us to fall ever further from being a democratic Republic under the Constitution to becoming a collectivist tyranny run by an Elite that serves its own interests and not the interests of the people.

Therefore, to overcome the Crisis, we must first understand the mindset of those who seek to use it to their own advantage, regardless of how many it hurts, what values it destroys, and what freedoms it seeks to obliterate. To do that, we must understand the history that drives it forward.

Since the end of the Second World War, this country has effectively been ruled by this Duopoly—two parties driven by two supposedly different concepts regarding the size and scope of governmental power vs. the primacy of Individualism and the Ordered Liberty that makes it possible.

In theory, the Republican Party represents the "conservative" or "right wing" party, favoring smaller government, traditional values, incremental, gradual change and free markets primarily dedicated to private profit and the idea that a strong national defense is the best way to insure peace; its counterpart was the Democrat Party, the party of larger government, progressive values, impulsive revolutionary change and government regulated markets primarily dedicated to serving the interests of society at large and the idea that negotiation and global agreements are the best way to avoid war. To the general public, the concern of American politics is the debate between these two general views. The reality is far different. Our system is not about a struggle between two political parties where one fights to maintain and strengthen the rights of the Individual and the other seeks to increase the power of the State; it is not about two parties struggling to decide between maintaining support for long-held traditional religious and family values and those who demand a secular, values neutral, politically correct culture; it is not about one side defending Ordered Liberty and National Sovereignty, while the other side aggressively pushes a form of neo-Fascism dressed up as Socialism in the service of a globalist Transnational Progressive order, which can supposedly bribe and appease its way to world peace. It is rather about two parties that are more or less dominated by those who *openly* reject individualism, tradition, religion, Ordered Liberty and National Sovereignty and those who, while mouthing empty platitudes in support for them, *clandestinely reject them as well.*

That is, we have now come to the point where the Democrat Party has all but abandoned any pretense that it supports those values and even more openly campaigns on the need to reject them in favor of their Statist, collectivist opposites; any pretense of support for Capitalism, traditional values, a strong sense of nationhood and the will to defend it have been joyfully rejected by a Party now controlled by a Base dedicated to Socialism, secularism, constrictive politically correct dogma, multiculturalism and, most importantly of all, Transnational Progressivism.

Transnational Progressivism is an elitist ideology that rejects all the stabilizing morals, politics and traditions of the past in favor of a radical new governing order that rejects National Sovereignty, national community, national culture, individual achievement, traditional religion, Judeo-Christian moral-ity, Enlightenment ethics and free-market Capitalism. It seeks to replace the current order with a post-national Globalist society governed by an interna-tional Corporate cabal operating through institutions such as the E.U. or the U.N. with open borders, Identity Politics, a multicultural society, advocacy of collective achievement over individual accomplishment, favored interest over merit, and the promotion of atheism or a form of pagan "Gaia Worship." It promotes relative morality, situational ethics and a neo-Fascist economic sys-tem hiding behind a Potemkin Village composed of empty Socialist slogans and meaningless Leftwing bromides.

Transnational Progressivism… and the rich and powerful people such as George Soros (and before him, David Rockefeller) who run it from behind the scenes… represent a great magnitude of influence and control over those in governments around the world who are essentially on their payroll. Even if it is largely unknown to the general public, it is in many cases the driving meta-reality above and behind what most people think of as "politics."

Despite the appearance of a difference between the two traditional politi-cal parties, there is, in fact, no difference between those elements in the "lead-ership" of both parties that adhere to an anti-Liberty agenda. However, while the Democrat Party is now openly celebrating its release form the ideological closet of having to feign support for anything smacking of a "Liberty" agenda and instead condemns any idea associated with such an agenda as greedy, rac-ist, exploitative, mean-spirited, aggressive and warmongering, the Republican Party is mired in a dilemma. Although most of its party "leadership" prefers to continue to profess support for Capitalism and the Constitution, it is in actuality an ally of the Transnational Progressive forces that provide the funds for them to stay in office. But as far as the ideological purists in their Base are concerned, the Democrat "leadership" cadre is considered too weak, too old and too slow at implementing the utopian collectivist designs that are at the heart of Statist thinking. These groups are now rapidly moving to take over the Democrat Party and transform it into a New Socialist Democrat Anti-Semite Party.

But while the N.S.D.A.P. is unified in its detestation of the Liberty Agenda, the attacks on that agenda, both overt by the N.S.D.A.P. and covert by the Establishment Republicans-In-Name-Only, "RINOS," this increas-ingly open attack on it has not only driven the Base of the Republican Party to the Right but has also driven many groups that have long identified with the

Democrat Party toward the Right as well (i.e., union workers, manufacturing workers, traditional ethnic groups who oppose secular attacks on religious values and increasing numbers of Jewish voters who are upset with the anti-Israel sentiment and rank anti-Semitism of the modern N.S.D.A.P.) Further, the advent of Donald Trump and his program of Nationalist Populism has made it much easier for many among the former Democrat voting blocks, who were long suspicious of all Republicans, to tentatively align with Trump's Republican Party.

The reaction of the Establishment RINOS has been fierce; the angry harangues against the Trump Administration from the "Never-Trump" RINOs has barely been able to contain itself from condemning Trump on all levels: he isn't presidential, he isn't a real conservative (as if they were!) he is crude, he is authoritarian, he is an isolationist, he is a "divider" and, of course, he is a "racist." Despite Trump's great policy successes, the RINO wing of the Republican Party cannot, as the Whig Party also couldn't do in the 19th Century, accept that the grassroots of the Party are currently moving past silently suffering their flaccid RINO "leadership" as well as their continual sellout of the Liberty Agenda. Exactly how long is the Conservative Base of the Republican Party going to tolerate suffering electorally fatal subversion by so-called "moderate" RINOs? How long will it tolerate being politically debilitated by a disease caused by an internal enemy consisting of a disloyal collection of subversive "Republican" progressives who are, for all intents and purposes, looking to either ideologically mutilate their host body beyond all recognition or to kill it outright? The RINO betrayal is nothing new. It has been able to periodically weaken the Republican Party because RINO-ism has been a congenital condition that has existed within the body of the Party since its birth in the mid-19th Century. RINO-ism is like an inherited disease, which passed to the Republican Party from its parent, the equally Statist, corrupt and sclerotic "business oriented" Whig Party. The ill-effects of this inherited disease sometimes lay dormant. But when they become active, they have proved to be historically devastating not only to Republican electoral hopes, but have also proved to be spiritually devastating to the very soul of the Party and everything for which it's supposed to stand. This legacy of subservience to plutocratic corporate interests has subverted the desire of the overwhelming majority of the Republican Party for small government and Ordered Liberty since its inception over a century ago *and the center of this plutocratic infection is found in the so-called "Eastern Establishment."*

THE EASTERN REPUBLICAN ESTABLISHMENT

Again, it cannot be stated strongly enough that there are really *two* Republican Parties. At the top is a very small minority group, national in scope but historically based in the Northeast, which is able to exercise great influence on the workings of the party by using both its considerable finances and long-established influential connections with power players including Big Business, High Finance, Elite Academia, powerful Foundations (such as the Ford and Rockefeller Foundations), important members of the news media and the Foreign Policy establishment, which includes powerful organizations such as the Council On Foreign Relations. This elitist group has always pushed the Republican Party away from being the party of small government while trying to maintain the fiction to the grassroots that they were its champion. While it appears to be counter-intuitive that the party of small government should support increased Statist interference in our private and business lives, one must realize that this elitist group of Plutocrats cares *nothing* for the principles of small government and Capitalism because such principles limit their ability to control. They detest competition and they want to control market forces in order to bend them toward their own narrow interests, not allow them to create wealth for a wide section of society in general as the forces of Liberty always prove to do if left to work with a minimum of interference.

The Plutocracy would be much happier with a powerful central government, putatively acting in the name of "fairness" and "egalitarianism" and "sharing the wealth" that in reality carries out an agenda which favors them and their interests. They are not interested in any "principle" *other than the principle of controlling power* behind the mask of a "moderate," supposedly altruistic policy that favors giving a break to the type of "little guy" they only see in their own lives when they acknowledge the servants waiting on them.

Unlike those modern Liberals who push "progressive" socialist policies from the Left, for whom such change cannot take place fast enough, the RINOs in the Eastern Establishment prefer a slower, more incremental approach, one less likely to produce a backlash which threatens to undo years of patient clandestine work and which tries to avoid anything that threatens to throw a wrench into their plans (as happened in 1980 with the election of Ronald Reagan.) The Eastern Establishment has been around for a long time, working behind the scenes while posing themselves as simple businessmen seeking the same freedom from Big Government to run their lives and businesses without interference of the type of excessive Governmental control that has been antithetical to the American way of life since its birth. To see this one must understand the difference between the mindset of a Plutocrat and the mindset of a Constitutional Conservative.

Let us be clear: *we are not talking about the average American businessman or corporation.* These people and organizations are the backbone of American Capitalism and the source of the massive amounts of wealth this country has historically produced. They support a small government, less bureaucracy and low taxes. They are the very image of the free-enterprise system that values individualism and which rewards hard work, merit, initiative and innovation. They are more than willing to take their part—and their chances—in what Joseph Schumpeter describes as the creative destruction process of Capitalism. They know that no one is "too big to fail" and that along with reward for success there is always the risk for failure. Most importantly, they understand that reality dictates that there are no perfect solutions or social utopias, only options that are less bad than others.

The truth is that in its essence, the Statist RINO agenda is, albeit moving in slower motion, exactly the same as that of those Democrats who have openly and actively supported an ever-increasing role for Big Government, as fast and as much as possible, in the service of the advancement of the type of collectivist policies an ever larger central government is prone to enact. The RINO Establishment is not opposed to this view, but reacts negatively to the speed with which its proponents (now found in the Progressive Liberal wing of the Democrat Party) seek to put it into effect. The only thing that is "conservative" about this Plutocratic Elite is the rate at which they want to travel the road to the same collectivist goals as their supposed "rivals" in the opposition party. In order to understand how we arrived at this confused situation, one must examine the history regarding how the Progressive Democrat / RINO Republican Duopoly which rules us came into being, evolved and ultimately came, among the Republicans, to largely control a Party in which it is a minority and which ideologically disagrees with an overwhelming majority of its members.

In the beginning, there were the Whigs, a 19th Century political party formed in opposition to the Democrat-Republicans, the ancestors of the modern Democrat Party which at the time championed small government. The Democrat-Republicans were a Jeffersonian party of "Classical Liberals" (such as Adam Smith, Edmund Burke and others associated with the rationalist

English Enlightenment and its ideas about the morality and utility of the concept of "Ordered Liberty") that had defeated—and ultimately destroyed—their rivals, the neo-aristocratic Hamiltonian Federalist Party, which favored a strong Federal Government and far more Statist policies designed to help the business class (or, as they were known at the time, the "Manufacturer" class.) Whigs sought to promote American business interests by using the power of the Federal Government to advance such policies that they believed would accomplish this. They believed in protecting American products from foreign competition through high tariffs that put foreign wares at a price disadvantage to domestically produced goods. They preferred a growth-oriented monetary policy set by the type of government sanctioned Central Bank (the Bank of the United States) that their arch-rival, Andrew Jackson, had destroyed as an anti-democratic tool of rich and powerful elites. They advocated the Federal Government financing what Henry Clay called the "American System," which was a vigorous mercantilist economic program of "internal improvements" to build canals, roads, and railroads, funded by the sale of public land. The Whigs promoted public schools, private colleges, charities, and cultural institutions. Most important of all, they wanted to preserve the Bank of the United States. Those who favored the Jeffersonian model of a small, agrarian republic bristled at what they viewed as a push toward a more powerful central government which, along with a Central Bank the elites would control, they saw as a threat by a powerful class of rich businessmen-aristocrats who were dedicated to subverting the ideals of the democratic Republic founded in 1776. Whigs proposed a counter-vision based in the Hamiltonian/Federalist desire to tie banks, industrial interests and taxpayer-funded public works required to build the infrastructure to support them by deepening the ties between business and the Federal Government. The party generally split along sectional lines as the Civil War drew closer until many of the Northern Whigs, who hated those Whigs that sought conciliation with the South in the name of good business, formed a new party—The Republican Party—in 1854 consisting of Northern Whig businessmen, abolitionists and other reform minded modernizers.

The Northern victory in the Civil War crushed their Democrat Party rivals and opened the way for 50 years of almost uninterrupted Republican Party dominance. During that time Republicans relentlessly pushed through their program of industrializing and "modernizing" America. Of course, the backlash against the excesses of this industrialization and the social disruption the modernization process entailed, eventually resulted in very serious workers' riots (such as occurred throughout the country in 1877.) Worker and Farmer discontent with a central government that was too weak to control Big Business, moved to form the Populist Party, which embraced the radical socialist and neo-socialist attempts to "reform" the power of "Big Business" that were gaining popularity among radicals in Europe. The Republicans reacted by pointing out just how dangerously radical many "Populist" ideas were and assured the public that Democrat / Populist schemes to use the government to enforce "progressive" social and economic policies would result not only in economic disaster but would also result in a dangerous loss of the individual freedom that was considered absolutely basic to the American way of life. Hence, the Republican Party used the defense of "small government" opposing Democrat-Populist advocacy of "big government" as an excuse for continuing to support the interests of Big Business; any government big enough to enact "progressive" policies was a threat to the Big Business interests that depended on a compliant government largely in their employ, which existed to serve and be controlled by the business interests that largely owned it. The problem for the Plutocrats was absolutely not a problem with government; it was with a government that wasn't the sycophantic puppet of the Business Elite. They understood well the animus and distrust Americans had for a strong central government and they used this animus and distrust to fight those in the Democrat Party who sought a strong central government to serve *their own* interests, using it to buy the votes of the masses as well as seducing them with socialist egalitarian economic fantasies and promoting class warfare.

Both the Democrat Party and Big Business Republicans favor a strong central government for their own reasons; the former to finance and enforce the social revolution that justifies the need for the bureaucratic power required to control it and dole out its benefits at the taxpayer's expense to its supporters, and the latter so that it can use the government's coercive power to destroy competition, increase their profits and preserve their dominant position in society.

While neither wants a small government, the Big Business Republicans have a vested interest in maintaining the fiction that they do. This is why the Democrat Party, born of a Jeffersonian desire for small government that allowed independent citizens a maximum of freedom from government interference and the Republican Party, who's ancestry lies in a Federalist / Hamiltonian / Whig desire for Statist intervention on behalf of a quasi-aristocratic Plutocracy composed of "manufacturers," switched places in modern times to become the advocates for the exact opposite of what they originally stood for! While the problems connected with the Democratic switch are manifold and extraordinarily dangerous, the legacy of Big Business control of the Republican Party and their desire to control it through RINO "moderates" is perhaps even worse because it is not as open about its own anti-Liberty agenda as the Democrat Party.

TEDDY ROOSEVELT AND THE NEW NATIONALISM

There is much to admire about Theodore Roosevelt: his vitality, his patriotism, his courage, his fortitude, his concern for protecting the natural environment and his devotion to the idea that all Americans deserve a "Square Deal" regardless of their class status. However, there is a dark side to Roosevelt which fully emerged after his term as president, a period during which he identified with the so-called "Progressive Movement" that influenced the direction of both the Democrats and Republican parties. This Movement sought to contain the abuses of Big Business caused by their long hold on the levers of political power after the Civil War, and was aided by reform-minded intellectuals who were heavily influenced, as they are today, by the ideas of European Socialism and Marxism, which they saw as the key to a more egalitarian future society. These groups sought to expand governmental power and use it to limit the power of the rich as well as ameliorate the bad conditions suffered by the poor when the Industrial Revolution came to the United States in the post-Civil War period.

The Democrats responded to this "Populist / Progressive" movement with Woodrow Wilson's seeking to co-opt it with his "New Freedom" program, which claimed it was going to bring about a "second emancipation" of the workers and farmers from the clutches of corporations and trusts just as the "first emancipation" freed the slaves from the slave owners. Populist Democrats sought to move away from their individualist Jeffersonian roots and become the Party of activist big government working on behalf of farmers, workers, the dispossessed and the powerless (that is, as long as they were White.) Wilson said: "…there is one principle of Jefferson's which no longer can obtain in the practical politics of America. You know that it was Jefferson who said that the best government is that which does as little governing as possible… but that time has passed. America is not now and cannot in the future be a place for unrestricted individual enterprise."

Teddy Roosevelt had a slightly different view. He was so concerned that his hand-picked successor, William Howard Taft, had abandoned his policies of vigorously using government power to intervene with what Roosevelt saw as excesses of Plutocratic influence and power as well as the pervasive lawless violence caused by radicals in the Labor Movement, that he decided to seek the nomination of the newly formed Progressive Party to run for president in 1912 in order to prevent the Democrats from seizing the issue for themselves. Roosevelt was the advocate of what might be called "the Omnicompetent State," which would guarantee new social benefits to the American people but would also make new demands for sacrifice that would impinge on traditional American concerns for their individual liberties. He saw government as the square-dealing arbiter between the Corporations and the Workers. While he would use government power to protect workers from Corporate attempts to pay subsistence wages and prevent the formation of unions, he also strongly maintained that he would not allow the kind of riot, disorder and possible socialist revolution that threatened the country in the late 19th century, which saw widespread industrial violence across the nation. He would protect the owner's right to their profits, but insisted they "deal fairly" with the just demands of those who worked for them. In essence *he, and the government he ran*, would make sure that in the class war between Capital and Labor, the national interest—as *he* saw and defined it—would take priority. Roosevelt would protect the Nation from both radical Jacobin demagogues in the Labor Movement as well as reactionary Conservatives in the Republican Party, which he saw as heirs to the pro-Confederacy "Cotton-Whigs" who cared more about their private profits than those "true Republicans" that followed Lincoln and joined him in giving priority to the national interest of maintaining the Union.

Roosevelt's ideas were most influenced by the American social philosopher, Herbert Croly. In Croly's 1909 book, "The Promise of American Life", we find the ideas that made up those which Roosevelt supported in speech after speech when discussing his "New Nationalism" ideology. Croly believed that Jefferson was a panderer to the masses. He felt Jefferson was wrong to advocate a government of and by the people when he should have advocated, according to Croly, "*a government for the people by popular but responsible leaders*". He went further to contend that the worst mistake Jeffersonian political philosophy made was that it supposed that "the people were to guide their leaders, not their leaders the people." He castigated Jefferson and Jackson's concern for individual rights as fetishism that held back reform and modernism; Lincoln, according to this view, instead correctly used the power of government to rally the country to a sense of its responsibilities, regardless of how implementing this view trampled on the rights of private citizens or individual states. Croly saw the Civil War as a great opportunity to end provincialism and outdated concepts of individualism so that it could be replaced with a *national* purpose run by a much more powerful Central Government, but was stymied by the subsequent class warfare that ensued in the industrialization process that swept through society after the war ended.

This was the essence of Teddy Roosevelt's "New Nationalism"—using the power of government in a way that was not accepted by those corporate interests who championed (at least in principle) the idea of a small government that didn't interfere in private enterprise. Plutocrats were very happy to have a compliant government just strong enough to do their bidding but not one strong enough to regulate their business or class interests. Roosevelt disagreed. He said that "The man who wrongly holds that every human right is secondary to his profit must now give way to the advocate of human welfare, who rightly maintains that every man holds his property subject to the general right of the community to regulate its use to whatever degree the public welfare may require it." TR believed that "social efficiency" required society to have the "*capacity to subordinate the interests of the individual to the interests of the community.*"

Roosevelt's philosophy of the "New Nationalism" sought to use governmental power to enforce his own concept of class stability in the service of national goals set by... him. He was alarmed by the power of both Business and Labor; he feared Jeffersonian individualism almost as much as he feared socialist revolution; he had great faith in a strong, centralized, "omni-competent" State and saw nothing wrong with building a personality cult around the Presidency to increase the Chief Executive's popular power to enforce his will over and against the individual States, the Congress, the Courts, the Trusts, the Unions and, of course, those individuals that dissented from this Statist policy, especially in the Press. One does not have to be an alarmist to see just how dangerously close this view of government is to the Corporatist politics of the later 20th century phenomenon of Fascism as practiced in Italy or Germany as well as in the United States by Theodore's cousin Franklin Roosevelt and his "New Deal". This view was diametrically opposed to the entire history of Ordered Liberty and limited government in the USA, but was also a direct threat to the Plutocracy's manipulation of government power to achieve its own ends. Classical Jeffersonian Liberals were horrified by the movement, which caused them to become increasingly identified *not* as "classical liberals" but as "Conservatives" trying to maintain the pre-existing economic and social status quo in favor of individual achievement without government interference. They viewed Roosevelt as a "Tammany Nietzsche" whose hyper egoism and intemperate will to power rendered him incapable of drawing a distinction between himself and the nation he governed. The supporters of Taft were therefore rather clumsily cast as the "conservatives" in the 1912 election running against progressives in both the Democrat and Progressive Parties (The Progressives were also known as "The Bull Moose" Party, so named after Roosevelt's assessment of how healthy he was to run—"I'm as healthy as a bull moose!")

For what would later become an almost regular RINO occurrence, Teddy Roosevelt split the Republican vote, receiving so many votes that might have gone to the uncharismatic Taft that he caused Wilson to win thanks to the ideological split between the former Republican running mates. But TR's philosophy found a home in the "moderate" wing of the Republican Party and lived on long past his defeat in 1912. The "New Nationalism" was nationalist in that it maintained the right to control business in the name of the greater good of the nation over the individual and his private property and needed to greatly expand governmental power to do so. Again, as proved to be true later in the 20th century in Europe, this mixture of big government policy combining nationalism and socialism—especially in Germany and Italy—made for a toxic, deadly cocktail of tyranny capable of crimes beyond the imagining of those who thought such power could be directed towards regulating society for the better during the turn of the century.

Minor rhetorical differences aside, the policies favored by Wilson and Roosevelt differed very little from each other. Both believed in the power of Big Government to affect positive change. Both were imperialistic in foreign policy seeing war as an edifying, glorious experience that was necessary for a vibrant, virile society to advance and win in the worldwide Darwinian struggle of "survival of the fittest" (which was not, in fact, a phrase coined by Darwin but by the philosopher Herbert Spencer). Both believed that if so empowered the State could create a new, fair, egalitarian society on earth such as the one traditional religion promised to create but never delivered on and therefore deferred to the afterlife. Both chafed under the restrictions placed on the State by constitutional checks and balances and saw it as an outdated impediment to the fulfillment of their utopian plans to re-make society. Wilson mocked concern for constitutional checks and balances as "Fourth of July sentiments" and believed in a Darwinian "evolution" of the Constitution whose interpretation should reflect the changes in society and not be interpreted for all time strictly as it was written. This was the genesis of the idea of the Constitution as being a "living document" subject to radical and far-reaching "interpretation" to the extent of discovering constitutional "rights" in it that are not even mentioned, found only in the "light" of living in the more tolerant sunshine of the modern world. Roosevelt had a similar disdain for constitutional limits on the power of the State, which he saw as "lagging behind" the reality of modern society and over concerned with individual rights over "popular" or the Public's "rights"… as defined by Teddy Roosevelt.

Both Democrats and Progressives encouraged personality cults to be built around Wilson and especially around TR. Both Democrats and Progressives hated the idea of the increasingly materialistic, money worshipping America being established by the Plutocrats who owned the Trusts and Corporations, which was driving the country to the kind of violent class warfare that often erupted in the period lasting from the late 1870s through the early 1900s.

Thus was born the Duopoly, which perpetually passed power from one Party to the other in order to supposedly reign in the plutocratic elites but was, in actuality, an instrumentality that served it.

While Roosevelt represented the more masculine version of the two, demanding people take up the burdens of the "strenuous life" required by an aggressive Nationalist government, Wilson represented the social reformers who sought to alleviate society's problems by handing them over to maternal "nanny state" socialistic "experts"—social workers, reformers and government bureaucrats for resolution. This mix of nationalism and progressive reform sank deep into both parties and re-emerged in much stronger forms later in the 20th Century; as the increasingly more open socialism of the New Deal among the Democrats and as the RINO "progressive moderates" centered in the Eastern Establishment of the GOP.

HERBERT HOOVER

After two Republican administrations tried to return America to Limited Government "normalcy" after the First World War, a third Republican president was elected in 1928.

Despite the mythology, Herbert Hoover was no paladin of laissez-faire economics. While the causes of the Great Depression are beyond the scope of this work, it is interesting to note that Hoover, a man closely associated with championing small government and "Rugged Individualism," massively interfered in the economy in an attempt to deal with the Depression's effects. All sorts of "emergency" measures—from the bolstering of wage rates and the imposition of price controls, to the expansion of credit and the propping up of weak firms as well as a sharp increase in government spending (e.g., unemployment subsidies and public works) were all taken up by Hoover in his attempt to end the Depression through governmental action rather than let the economy take its natural course and allow it to self-correct as it had *always* done in the past. Throughout his career, from his work as a food administrator in WWI, wielding autocratic power over his bureaucratic fiefdom as well as his tenure as Secretary of Commerce under Harding and Coolidge, Hoover favored a corporate state system of forming cartels in both industry and agriculture which would be controlled and coordinated by the Federal Government. They would also provide the coercive power required to enforce the compliance of its dictates to private enterprise.

It is therefore no surprise—except to those who have been fed the mythology of the Hoover Administration as one dedicated to "Rugged Individualism" and "hands-off" laissez faire economics—that Hoover advocated all sorts of Statist interventions to try to resolve the crisis. Hoover used every measure later taken to even further extremes during the New Deal: wage controls, public works, unemployment relief, inflationary monetary policy, large federal loans to shaky businesses and farm price support programs. He insanely supported a tax hike during a severe depression and also kicked off a mutually fratricidal international trade war by supporting the Smoot Hartley Tariff. As is routinely the case of Government interference in the natural processes of a free economy, it not only failed, it made matters *much* worse. Capitalist economies found in societies structured on Ordered Liberty succeed because they naturally reflect the free human beings that compose them.

Terrible as they are, recessions and depressions are the results of the bad economic decisions and poor investments made by fallible individual human beings. There were depressions in the United States before 1929; left alone by the Federal Government, they all righted themselves in a short period of time. However the large amount of interference in the economy by Hoover only exacerbated the problem; the even more massive interference of the New Deal under Franklin Roosevelt kept the economy in Depression *for almost 10 years*, the longest time the country ever spent in severe economic depression. Only WWII pulled the country out of its economic woes and victory in that war—which saw all our competitors bankrupted and our enemies destroyed—established a post-war prosperity that America rode for decades. But the Statist poison had reached deep not only into the American economy but into the American psyche as well.

Both political parties accepted the New Deal as permanent and Republican politicians were apparently more than content not to upset what they saw as a governmental applecart that supported their petty political re-election concerns. By being faithful junior partners with the so-called "opposition" party and using abundant taxpayer dollars tossed to them by the Democrats to bribe the voters back home with governmental largess—as well as provide access to government spending programs to the corporate sponsors that financed their campaigns—they could ensure themselves almost eternal re-election. Sure they paid lip service to Capitalism and Individualism, but in practice Teddy Roosevelt's "New Nationalism" evolved into a barely concealed desire to use the power of government to pay back those whose political contributions were essential to Republican (and Democrat) election. The Duopoly thus became an all but permanent feature of the American political system. In the end, it was the Corporate State Plutocracy—and to a lesser extent, Big Labor—that most benefited by the concentration of power in Washington. Formerly, the Plutocrats controlled a government they preferred be relatively weak so as not to threaten their interests; now, by pulling the strings of the politicians with their hands on the levers of power, they controlled a massively powerful central government that did their bidding much more effectively by hiding behind a mask of egalitarianism, fairness, equality and a desire to promote "social justice," all found in the socialist and neo-socialist rhetorical bromides uttered by their tethered creatures and puppets in both parties.

THE FAILED COUNTER-REVOLT OF ROBERT TAFT

Robert Taft, the son of Teddy Roosevelt's successor, William Howard Taft, was the senator from Ohio from 1939 to 1953 and was considered the leading voice of conservatism in the Republican Party, who, like many Americans prior to the attack on Pearl Harbor with sour memories of our intervention into WWI, opposed further U.S. intervention in European affairs. He was opposed by the so-called more "moderate progressive" wing of the Republican Party, which both opposed what has become known as foreign policy "Isolationism" and embraced a more "Interventionist" policy for the United States in the world (especially in Europe.) "Moderate" Republicans were also favorable to a solution provided by a much larger, much more powerful, socially intrusive central government at the expense of the individual states regarding issues concerning economic and social justice. Following the tradition of Theodore Roosevelt, these progressives included people like Wendell Willkie, a corporate executive who was a former Democrat and Tom Dewey, the moderate Republican governor of New York. In 1940, the "moderate" Willkie lost to FDR, as did the "moderate" Dewey in 1944. Dewey, who was opposed by Taft in the quest for the1948 Republican nomination, was subsequently defeated again that year by Harry Truman in a race most thought Dewey would win. Taft was a strong opponent of the New Deal and many liberal Republicans opposed his run for the presidency in 1952 as strongly as conservatives looking to roll back 20 years of Democrat policy supported him. Given the Republican Party's penchant for nominating those "whose turn had come" Taft was viewed by many observers as the front runner for the nomination.

However, Liberal Republicans were more than comfortable with the Statist policies of the New Deal and were quite satisfied with the gigantic government that had grown up during WWII and the early Cold War. Whether it was due to access to lucrative government contracts or a desire to see the "progressive" social views of the country-club crowd they ran with prevail, "moderate" Republicans were desperate for an alternative to what they saw as a reversion to the "Neanderthal" conservative policies favored by Taft. They found their candidate in the highly popular WWII general Dwight Eisenhower. Having not even indicated his party affiliation as late as 1951, Eisenhower was courted by both Democrats and moderate Republicans. The moderate wing of the Republican Party, led by prominent liberals including Senator Henry Cabot Lodge and N.Y. Governor Tom Dewey convinced him to run as a Republican. Their rationale to the Party faithful was that a war hero like Eisenhower was far more electable than the bland, uncharismatic Taft. Further, with the Cold War threatening in Europe and the Korean War raging in Asia, Eisenhower's military expertise and interventionist stance of containing the spread of Communism overseas were far more in tune with the times than Taft's neo-isolationism.

Ike announced that he would accept the Republican nomination if offered to him on March 12, 1952 and his battle with Taft for the GOP nomination was very close and very nasty. It opened with Ike and Taft running neck and neck for delegate votes, but the Eisenhower forces were able to out-maneuver those supporting Taft and Ike was nominated. So divisive was the convention that many felt Eisenhower's election might be threatened if Taft supporters sat on their hands. Meeting personally in September 1952, Eisenhower and Taft worked out an agreement to gain Taft's support by promising him that he would cut federal spending and fight "creeping socialism in every domestic field."

Eisenhower followed what by today's standards would certainly be considered a moderate, Establishment Republican course. During his administration he funded massive federal spending programs such as the Interstate Highway System (which he presented as a national security measure) and appointed liberal judges to the Supreme Court including the ultra-liberal Republican Earl Warren, Potter Stewart and the radical William J. Brennan. He was not opposed to using Federal power to enforce Supreme Court decisions at the expense of the individual states. Most importantly, he continued and even augmented all the major New Deal programs of FDR including the creation of a massive bureaucracy, the Department of Health Education and Welfare, as well as pushing for the extension of Social Security benefits to an additional 10-million workers. While Eisenhower was certainly no liberal in the current-day sense, he was also certainly no conservative. He was quite comfortable with Big Government policies. His Vice President, Richard Nixon, was even *more* of a Statist, Corporate Republican, than Ike himself. The success of Eisenhower convinced moderate Republicans, as well as the liberal Eastern Establishment that supported and controlled them, that they had found the winning formula. Just as the Plutocracy allowed the Democrats to don the disguise of a "liberal, socially conscious progressive reformer," a Republican could put on the mask of a Conservative when running for office. When the election was over, they simply removed the mask and governed as liberal Corporatists once they were in power. They doled out government contracts at the taxpayer's expense to their corporate and banker owners in the Eastern Establishment in return for ample campaign contributions; then repeated the process using fear tactics during the next election cycle.

But they didn't count on a backlash of disgust and anger from the overwhelming majority of average Republicans who comprised their Conservative

Base, who they disdained and looked down on as unsophisticated, benighted sheep to be sheared for taxes and votes and then discarded. And they didn't count on them finding someone like Barry Goldwater to represent them.

THE GOLDEN AGE OF THE DUOPOLY

Republican capitulation to New Deal domestic polices during the 1950s and early 1960s was total. After all, the mainstream New Deal consensus agreed with literary critic Lionel Trilling who echoed the thoughts of many politicians and intellectuals when, writing in 1950, he noted "in the United States at this time liberalism is not only the dominant but even the sole intellectual tradition.... It is the plain fact there are no conservative or reactionary ideas in general circulation" but only "irritable mental gestures which seem to resemble ideas." The historian Richard Hofstadter agreed with Trilling, portraying Conservatives as cranky, angry reactionaries who were people, as the *Washington Post* put it, that "complain about the twentieth century" and irrationally sought to repeal it. Such types were not to be taken seriously and, faced with this reality, the Republican Conservative Base found itself firmly under the control of go-along-to-get-along Republicans In Name Only (RINOs—or as Eisenhower called it "Modern Republicanism") who ushered in a golden era of bi-partisanship. In basic agreement that "Isolationism" was a dangerous foreign policy, both Republicans and Democrats recognized the Cold War required a vigilant and active policy to contain the danger of Communist Imperialism. Democrat Cold Warriors such as Truman, John Stennis and John F. Kennedy were often even more anti-Communist than were many Republicans. Both Parties agreed that Statist intervention in both economic and social policy was the key to a stable and prosperous society. "Moderate" Republicans coalesced around not only Eisenhower, but around those RINOs who provided the intellectual basis of his polices. These were found, not surprisingly, in the Eastern Establishment located in New York City and Washington DC and they were led by Nelson Rockefeller.

The Rockefellers were the financial and social scions of the Eastern Establishment. They were not only ultra-rich, with mega-fortunes tied up in Standard Oil (long ago re-named "ESSO" and later "EXXON" in a clever but dishonest public relations attempt to put some distance between the company and the Robber Baron reputation it acquired when it was known as "Standard

Oil") and in the powerful international bank, Chase Manhattan. Moderate "Rockefeller Republicans" supported all the Statist policies that grew up in the shade of the New Deal and WWII including expanding social welfare programs, Federal Civil Rights legislation, high rates of taxation and public works spending (especially those concerned with highway expansion and other infrastructure projects.) The only difference between Rockefeller Republicans and their so-called rivals in the Democrat Party was that the RINOs maintained they, as people with stronger business backgrounds, would be able to administer the Government Leviathan more efficiently than Democrats. They had no problem keeping "good" New Deal measures—as long as they were run "efficiently." RINOs paid lip service to Ordered Liberty and they pretended to have more respect for States Rights and private enterprise than Democrats, but recognized that the New Deal—and all the bureaucratic meddling it represented—was to be permanent. Combined with a vigorous Interventionist foreign policy that they justified as a requirement for the "containment" of Communism, RINOs insisted that this was the *key* to the electoral success that was denied them during their years in the wilderness under FDR and Truman.

But the level of sacrifice required for the Eisenhower era was high since it caused the Republican Party to basically make itself a virtually irrelevant afterthought to Democrat/Liberal ideology. In the name of getting elected, the RINOs became "Democrat Light," which was a confection that usually resulted in minority status, given that the voters could get the undiluted version by pulling the lever for their Democrat opponents.

Disgusted with the complete abandonment of any type of Conservative agenda worthy of the name, something of an intellectual rebellion broke out in various precincts on the Right. In 1955 William F. Buckley launched a small but influential periodical called *National Review*. Rebelling against the idea that Conservative thought was an irrelevant anachronism, Buckley shed the Old Right's addiction to isolationism and embraced the concept that the cause of Ordered Liberty and a stable world order depended on a militarily powerful United States capable of intervening in the Cold War in order to respond to Soviet aggression. Conservatives despised the fact that the RINOs had created a role for the Republicans that left them in permanent minority party status where they meekly rubber-stamped the New Deal Democrat conception of an increasingly powerful central government. Buckley's *National Review* roundly rejected what it found to be the morally repugnant RINO dedication to "moderation" for its own sake at the cost of all political principle... as well as any meaningful political influence on major issues. In an effort to build a respectable intellectual base for modern Conservatism, Buckley waged a vigorous campaign to purge the Right of its fringe elements including isolationists, anti-Semites, extreme Nativists and conspiracy theorists. Buckley's magazine effectively promoted Conservative ideas that challenged both Liberal Orthodoxy and the "well-fed" RINOs who feasted on the political crumbs it was thrown by it. Within a few years, it became one of the most important intellectual voices of the new Conservative movement it helped to birth.

Although no Conservative, the philosopher and novelist, Ayn Rand was largely responsible for another strong intellectual current that Rand herself, ironically, rejected: Libertarianism. The Libertarian movement was dedicated to as small a government as possible. Although some of the more exotic libertarian theories postulated a form of "anarcho-Capitalism" in which *all* functions of the state, including the army, police and courts, were privatized, most libertarians accepted Rand's definition of the proper role of government. Rand herself rejected both Conservatives—who she condemned as basically flawed because they accepted altruistic morality based in religious doctrines that she thought irrational—and Libertarians, whom she thought were irresponsible intellectual "hippies" advocating impossible free-market utopias built on pure voluntary association. However, what brought Rand and the large numbers of Libertarians and Conservatives she influenced together through novels such as "Atlas Shrugged" published in 1957, was the desire to limit government's role in society to that of a "negatively regulative" force; that is, it should regulate only those things which required the legitimate use of force or state coercion. These functions would include providing armed forces to protect society against foreign invaders, a police force to protect society against criminals, and a court system to adjudicate legitimate differences between law abiding citizens. But when the government became "positively regulative" it engaged in trying to regulate functions for the betterment of society. These would include public welfare, public education, socialized medicine and all the other myriad social engineering policies associated with the Welfare State. Rand maintained that when government was given the power to engage in "positively regulative" functions it not only produced counter-productive results and exacerbated the problems it was trying to solve, but also was dangerously corrupted by the power it was granted. Such corruption inevitably led it to become more and more oppressive in the pursuit of its goals, always maintaining that it was acting in the name of some greater collective good—the Race, the Workers, the

71

Environment… *The People*—when in actuality it was increasing its power to engage in tyranny over individual citizens. To Rand, the principle of individual rights was paramount. Like the Conservatives she routinely criticized for not being the "radicals for Capitalism" she maintained it was necessary to be in order to defeat Statism, she understood that the Constitution is a limitation of *government*, not private individuals; that it was not a charter for governmental power but *a bulwark for the protection of citizens' rights against the power of the State*. Rand saw the free market—as exemplified by laissez-faire capitalism—as the best system for opposing the creation of the kind of collectivist dictatorships which blossomed like poisonous weeds around the world during the 20th Century… and which took root in the United States in the form of the New Deal programs supported by both Democrats and RINOs.

This outlook, which was supported by free-market economists such as Milton Friedman and Friedrich Hayek, who further influenced the conservative intellectual revolt against the power of the Welfare State which was, by the mid-1950s, almost unchallenged among "mainstream" intellectuals in Academia and Government. Libertarians differed from Conservatives in that they rejected the need for religion and traditional values to form a stable society. Rejecting all power by government as interfering with non-violent individual action, they had no problem with such issues as atheism (Rand herself was an atheist), personal life-styles and sexuality, prostitution, private drug use or naturally occurring monopolies. More controversially, more radical Libertarians even rejected the modern Conservative impulse to oppose Communism through a policy of military and economic containment as one that fed an unhealthy growth of State power. These libertarians, such as the economist Murray Rothbard, favored a return to the Isolationist policies of the pre-WWII "Old Right" rather than a continuation of the "Welfare-Warfare" state and its attendant Military-Industrial complex. However, their strong support for low tax rates and restricted government spending was extremely influential on what became known as "fiscal conservatism," with its strong support of Free Market solutions to problems, eschewing governmental intervention and all the negative baggage associated with it.

These intellectual forces came together in the early 1960s to threaten to dethrone the power of the Eastern Establishment represented by RINOs then known as "Rockefeller Republicans," after their titular leader, Nelson Rockefeller. Rockefeller Republicanism was the personification of the idea that both Democrats and RINOS all believed in: that *all* problems could be solved by a disinterested application of managerial expertise backed by the coercive power of big government. In foreign policy, Rockefeller Republicanism accepted every aspect of the Cold War paradigm that Harry Truman, John F. Kennedy and Lyndon Johnson did, including the need for a containment policy backed by military intervention, mutually assured destruction (M.A.D.) massive foreign aid and an almost mystical belief in the power of the United Nations to resolve international problems. It is the reason behind the Chimera of a rivalry between the two parties and it is why governmental policy usually results in a growth of government and a reduction in individual Liberty no matter what Party is in charge of administering the government.

Though nowhere near the level of financial and institutional power of the Eastern Establishment, a counter-force of nouveau-riche forces, mostly based in the Southwest, decided to commit their resources to supporting the forces stirred by the intellectual Conservative counter-revolution. These forces were much closer philosophically and politically to the values held by the numerically superior Conservative Base because the counter-revolutionaries themselves were not generations removed from the Middle Class as were the Plutocrats led by Rockefeller. Instead they tended not to be scions of corporate wealth but rather very successful small businessmen who struck it rich. One such was Holmes Tuttle, who owned a series of Ford dealerships in California and Arizona. Others included publisher Henry Regnery, land developer William A. Wilson and Justin Dart, of Dart Industries and Kraft, Inc. This was a class based on those who had acquired wealth in the oil, natural gas and aviation industry as well as those industries serving the requirements of the WWII and Cold War military effort based in the South and West centered in Texas and southern California. The emergence of this group made it possible for those in the Conservative Base whose values were long ignored and marginalized by the RINO elites to make itself felt in the political nomination process instead of simply being required to rubber-stamp the choices made by that elite, which was looked on as increasingly out of touch with the majority of the Party and, in fact, as traitors working in the service of the other side. The Conservative intellectuals and their financial backers detected deep flaws in the Trilling-Hofstadter analysis that dismissed their movement as part of the "kook fringe." By the early 60s a strong base of support for the Conservative Resurgence was growing in the Southwest. The Old Money Eastern Establishment which, through its wealth and influence, controlled the financial institutions, the large foundations, the most influential print and broadcast media and Ivy League academia that had dominated the Republican Party for almost its entire existence, was facing a popular revolt on the Right fueled by new ideas and new money. Growing numbers of businessmen and politicians, who became rich during the economic expansion after WWII, wanted to exert greater influence in national politics and were prepared to spend money to fight for it.

The very nature of the Eastern Establishment: Ivy League, cosmopolitan, Anglophile, very liberal, internationalist, possessed of a sense of noblesse oblige regarding their patronage of the arts, made them anathema to the Conservative Base of the Republican Party which was overwhelmingly middle-class, chiefly small town, Mid- and South-Western and who provided Republicans with electoral victories. But the Base found it almost impossible to nominate those who identified with its value set, especially on the presidential level, because the financial power required to secure nomination to national office was largely owned by an Eastern Establishment centered on Wall Street. The core, base support for the Republican Party has always come from the middle classes, while that of the Democratic Party found its base of support in organized labor, the intellectual elites the very poor and the very rich. In general, aristocrats have tended to move toward the Democrats, while semi-aristocrats, such as those nouveau-riche businessmen who backed the Conservative Resurgence, often remained Republican. With their affinity for the traditional middle class values of free enterprise, anti-Communism, and the primacy of the individual against the state (that is, Ordered Liberty) Conservatives began to band together around candidates who would form a variety of challenges to the stale ideas and political collaborationism of the RINOs with the Democrat power structure in Government, Media and Academia.

Rightly fearing that the growing power of the Conservative Movement was influencing the far more numerous Conservative Base of the Republican Party, the RINOs realized that those numbers could trump the financial and institutional influence held by the tiny group at the top of the Republican Party pyramid. Therefore, a counterattack was deemed to be in order. The Conservative Resurgence was portrayed as wild-eyed, fanatic and reactionary. It was tarred as part of a dangerous trend which fueled hatred and social division. The charge of "extremism" in both domestic and foreign affairs (which bizarrely included the idea that President Kennedy was killed by a cabal of "rightwing" conspirators even though his assassin was an open Marxist-Leninist) was the basis of the RINO response to the Conservative Resurgence and it would later find its first major target in the form of the symbol of that resurgence: Senator Barry Goldwater; but he would not be the last.

1964: FINDING VICTORY IN DEFEAT

So dangerous to the RINOs was the Conservative Resurgence that their leader, Governor Nelson Rockefeller of New York, led the charge against it by seeking to deny the Resurgence candidate, Senator Barry Goldwater, the 1964 Presidential nomination and secure it for himself. But Rockefeller faced two difficult hurdles, one personal the other political.

The personal problem was that Rockefeller, recently divorced, in May 1963 married his mistress of 5 years, Margarita "Happy" Murphy. While this situation appears morally innocuous by today's more lax standards, at the time this resulted in a public scandal that was exacerbated by the fact that Murphy surrendered custody of her four children by her first marriage. Rockefeller's divorce and re-marriage outraged a public morality still steeped in the bland, morally conventional, bourgeois ethos of the pre-1960s, especially in the Republican Base that was already disgusted with the arrogant RINO dominance of their Party, which sneered at them from their intellectual salons and country clubs. Although his poll numbers plummeted, Rockefeller forged ahead in his quest for the Republican nomination and tried to stir up the heat regarding his problems with the Conservative Base as one anchored in his RINO corporatist opposition to what they termed "extremism." Led by Rockefeller, the RINOs put all their considerable money and influence at work to portray Goldwater, with his support for tough Cold War policies against the Soviets that favored military strength over diplomatic accommodation, his call for low taxes and a rollback of New Deal social engineering programs including Social Security, as a "reactionary kook." Further, Goldwater championed respect for States Rights. His views became the symbol of all that was "extremist" and "out of date" to the Rockefeller wing of the Party. Goldwater was excoriated by the RINOs as reckless, dangerous and out of touch not just with modern times but with reality itself. Rockefeller summed up his thoughts about the Conservative Resurgence when he stated "Americans will not and should not respond to a political creed that cherishes the past solely because it offers an excuse for shutting out the hard facts and difficult tasks of the

THE SEVENTH CRISIS

present." Goldwater had an answer for this argument. What he wrote in the introduction to his book "The Conscience of a Conservative" would also serve as a rejection of arguments made by current-day RINOS, who today make the same case Rockefeller made in 1964:

> "The charge is preposterous and we ought boldly to say so. The laws of God, and of nature, have no dateline. The principles on which the Conservative political position is based … are derived from the nature of man, and from the truths that God has revealed about His creation. Circumstances do change. So do the problems that are shaped by circumstances. But the principles that govern the solution to the problems do not. To suggest that the Conservative philosophy is out of date is akin to saying that the Golden Rule, or the Ten Commandments or Aristotle's Politics are out of date."

Realizing that RINO control over the Party was in deep trouble, Rockefeller well understood that if he lost the nomination to Goldwater, their only salvation lay in a Republican defeat in 1964. As has become standard operating procedure for RINO subversives to this day (as recently demonstrated by RINOS in the so-called "Never Trump" movement in the 2016 and 2020 election… and beyond) Rockefeller worked hard to lay the groundwork for his party's defeat at the 1964 Republican Convention. He relentlessly bashed Goldwater during the primaries by indicating he was a reckless extremist who didn't have the temperament to be President. The Eastern Establishment went all out in its determined and highly expensive negative campaign to defeat Goldwater. Campaign literature caricatured Goldwater as a mad-bomber who couldn't be trusted with his finger on the nuclear button. Outraged by these tactics, the Conservatives responded by contrasting Goldwater as a family man and Rockefeller as a middle-aged philander. It was a viscous campaign that left both sides looking for blood by the time they got to the convention, where Rockefeller delivered a blistering attack on the forces of the Conservative insurgents that supported Goldwater and were seeking to overthrow RINO domination. With Goldwater forces drowning out his supporters with boos and catcalls, Rockefeller all but declared war on the Conservatives:

"During this year I have crisscrossed this nation, fighting ... to keep the Republican party the party of all the people ... and warning of the extremist threat, its danger to the party, and danger to the nation... These extremists feed on fear, hate and terror; they have no program for America and the Republican Party... [they] operate from dark shadows of secrecy. It is essential that this convention repudiate here and now any doctrinaire, militant minority whether Communist, Ku Klux Klan or Birchers."

Having been slanderously compared to both Communists and Fascists, the Base went berserk with anti-Rockefeller animus. It led Goldwater to ride the wave of anti-Establishment feeling at the Convention to the nomination, but it also led to his greatest mistake. Wearing RINO antipathy as a badge of honor, Goldwater crossed the Rubicon on the "extremist" issue when he all but embraced it by saying "I would remind you that extremism in the defense of liberty is no vice -- and let me remind you also, moderation in pursuit of justice is no virtue." It won him the nomination battle, but it lost him the electoral war.

Lyndon Johnson and the Democrats picked up where Rockefeller left off. Realizing the RINOs had a vested interest in allowing the Conservatives to lose in order to have any hope of regaining control of the Republican Party, Johnson's campaign openly demonized Goldwater. Johnson's campaign echoed all of the Rockefeller attacks on Goldwater and even upped the ante. He was the tool of paranoid Right-wing conspiracy theorist kooks in the John Birch Society; he was a tool of Segregationists and a favorite of the Ku Klux Klan in the South; he would repeal Social Security (actually, Goldwater wanted to make it voluntary); indeed, he would repeal the entire New Deal; he was a tool of Wall Street; he was anti-Labor and was a danger to labor unions; he would exacerbate sectional differences in the country dividing North from South and Urban from Suburban and Rural; he would recklessly inflame the Arms Race; he would get us more deeply involved in Vietnam and, most dangerous of all, his recklessness would lead us into a nuclear war with the USSR. This point was driven home in the infamous "Daisy Girl" campaign commercial which has gone down in history as the most vicious example negative campaigning ever produced, portrayed a little girl picking the petals off a daisy innocently counting them; a few seconds into the commercial a stern, metallic-sounding man's voice is heard counting down a missile launch. The little girl looks skyward and when the count reaches zero a nuclear bomb explodes into a terrifying mushroom cloud.

The commercial only ran once, but that's all it took; Goldwater's image as the man who would start WWIII if elected was indelibly impressed on the national consciousness.

Conditioned by months of negative RINO campaigning stressing exactly this point, the commercial symbolized everything people feared about Goldwater and his policies. Combined with Johnson's happy talk about his *"New"* New Deal—his socialistic "Great Society" domestic program—was his dishonest pledge not to get further involved in Vietnam, which was exactly what he was preparing to do even while making campaign speeches that promised "American boys" would not be sent to fight wars that "Asian boys" should be fighting themselves.

Goldwater and the Republican Party were annihilated in the 1964 elections. They not only lost their bid for the White House, but they also suffered terrible losses in the House and Senate, both of which were dominated by large Democrat majorities as a result. Liberalism reached its highwater mark with the help of RINO subversion. The Conservatives had delivered a catastrophe; the Republican Party was pronounced dead and its obituaries were found in every newspaper, in every magazine and on every TV news program. But, all the obituaries missed an important fact: while the Duopoly was strengthened by the election, it was not the Conservative Base that was dead; *it was the unopposed RINOs domination of the Republican Party that had existed since the 1940s.* The RINOs themselves survived, but realized they could no longer operate openly as Liberals and remain as leaders of the party.

The Republicans were buoyed by Southern Dixiecrats opposed to Johnson's pro-Civil Rights legislation and by conservative working class Democrats in the North who had many problems with Johnson's domestic policy of requiring high taxes to pay for what was viewed as parasitical social welfare by traditional Union members. The result was that the Conservative Base of the Republican Party didn't shrink in the wake of its 1964 debacle, it grew. It had learned a great deal about the dos and don'ts of modern national election campaigns and the power as well as the sham objectivity of the liberal media. For example, while considering the Conservatives in the Republican Party, columnist Drew Pearson said that the "smell of fascism" was in the air; Norman Mailer compared the Republican Convention to a Nazi rally in *Esquire* magazine; *The New York Times* reported that Roy Wilkins of the NAACP said "a man came out of the beer halls of Munich, and rallied the forces of Rightism in Germany; all the same elements are there…"

The Conservative Base grew even further as Johnson's Vietnam War policy was revealed to be the utter disaster it was. Too arrogant and stupid to avoid getting into the war, Johnson and the Cold War liberals around him were too weak and fearful of the political consequences to take the necessary steps required to win it. Many of those families that had traditionally voted Democrat in both the South and in the working class North now saw their sons being shipped off to a no-win war while the children of the elites carried Viet Cong flags at anti-American rallies held on the college campuses that provided them with student deferments. They worried about an economy highly overheated by the massive spending required to pay for Johnson's insane Guns *and* Butter combination of a foreign war and a utopian "Great Society" social welfare program. They rejected the coddling of criminals by a Liberal Supreme Court and a mindset that sought to "understand" crime rather than fight it; they rightly feared what soon became an annual cycle of increasingly deadly urban race riots that no amount of naïve liberal do-good legislation seemed to be able to resolve. Crime rates soared, campus violence became pandemic and the Liberal Era, which appeared so permanent in 1964, melted away like a spring snow. The people wanted a change; the Conservative Base was ready to provide it. But who would carry the banner?

1968: NIXON AND THE CREATION OF THE CONSERVATIVE MASK

An old Cold Warrior, militant anti-Communist and a nasty political infighter, Richard "Tricky Dick" Nixon was despised by the Left. But for all his darkly bombastic rhetoric and scheming personality, Nixon was essentially attached to the Eastern Establishment throughout his term as Eisenhower's Vice President. Nixon had to resolve a problem his previous failed 1960 run for the White House had caused with Conservatives in order to unite the Party behind him; strengthened by the defections of Southern and working class conservative Democrats to the Republican Party during the chaos of the Johnson years, the Base constituted the overwhelming majority of the Party. But the RINOs, though muted, remained in the Leadership positions.

Conservatives had little to trust when dealing with a Machiavellian manipulator like Nixon. Just before the 1960 convention he cut a deal with

Rockefeller after a marathon 8-hour meeting at Rockefeller's apartment in New York City, which became known as the "Compact of 5th Ave," or, as Goldwater termed it, "the Munich of the Republican Party". Desperate not to split the Party as the Conservatives would later do in 1964, the cynically pragmatic Nixon accepted all 14 changes Rockefeller and the RINOs demanded be made to the Republican Platform. Nixon ordered the Platform Committee to comply. Nixon sold his independence through this servile act of appeasement but headed off a challenge by Rockefeller for the nomination and also gained the acceptance of the RINOs who hitherto were as distrustful of him as the Conservatives were. In 1960, he lost in the closest election in American history up to that time to Cold War Democrat John F. Kennedy; he was determined for it not to happen again, no matter who or what he had to traduce in order to be elected. While nominally supporting Goldwater in 1964, Nixon was relatively silent during the campaign. After Goldwater's defeat, Nixon spent much time building up support by campaigning around the country for many local Republican candidates. By 1968, he was the frontrunner for the nomination, certain he had learned all the lessons his previous bitter failures, both in the 1960 Presidential race as well as his disastrous run to become governor of California in 1962, had taught him. Having placated the Left of the Party in 1960 with the Compact, in 1968 he not only surrounded himself with cynical, professional political operatives such as corporate lawyer John Mitchell, but with true-believing Goldwater Conservatives such as speechwriter Patrick Buchanan. He also made a highly important concession insisted on by the Eastern Establishment: he chose Rockefeller's close associate and foreign policy advisor, Henry Kissinger to be his National Security Advisor, though he acted with the powers and portfolios usually reserved for the Secretary of State during Nixon's first term.

Nixon knew he had to get the Conservative Base to support him or he had no chance of victory. He knew that George Wallace, the populist segregationist governor of Alabama was considering an independent run on a third party ticket that would draw enough conservative and blue-collar votes away from him (especially in the critical area of the South) to ensure his defeat despite the anarchy that reigned in the Democrat Party, which was ripped apart by internal disagreements over Vietnam. So, in the riot and war-torn political landscape of 1968, he ran as a law and order Conservative. He would clamp down hard on crime and riots and restore calm to the streets; he indicated that he had a foreign policy plan to win "Peace with Honor" in Vietnam; he would move away from the neo-socialist policies of the "Great Society"; he would "get tough" with the Soviets and Red Chinese; he would return power to the States, which was taken as a go-slow policy on Federal support for Civil Rights issues such as forced bussing and instead foster "Black Capitalism" in urban areas; he would heal the deep divisions in American society and, as he said, "bring us together".

The election was close, but even with Wallace drawing off Conservative votes and carrying much of the South, Nixon was able to hold enough of both RINOS and Conservatives to squeak out a very, very narrow victory (43.4 per cent to 42.7 per cent) over the hapless Democrat candidate, Johnson's syco-phantic Vice President Hubert Humphrey. But the strategy had worked: he had placated *both* wings of his Party.

Four years later, the Conservative mask was not as essential to disguise the Statist face beneath it. Nixon came down hard on domestic terrorism through a vigorous crackdown of questionable legality carried out by the FBI called the "Co-Intellpro" program. Urban riots tapered off. Nixon's new Supreme Court Chief Justice signaled a harder line against crime. Far-reaching arms agreements were concluded with the Soviets; Chinese fears of Soviet attack allowed Nixon and Kissinger to "open the door" to much better relations with China. "Peace with Honor" was achieved in the Vietnam War, which was ended through a combination of severe military action taken in conjunction with diplomatic efforts to deny support to North Vietnam by its sponsors in the USSR and China. On the political front, George Wallace was forced out of the 1972 Presidential race due to severe injuries suffered in an assassina-tion attempt, leaving the South almost completely Nixon territory. A coalition had come together consisting of a core Conservative Base infused with what would later become known as Religious Right or "Social Conservatives" who were mainly evangelical Southern traditionalists upset with the moral direc-tion of the country caused by the upheavals of the 1960s. These people were former Democrats and like many of their politicians, switched sides from the Democrat to the Republican Party. Urban union workers similarly upset with what they saw as a radical anti-Patriotic trend in the Democrat Party joined Republican ranks in supporting Nixon, Also coming on board from even fur-ther Left Democrat precincts were the so-called neo-Conservatives, brought in by their fellow intellectuals such as William F. Buckley.

The Democrats, indulging themselves in the fever swamps of leftwing ideol-ogy, nominated a totally inept candidate, Senator George McGovern, the Party's most vocal critic of the Vietnam War. Horrified by the far-left candidacy of McGovern, the Conservative Base, though suspicious of Nixon, remained solid for him. McGovern proved to be a very weak and clumsy candidate who faced an impossible uphill battle against a sitting President that could point to a series of impressive accomplishments especially in foreign policy. Unsurprisingly, McGovern lost in a landslide of historic proportions in the 1972 elections. Nixon apparently felt he no longer needed to bend a knee to the Eastern Establishment… and this hubris was inevitably followed by nemesis.

THE WATERGATE DEBACLE

Within two years of his historic success Nixon was not only a pariah who had been forced to resign from office in disgrace, but almost his entire senior staff, including Vice President Spiro Agnew and Attorney General John Mitchell, were forced by various associated scandals into either resignation or jail. Over 70 people were convicted or pled guilty to Watergate-related crimes. Interestingly, two of those few important Nixon staffers who did not were both long-time Establishment RINOs: Henry Kissinger and his deputy Alexander Haig.

Nixon's second VP, Gerald R. Ford, was an amiable, inoffensive but compliant RINO puppy who spent years very comfortably berthed as a "Me Too" Republican, happily accepting crumbs tossed from the Democrat table during their fat pre-Nixon years. Pressured to get the entire scandal behind him, he pardoned Nixon and saved him from potential prosecution. Facing a Democrat Congress that correctly saw him as a weakling based on his 25-year performance in the House of Representatives (eight of them as House Minority Leader where he was well-schooled in accommodating and kow-towing to the Democrat majority), Ford was neutered by both public disgust with Republican scandals as well as by the 1974 mid-term Congressional election victories, which granted the Democrats an additional 49 seats in the House, increasing their majority above the two thirds required to override any presidential veto. Republicans also lost five seats in the Senate. Hammered by scandal and defeat, Ford could do little more than watch what basically turned into Congressional Government. Liberals ran rampant, emasculating the CIA in the middle of the Cold War and betraying solemn American commitments to South Vietnam, which resulted in the country being overrun by the North Vietnamese Communists. A Communist conquest of all Indochina soon followed as the much-derided Domino Theory was proven true with deadly accuracy. At least 4-million people were murdered by the Communist forces in Cambodia, Vietnam and Laos resulting in the displacement of millions more as pathetic refugee "boat people." In response to the deep 1974—1976 recession, Congress passed many budget-busting appropriations bills to "stimulate" the economy. Once again, Big Government economic nostrums that were put into effect to fix the "emergency" exacerbated the problem by a quantum leap. Further, these disastrously stupid policies led to a raging fire of inflation. Ford assumed the presidency at a point when consumer prices were rising at an annual rate of more than 12 percent, which was the first time in 30 years that the economy suffered double-digit inflation. Nixon, who had announced to the delight of RINOs everywhere that he was, in fact, an economic "Keynesian," had tried to reduce inflation through the imposition of wage and price controls. This effort in pursuit of the type of Statist economic programs favored by both Liberal and RINO corporatists not only failed to halt inflation but instead caused it to explode. With inflation roaring out of control, the new president issued a response that became infamous as a perfect example of ineffective, weak, out of touch leadership. In October 1974 Ford proposed in a speech before Congress that to reduce inflation there should be a one-year 5 percent surcharge on corporate and personal income taxes and a deep cut in federal spending... as well as a laughable proposal that citizens join the fight against inflation by wearing buttons that said "WIN"—standing for "Whip Inflation Now." This ludicrous response to a serious economic problem was met with extreme derision on the part of the public.

Ford's problems weren't limited to the Democrats. Holding no brief for another president with too independent a streak, the Eastern Establishment surrounded Ford with ex-Nixon advisors from their camp, most notably Kissinger, who essentially took over all issues dealing with foreign policy. Kissinger used this power to formalize the policy of "détente" with the USSR. This long-time goal of the Eastern Establishment was accomplished with the signing of the Helsinki Accords in 1975; the treaty formally recognized Soviet control over Eastern Europe. Containing clauses regarding the inviolability of national borders and committing the United States to respect the territorial integrity of the occupational gains made by the USSR in Eastern Europe following WWII (most notably including the division of Germany) the accords ended long-time official U.S. government support for the liberation of the so-called "Captive Nations." With Kissingerian "Real Politique" running foreign policy, Ford's utter capitulation to the Eastern Establishment was completed by the appointment of its leader, Nelson Rockefeller, as Ford's Vice President. With his acolyte in charge of foreign affairs, Rockefeller insisted that he be given a large role in formulating and directing domestic policy and brought many of his N.Y.-based advisors and specialists with him.

It was a trifecta of weakness: a feckless Congress mis-running the government, Kissinger running foreign affairs for Rockefeller, and Rockefeller running domestic policy for the Plutocracy. Even Nixon was being closely watched in his exile. Although he yearned to return to California, he was moved to a town house in Manhattan… living under de facto house arrest next door to Nelson Rockefeller's brother, David, the CEO of Chase Manhattan Bank who himself was a powerful leader of the Eastern Establishment through his associations with the Council on Foreign Relations and the Tri Lateral Commission (the latter being instrumental in advancing the career of an unknown but up-and-coming Georgia Governor, Jimmy Carter). Despite a personal affection for him as the "anti-Nixon" in terms of his open and pleasant personality, Ford's presidency was plagued by weakness, dithering and embarrassing faux pas. Ford sealed his fate with the dismal performance he gave in the presidential debates with his Democrat rival, Jimmy Carter, where he made incredibly stupid remarks regarding foreign policy (by indicating that Eastern Europe would not come under the control of the USSR). Only 4 years after their greatest triumph, Republicans had reached the nadir of their power and influence… and the RINOs were there every step of the way pushing it along.

Nixon was in exile, the Republican Wing of the Duopoly was disgraced and out of power and its counterpart in the Democrat Wing of the Duopoly was back in control of the government, re-positioning the chairs on the American Titanic to ready it for the next meaningless transfer back and forth between the Parties that administer the State for their corporate owners, so that they could create the next "emergency." Carter, a pawn even more compliant and dishonest than Ford, would prove to only be a change for the worse.

THE REAGAN REVOLUTION—THE RINOS DEPART

Incredible as it seems, the Presidency of Jimmy Carter was so weak, so inept and so riddled with failure in both foreign and domestic affairs that it actually managed to outdo Ford in its ability to wreck almost everything it touched. It was such a dismal failure that it provoked a presidential primary challenge by the late president's brother, Senator Edward M. Kennedy.

In the Republican Party, disgust with the dangerous direction Carter was taking the country was as palpable as was its desire to finally free itself of RINO domination. The popular Governor of California, former movie actor Ronald Reagan, seemed to fit the bill as the person to lead the charge for the Conservative Base. On intimate terms with leaders of the Conservative Resurgence in the 1950s and early 1960s, a strong Goldwater supporter and an effective speaker, Reagan was no stranger to bids for the Presidency. His name was floated as a conservative alternative to Nixon in 1968; but RINOs objected and insisted he represented a repeat of the Goldwater debacle still fresh in the minds of the Party faithful. Reagan, they said, was even *more* conservative than Goldwater and therefore was *too "extreme" to be even considered.* In 1976, Conservatives were utterly disgusted with Ford's weakness and passivity in the face of RINO domination, his supine posture with regards to the Democrat-controlled Congress and his almost obsessive devotion to appeasing the USSR via Kissinger's detente policy. The leaders of the Conservative movement convinced Reagan to launch a primary challenge against Ford, promising a new era devoted to Conservative foreign and economic policy that didn't bow to or beg favors from either the Democrats or the Rockefeller Republican RINO "moderates" based in the Eastern Establishment. Reagan's challenge initially went well. He won in North Carolina, Texas, and California, but lost in New Hampshire and Florida. In a futile attempt to reach out to the RINOs, Reagan chose a moderate Republican Senator Richard Schweiker of Pennsylvania as his running mate. Depicted by the RINOS as *too "extreme" to be nominated*, Reagan lost the nomination to Ford.

But Carter's abysmal failure gave Reagan another chance four years later in 1980. After several primaries, including one where he badly defeated RINO favorite George H.W. Bush, he was clearly the front runner. Determined not to allow a candidate they now portrayed as *too "extreme" to be elected*, the RINOS pulled out all the stops and openly sought to sabotage Reagan's chances by dividing the vote and running a "moderate" independent against him. They found their cat's-paw in John B. Anderson, a little-known member of the House of Representatives from Illinois and a First Class, full blooded RINO. A graduate of Harvard Law, who was initially aligned with the conservatives, Anderson soon found his true calling as a proud "Rockefeller Republican." Despairing of the Conservative drift of the Party during the

1980 primary campaigns, he tossed his hat into the ring as a "moderate" alternative to Reagan. When it became clear that Reagan was going to be nominated, he showed his true loyalty to the Republican Party in the manner Republicans had become masochistically tolerant of since Taft was sabotaged by TR: he attempted to subvert their election prospects, this time by running as a "progressive" "Independent". In a 1999 PBS interview with Jim Lehrer, Anderson said:

> "I had taken diametrically opposed positions to Reagan on National Security issues, on the energy problem, on his tax policy. I had adopted the language of his erstwhile opponent, Mr. Bush that it was "voodoo economics…" Further, he supported a Ford-Kissinger "détente" policy with the USSR.

These policies were the polar opposite of Reagan's message regarding the need for a more muscular foreign policy built on a strong military. Echoing the same hysterical talking points uttered by RINOS since their leaders first directed them against Goldwater, Anderson proved himself to be the essence of RINO moderation in opposition to Conservative "madness" and "extremism." Regardless, Anderson remained in the race, choosing a two-term *Democrat* ex-Wisconsin governor Patrick Lucey, as his running-mate. Anderson managed to get on the ballot in all 50 states and stayed in to the end, hoping his single digit poll numbers might make a difference in a close election to ensure a Carter victory. Anderson was elitist Rockefeller Republicanism to the core. As the *Atlantic Monthly* noted in February 1980:

> "These days, Anderson is Washington's favorite Republican… Anderson appeals to that elitist strain among Washington thinkers which asks the great unwashed of the electorate to send forth statesmen, not grasping, ambitious politicians."

Yes, the "Great Unwashed"—or as they are known outside the RINO country club: the Constitutional Conservatives who comprise the majority of the Republican Party. The RINOs themselves hedged their bets by trying to saddle Reagan with a RINO running-mate at the Republican Convention. When Reagan was out of the building the 1980 convention was held in, former President and eternal RINO lap-dog Gerald Ford appeared in an interview with news veteran Walter Cronkite to announce that he would be open to a "dream-ticket" acting as Reagan's Vice president. However, his price for this was to be a "co-president" basically in charge of foreign policy—that is, being able to appoint someone like Henry Kissinger, whose policy of one-way "détente" was a central target of Reagan's proposed "get tough" foreign policy. Reporters in the liberal media, panting with excitement over the possibility the "extreme" cowboy Reagan would be reined in by the more "moderate" "experienced" and "thoughtful" doyens of the Eastern Establishment joined the RINO stampede, picturing the Ford offer as "a done deal."

While much of the mainstream Establishment Press of the time—*The New York Times, The Washington Post, the L.A. Times, Time Magazine, Newsweek Magazine*, the CBS, NBC and ABC television networks - had long been editorially Liberal, at this point there was still some effort to maintain a divide between straight reporting and editorial opinion. This began to change in earnest with the rise of Ronald Reagan and certainly took hold during his presidency. Unlike the type of Establishment Republicans (with the exception of Goldwater) that the Mainstream Media was used to, Reagan was not only a Conservative, but a Conservative who, unlike Goldwater, had a good chance to win against a clearly ineffective opponent. Hence the Mainstream Media abandoned its role as an unbiased "watchdog" on all political parties and became a partisan… and then the virtual public relations arm… of the Democrat Party that it aligned with in its network boardrooms and on its editorial and opinion pages. Further, in opposing Reagan, it opposed the Conservative movement that coalesced around him and saw its new role as not simply being an unbiased arbiter of the truth or of speaking that truth to power, regardless which party held it, but to be the *enemy* of everything Reagan advocated, did and represented. The Mainstream Media correctly saw that Reagan would upset the entire inert, self-serving, elitist Duopoly apple-cart and replace compliant RINOs gathered around flaccid, "go-along-to-get-along" hacks like Gerald Ford with the Conservative activists that followed in Reagan's wake and who demanded change. The threat posed to Duopoly power by a Reagan Presidency over-rode all previous journalistic boundaries, rules and protocols followed by the Liberal Media, which all but dropped any pretense to journalistic fairness or unbiased, fact-based reporting and instead adopted the stance of being the enemy of a Conservative Movement that they saw as a threat to their ability to set the narrative and their control of what might be called an "Information Hegemony" over the American people. They even ceased to be an "Opposition Media" that once legitimately voiced its editorial comments as the Liberal opinions they were and began incorporating Liberal political bias into what was supposed to be straight reporting of the news. They adopted the role of the Enemy of Conservatism and transformed from a "Watchdog" media to an "Opposition" media to an "Enemy" media... viz. an "*Enemedia*".

This attempt by the Establishment to use the Enemedia they had become to end-run Reagan's ability to control his choice when picking a running mate resulted in Reagan's strong refusal to have his presidency held hostage to the good will and approval of an elitist establishment that he had spent his entire career opposing was clear and definitive. Blindsided by this arrogant and under-handed sucker-punch, Reagan cleverly responded with an ultimatum of his own: respond in one-half hour agreeing that if Ford were to be on the ticket it would be as "Vice-" *not* "Co- president", or the deal was busted. Ford let Reagan's deadline slip, but didn't have the spine to continue the charade any longer, even though the press continued to flail the story. Then Reagan sealed Ford's fate by choosing George H.W. Bush (who was himself a member in good standing with the RINO elites) with the understanding that he was clearly NOT to be a co-president. This move staunched further RINO sub-terfuge and quieted Conservative fears about RINO machinations. Despite all the RINO subversion via Anderson and Ford, Reagan handily beat Carter in November, and to the chagrin of both the Democrat and Republican Left put the Conservative policies he supported into play. Despite heavy criticism from the Left and the RINO Establishment, he remained firm in his policies through the tough early years of his Administration.

However, Democrat criticisms of Reagan, were echoed endlessly by a severely hostile media—that he was an intellectual lightweight; that he was too old and tired to deal with the rigors of the presidency; that he was a reck-less cowboy that would cause WWIII; that his Strategic Defense Initiative was a pipe dream that wouldn't work or influence the Soviets to negotiate seriously; that it was as dangerous as it was ridiculous to think any U.S. poli-cies could bring about the fall of the USSR; that his economic policies were a throwback to the heartless era of the Robber Barons and would cause another Great Depression; that his policies were inflationary and that his "simplistic" views of the world were out of date in the modern world. All these criticisms were proved wrong.

Conservatives were convinced they had finally staked the RINO vampire once and for all with the Reagan presidency, the most successful two-term presidency in the 20th Century in both economic and foreign policy terms. Further, the Reagan promise of a turnaround from the failed policies of the Carter Administration revitalized the prospects of the Republican Party so much that it rode his coattails to regain the Senate in 1980 for the first time in decades. Reagan followed up his 1980 success with an even greater Presidential victory in 1984, burying his opponent, former Carter VP Walter Mondale in a 49-state landslide.

THE RETURN OF THE VAMPIRE

But the RINOs were not so easily put to final rest. They sank back, donned their Reagan masks and issued copious amounts of lip service about the need for small government while basking in Reagan's historic successes and biding their time. Their time came in 1988 when they basically ran Bush I as Reagan III—but the Gipper mask quickly fell off. Bush insisted he was a Conservative. He also claimed that he was "kinder and gentler" than Reagan and soon proved it by filling his administration with Eastern Establishment RINOs, raising taxes and speaking in sweeping terms about the inevitability of the United Nations leading a corporate, transnational, "New World Order." His record on conservative social issues was, at best, mixed. On the one hand, Bush was convinced by his RINO Chief of Staff, John Sununu, to nominate David Souter to the Supreme Court. Hoping to avoid a contentious nomination fight by putting forward a virtual unknown person without a long paper trail indicating strong political opinions, Bush sold Souter to the Party faithful as a "conservative". He was not, and both knew it. He turned out to be one of the most consistently liberal judges on the Court during his entire tenure there. As always, no matter which side of the Duopoly was in charge of an administration, the policies always leaned in the direction of increasing governmental power at the expense of Ordered Liberty; one didn't necessarily require a Democrat Administration to nominate an open Statist to the Supreme Court, when the Republican side of the Duopoly will nominate a crypto-Statist to the same position. No matter who wins the election, the Duopoly ensures that as the government expands, the people shrink.

Of course, Bush provided a true conservative Supreme Court Justice in the form of Clarence Thomas, though his nomination process was as brutally grueling as the Democrats in the Senate could make it and the nomination came very close to failing. The Democrats fought so hard because their Party is made up of many special interest groups that strongly desired social justice legislation so extreme that it could only be enacted into law by an activist, Progressive Democrat-dominated Supreme Court, which had a very elastic view when it came to interpreting the Constitution. But Bush's political fate was sealed when he definitively promised the country that he would hold the line against the endless Democrat pressure to raise taxes. When pressed he was adamantine in his resolve. No matter how many times the Democrats told him to raise taxes he would respond "Read my lips: No New Taxes!" This statement later came back to haunt him because he too-easily made a deal (which the Democrats quickly reneged on) to trade some tax hikes for prom- ised budget cuts that never appeared. "Read my lips" became a bumper sticker encapsulating Bush's weakness for a Conservative Base that had expected him to react with the resolve of Ronald Reagan instead of the dull spinelessness of Jerry Ford. Conservatives now realized that when reading his lips it was clear they were saying: "I'm an Eastern Establishment RINO internationalist whose conservative credentials can't be trusted."

In 1992, he faced a minor Conservative primary revolt in the form of Conservative pundit Patrick J. Buchanan who, though he lost, issued a blis- tering anti-RINO speech at the convention, much to the obvious disgust of Mrs. Bush, her family and faux "conservatives" in the Enemedia. Disgusted themselves with such attacks, dispirited conservatives stayed home on election day and allowed the supposedly "moderate" Democrat Bill Clinton to swing through the revolving doors and occupy the White House.

Unfortunately, the "moderate" politics Clinton espoused during the cam- paign were taken about as seriously by him as he took his wedding vows. He immediately launched a radical attack on traditional family values by pushing his policy regarding Gays in the military, demanding a confiscatory, job-kill- ing BTU Energy Tax and totally forgot about his pledge to end welfare "as we know it" (that is, as just another wasteful, ultra-expensive, ineffectively run, and ultimately counterproductive government boondoggle.) He supported the enactment of widely unpopular gun control laws. Most damaging of all, he appointed his wife Hillary to oversee a transparent attempt at socialized medicine billed as "Universal Health Care," which not only miserably failed to become law but also, due to the arrogant, secretive and high-handed way in which Ms. Clinton handled it, proved to be a public relations disaster.

THE GINGRICH CONGRESSIONAL COUP D'ÉTAT

The backlash was rapid and intense. In 1994, Newt Gingrich, a Republican back-bencher in the House of Representatives, led as purely a Conservative political movement as was ever put together to a victory even more sweeping than the election of Reagan's in 1980. Overthrowing the puppy-dog RINO appeaser Bob Michael as Minority Leader of the House of Representatives, Gingrich took a much more aggressively conservative position against the policies of Clinton and the Democrats who controlled Congress. In part using Ronald Reagan's 1985 State of the Union Address and the work done by various conservative think tanks such as the Heritage Foundation, Gingrich and other House conservatives put together a Conservative program and presented it to the country six weeks before the 1994 Mid-term Elections. It was a detailed plan designed to radically change the leftward drift of the country that had proceeded apace not only under liberal Democrats but also under RINO Republicans. The program was dedicated to the conservative principles of shrinking the size of government, enacting tort reform, lowering taxes, promoting entrepreneurial activity and reforming the totally dysfunctional social welfare system.

The Gingrich plan dealt in specifics. If elected, the Conservatives pledged to take specific actions such as balancing the budget, passing more stringent criminal control laws, cutting spending for welfare programs by discouraging teenage pregnancy through the prohibition of welfare to mothers under 18 years of age and denying increased Aid to Families with Dependent Children (AFDC) for additional children while on welfare. This reform also had a two-years-and-out provision with work requirements to promote individual responsibility. The contract provided middle-class tax relief by creating a $500-per-child tax credit and repealing the marriage tax penalty. The Contract sought to encourage job creation through a series of small-business incentives including capital-gains tax cuts, unfunded mandate reform and indexation. It passed tort reform by putting limits on punitive damages and various forms of frivolous litigation. It imposed 12-year term limits on members of Congress: two terms for Senators and six terms for Representatives. In foreign policy, the Contract

91

called for preventing American troops from serving under United Nations command and for integrating former Warsaw Pact nations into NATO.

Finally freed of toxic RINO influence, Conservatives swept to victory. Republicans won 54 seats in the House, destroying the record of domination the Democrats had held in the House for 68 of the preceding 72 years. Democrat Tom Foley became the first sitting Speaker of the House to lose re-election since the Civil War era. Majorities of many specific voting blocs: religious voters, white men, white women, college voters, former Perot voters went Republican. In 1994, Independents voted for Republican in large numbers, which would prove similar to what later happened with Donald Trump, who made significant inroads into longstanding Democrat voting blocs such as manufacturing workers in 2016. The Republicans captured 8 seats to re-take the Senate. The election victories spread to Governor's races where the Republicans, generally supporting the out-and-proud conservative agenda of Gingrich's Contract with America, picked up 10 seats in the 36 states in contention. State Houses followed suit with many state legislatures being taken over by Republicans. But had the Duopoly's lock on power been broken? Unfortunately, no.

It wasn't long before the "Gingrich Revolution" succumbed to the pressure of the Liberal Media to prove they were as "compassionate" and "tolerant" and "egalitarian" as the Liberals themselves never ceased to claim to be. Unable to bear newspaper covers depicting him as an angry, crying baby throwing a tantrum and television commentators reviling him as a heartless reactionary or worse, Gingrich caved and the Republican Congress moved away from its Reaganite principles at breakneck speed. They abandoned their Revolutionary character and became the very "mature governing party" they had revolted against. Like all denizens of the D.C. swamp, they realized that it was much easier to tax and spend and pander to special interests groups for short-term electoral gain rather than hold to principle in order to achieve long-term political success. Listening to beltway "consultants" and "policy gurus" they became that which they swore to destroy: big-government Statists who sought to use state power to get them perpetually re-elected at any cost to principle or commitment to the Conservative Movement's Cause they had formerly championed.

As Clinton struggled to convince the public he was "still relevant," a second attempt was made by Patrick J. Buchanan to run for the White House in 1996. Trying to capitalize on the resurgent Conservative feeling sweeping the country, Buchanan entered the primaries against the "moderate" RINO candidate Bob Dole. He totally upset Dole by winning the important New Hampshire primary. Buchanan also won three other states (Missouri, Alaska, and Louisiana). He did well in the Iowa caucus finishing just behind Dole. He sought to activate the grass-roots Conservative Base to do on the presidential level what they did on the Congressional level in 1994: finally defeat the RINOS in the Washington establishment (of which Dole was practically a metaphysical incarnation) that had exercised such control over the party for so long.

Dole had all the requisite qualifications: although he was, like George H.W. Bush, a genuine war hero who had proved many times over his personal military courage, but like all RINOs he lacked political courage. He was at home, as was Gerald Ford, with being a "me too," long-term, inside-the-beltway Republican who sought NOT to advance Conservative policies and programs but to simply administer a Statist agenda at a slower pace while remaining happy with whatever crumbs of pork that were tossed to him (and his RINO Senate colleagues) by the Democrats. He stood for nothing. He inspired no one. He motivated no one. His only support came from the RINOs... and those they pressured to join them including, amazingly, Newt Gingrich and many of the new "Contract Republicans" in the Congressional majority.

For whatever reason: political weakness, political bribes, political pressure, wanting to be seen as a mature governing majority rather than as an insurgent political force, or a desire to follow the fool's errand of trying to cultivate a perpetually hostile media, Gingrich and many others jumped on board the anti-Buchanan bandwagon and threw every shopworn, RINO shibboleth against him: he was too extreme, he was a warmonger (a claim later proved ludicrous given Buchanan's paleo-con opposition to both the Gulf and Iraq Wars) he was intolerant, he was ignorant, he was inexperienced in government, he was a bigot, he was a homophobe, he was a misogynist, he was a narrow-minded reactionary. Though an old trick even back then, the smear strategy proved to work so well against the Conservative Base that the RINOs later rolled it out, perfectly preserved, to launch at Donald Trump 20 years later, albeit with far less success. The charges against Buchanan, picked up by a liberal media ever ready to stymie and smear Conservative candidates, worked and Dole regained his footing, won the nomination and, like all openly RINO candidates, was immediately abandoned by the Media and lost the election to Bill Clinton. Four years later, debilitated by myriad scandals that produced an impeachment that resulted in, of course, too many RINOs in the senate failing to vote to convict, the public was suffering a severe case of Clinton fatigue. Clinton's robotic and lifeless Vice President Al Gore was pitted against George W. Bush, the former president's son in 2000. The election was so close that the recount process was ultimately brought into the Florida Courts by Gore, only to have him lose the case when it was appealed to the Supreme Court, thus giving Bush the victory. But the scars and division the weeks of uncertainty left the Democrats embittered and angry; conversely, the "victory" Bush won would ultimately prove pyrrhic.

In 2000, George W. Bush sought to avoid the mistakes made by his father and Bob Dole. He wore the Reagan mask well enough to barely get elected and indeed managed to keep it securely fixed on his face by rallying the country to arms after the 9/11 attacks on the United States. After again dodging the bullet in 2004 against the far left-wing Democrat John Kerry due to the absolutely essential support W. Bush got from so-called "values voters"—conservative members of the Religions Right—their help was, RINO style, promptly forgotten immediately after the election. Bush and the Congressional Republicans spent like drunken sailors—except that drunken sailors at least spend their own money. More precisely, *they spent like Democrats.* They doubled the national debt and passed exorbitantly expensive add-ons to already insolvent Governmental health care by loading Bush's prescription drug entitlement program on top of it. They hurt U.S. trade (via their support of Sarbanes-Oxley regulations) by putting the management of American corporations at a competitive disadvantage with foreign firms and drove businesses out of the United States.

So much for pro-Capitalist Republicanism; and, given the myriad instances of corporate corruption that the RINO Republicans winked at as well as the economic crisis that hit 4 years later, so much for the corporate owned Duopoly's ability to be "tough on corporate crime."

By 2006, voters had enough of Republican apostasy and threw them out of Congress in droves. In 2008 it was time to pay the piper for all the backsliding the RINOs engaged in, their dependence on political gunslingers and their reneging on their promise to make government smaller sullied the Republican brand so much that it almost destroyed the party. The Republicans in Congress lost because they deserved to lose for the same reasons they always lost: they had violated all the principles relating to the conservative ethos of governing and became the very panderers and conniving hacks whose malfeasance they were elected to correct, all in the pursuit of careers based on feeding off pork provided by the public purse. They had ignored the words of the great Enlightenment conservative thinker and advocate of Ordered Liberty, Edmond Burke, who wrote:

> "But when leaders chose to make themselves bidders at an auction of popularity, their talents in the construction of the state will be of no service. They will become flatterers instead of legislators; the instruments not the guides of the people. If any of them should happen to propose a scheme of liberty, soberly limited, and defined, with proper qualification, he will be immediately out bid by his competitors who will propose something more splendidly popular. Suspicions will be raised of his fidelity to his cause…. that will afterwards defeat any sober purpose at which he ultimately might have aimed."

JOHN MCCAIN

Surveying the shattered landscape of Republican fortune in 2008, the RINOs once again emerged from their ideological necropolis and found the field surprisingly devoid of Reaganite conservative candidates. Of course, all RINOS tried to put on the Reagan mask, but few were buying the charade. Thus the Party was presented with RINO extraordinaire, John McCain, the type of former military man that American Corporatists like to collect like toy soldiers, was the guy who was "next in line," a "moderate" and who was the candidate that "had the best chance to win." McCain was yet another in an already too long line of tired old men relying on their military record to cover up their lack of a political backbone; in sum, McCain was everything a RINO dreams of in a presidential candidate. He was against President George W. Bush's tax cuts; he supported amnesty for illegal aliens, he was against a border security fence until he was dragged kicking and screaming to give it the most grudging insincere support possible; he supported curtailing free speech with his futile McCain-Feingold campaign finance reform bill; he was insistent on "bi-partisanship" no matter how much it was used to rape conservative principle; he insisted on playing politics like an officer and a gentleman from the Country Club while the other side ran a candidate well-schooled in the political guerrilla warfare typical of those who hail from the fever swamps of the far, far Left. In essence, McCain was the epitome of the Republican flip side of the Duopoly and emblematic of why elections are held without effecting much change in overall policy direction.

The charismatic Democrat candidate, Barack Obama, was also engaged in his own bit of masquerade, posing as anything but the urban-based Socialist he had been from the time he began his political career in the home of Communist terrorist "Weatherman," Bill Ayers. He continued to pursue it as a "Community Organizer" following the playbook ("Rules For Radicals") of Saul Alinsky, which suggested using non-radical means (community organizing of the poor) to accomplish radical leftwing policy ends. In an introduction to Alinsky's 1972 interview with *Playboy Magazine*, the "The Progress Report" website (http://www.progress.org/2003/alinsky2.htm) describes Alinsky as having spent "nearly four decades of organizing the poor for radical social action." Following his stint as a "community organizer" in the Alinsky mold, Obama became an Illinois State Senator who later served 4 years in the U.S. Senate, where he spent the majority of his time devoted to preparing for his planned 2008 Presidential run. Devoid of any record of accomplishment or executive credentials that would qualify him for the job, Obama instead campaigned on a series of vague, empty liberal platitudes that were well disguised by his amazing gift to produce high-flowing rhetoric out of nothing. A relatively young man of bi-racial background, he held the promise for many as the living proof that America had overcome its past history of slavery, apartheid and discrimination.

The smooth and cool Obama was clearly a far better campaigner than the irritable and often nasty McCain who required the breathless liberal media to drool over him with praise and support for him to maintain his credibility. Obama seemed to be effortlessly gliding into the White House. Conversely, due his multiple apostasies, McCain was anathema to the Conservative Base, which was beyond disgusted with his nomination. McCain's record exemplified just how much the RINO Republicans, obsessed only with their political careers, cared *nothing* for those in the Conservative Base who they looked on as benighted boobs that had no other place to go to cast their vote. Again, they were wrong. Conservatives didn't have to go anywhere; *they stayed home.* Trying to somehow activate the Conservative Base, McCain's cynical gun-slinger consultants convinced him to shelve his own "bold" choice for Vice President (former *Democrat* Senator Joe Lieberman, with whom he was in *violent agreement* about everything) and instead take their advice by choosing a mixed-gender answer to Obama's breakthrough appeal as "The First Black President." This was accomplished by picking Sarah Palin, the largely unknown, recently elected governor of Alaska, as his running mate. Palin was a vibrant, young, folksy campaigner, with an attractive middle-class family that seemed to be prototypically American. She was a strong conservative and certainly no RINO. She electrified crowds and put McCain back in the race, boosting his sagging poll numbers to the point to where they were more than competitive to Obama's. In fact, the Base was so disgusted with the nomination of McCain that Palin often polled better than McCain did with voters. As a Rasmussen Poll on 11/04/08 showed "23% of Republicans say McCain was not the right choice for the party, while 18% say the same of Palin." But the Palin pick was not only too cute by half, in the end it also wasn't enough to save the day, especially when the economic crisis hit just before the 2008 election, which highlighted *everything* the public was tired of in "moderate" Bush Republicans: incompetent, dishonest, and owned by the Party's Corporate wing... *and McCain represented it all.*

GORED BY THE RINOS

The Republicans, once again led by a RINO, went down in flames losing the White House, the Senate and the House of Representatives. By embracing their role as a co-partner of the Duopoly, they had abandoned the winning formula developed after the Goldwater defeat, which had produced the transformational victories of 1980, 1984 and 1994. They abandoned Conservative principles that were devoted to traditional Judeo-Christian values, individual rights, low taxes and a healthy respect for the free market. They saw Big Government projects as their means to re-election, not as a threat to fiscal sanity and Ordered Liberty. They preferred to take the cheers of their Country Club corporate donors but paid the price for it by ignoring the anger of the Party's Conservative base.

They even failed to acknowledge the essential Conservative military value that wars must be fought with full vigor or not at all... and we can thank General Petraeus's "Surge Strategy" in Iraq for recognizing this and for the turnaround of our fortunes there, not the Republican Administration in Washington which waited far too long—at the cost of far too many lives—

before it understood that they only way to defeat the fanatic murderers pro-duced by Islamist Fascism was to fight them with overwhelming force (in Iraq's case, by focusing on smart counter-insurgency tactics) and not with impossible NeoCon panaceas such as "Nation-Building." Of course, after the election was lost, the RINOs re-appeared. Some blamed Palin for the loss. Many called for Republicans to "move forward" and "reach out" in the man-ner of the Democrat Party by pandering to minority groups and surrender-ing to what they saw as an inevitable demographic determinism that would ultimately destroy a "too White, too Male" Republican Party. It had to get in touch with issues that were important to Special Interest Groups: Women, Hispanics, Blacks, Gays, illegal immigrants and "young people." It had to be more "tolerant," more "inclusive," more "intersectional." It had to recognize that Reagan was dead and that Reaganism was even deader than he was. It had to practice a "transnational" foreign policy and stop making America act like an "international bully." It had to get more "modern," more "cool," more digital, more "YouTube." The RINOS demanded that the Base of the party had to realize that the American people wanted Big Government and that they wanted to be taxed higher to pay for it. It had to, in effect, hold their ideo-logical and policy relationship with their Democrat partners in the Duopoly *even closer*.

BASE VS. ESTABLISHMENT

The person most strongly out in front advocating this RINO position imme-diately after the election was former Secretary of State, Gen. Collin Powell, who, rose through the ranks as a "political general" starting in the Nixon Administration, where he became a favorite of its major Eastern Establishment figure, Henry Kissinger. Known as an intellectual and a moderate, Powell rose through the National Security hierarchy holding many important positions including National Security Advisor and Chairman of the Joint Chiefs of Staff. But despite a long association with the Republican Party, as late as 1992, people were so unsure of his Party status that he was considered a likely pick to be Bill Clinton's VP choice; the allusion to Eisenhower's own public ideological nebu-lousness is unavoidable. On 1/21/92, Liberal pundit Martin Schram wrote: "…on CNN's year-end edition of "The Capital Gang,"… I'd just revealed to my four co-conspirators in prognostication the identity of the person to whom the

1992 Democratic presidential standard-bearer (Bill Clinton) will offer his party's vice presidential nomination: Gen. Colin Powell… Powell rejected Bush's offer to be CIA director, says Bob Woodward's book, "The Commanders," because he was "troubled" by Bush's 1988 campaign exploitation of black murderer-rapist Willie Horton… In 1964, when Powell was driving from Fort Benning, Ga., to see his wife in Alabama and was stopped by a state trooper handing out Goldwater-for-president stickers; the trooper didn't take kindly to a black man in a Volkswagen with New York plates and an "All the Way With LBJ" bumper sticker… the Democratic nominee should offer Powell the vice presidency" However, when pushing hard for RINO Bob Dole in 1996, Powell had his Reagan mask firmly on his face when he told the Republican Convention: "I became a Republican because I believe, like you, that the Federal Government has become too large and too intrusive in our lives. We can no longer afford solutions to our problems that result in more entitlements, higher taxes to pay for them, more bureaucracy to run them and fewer results to show for it." It was pure Reagan rhetoric… and purely insincere on Powell's part.

In 2009 Powell had apparently once again broken out the RINO play-book and gone through its well-thumbed, dog-eared pages to regurgitate all the old calumnies against Conservatives… even though his presentation of them leaves anyone listening closely somewhat confused. Speaking to a con-ference in Washington on May 4, 2009, Powell savaged the Constitutional Conservative Base of the Republican Party. He said he hoped that the GOP will not keep repeating the mantras of the far right and warned that "The Republican Party is in deep trouble". The party must realize that the coun-try has changed. "Americans do want to pay taxes for services," he said. "Americans are looking for more government in their life, not less." Powell called McCain "a beloved friend" but had cautioned him during the campaign that the party had become known as being "mean-spirited" and more con-cerned with Conservative ideological economic dogma than the real economic problems faced by the American people. He brutally criticized Talk Radio host Rush Limbaugh, who was a key player in communicating the values promoted in the 1994 Contract with America: "I think what Rush does as an entertainer diminishes the party and intrudes or inserts into our public life a kind of nastiness that we would be better to do without," Powell said. Speaking on CNN two months later, Powell claimed that he believed all the things he said in 1996 "…but I also believe that we should have a government that works. I don't like slogans anymore like 'limited government'"

Powell's contention makes absolutely no sense. The Federal Government had always been historically SMALLER and more limited in the past than it has been in recent times. Even Reagan, hampered by a Statist Congress and a hostile liberal media, was only able to slow the inevitable rate of government growth. Certainly the government was smaller before 1933 and was smaller than that in the late 19th Century… *and even smaller than that in the early 19th Century.* Yet these were years when government clearly "worked' as evidenced by the explosive growth in the wealth and power of the United States to become the richest and most powerful country in the history of the world. So if, as Powell implies, government currently doesn't "work" it surely can't be the fault of a limited government that *doesn't exist* and *hasn't existed* in over 85 years! And what is Powell's solution to make government "work?" Why, to support the election of the greatest Statist ever to run for office and win: Barack Hussein Obama, a dyed in the wool crypto-socialist… whose ideology very quickly proved to be anything but deserving of the prefix "crypto." But "Limited Government" is no more a slogan than "Life Liberty and the Pursuit of Happiness" or "Government of the People, By the People and For the People" or "In GOD We Trust." The fact that Powell thinks that it *is* only a slogan says reams about him, not about the essential, sacred, fragile, Enlightenment concept of "limited government"… as does the fact that the man he disloyally supported for President in 2008 based his entire campaign on little more than the slogan: "Yes We Can." Yes, Powell is certainly the man to whom RINOs think the Party should be listen to so that they can continue to secure their favorite place as the Jr. Partner in the Duopoly. But the Base had other ideas.

The 2008 debacle produced by the RINOs was the last straw for many in the Conservative Base. Once again the RINO wing had not only forced the nomination of one of their own on the Party with the claim that he was "the only one who could win" and who ran on a platform that either paid cheap lip-service or openly betrayed many of their most core principles; Constitutional Conservatives rose up in an angry revolt that gave birth to the grassroots movement known as the Tea Party.

The revolt was not a "party" but a movement, whose name is the acronym for "*T*axed *E*nough *A*lready." It was comprised of many elements of the Base: Fiscal Conservatives, Social Conservatives, National Security Conservatives, Gun Rights Groups, Pro-Life Groups, Privacy Issue Groups and those opposed to the horror of Obama's socialized medicine "Obamacare" scheme.

It also included many Libertarians who supported what they correctly saw as a genuine, grassroots movement that was also dedicated to their Cause of Limited Government under the Constitution. They were all joined in unison in their disgust with the Establishment RINOs who had delivered defeat after defeat at the polls and who had kept so few of their promises (especially to the Social Conservatives and Pro-Life Groups, which had been waiting in vain for them to deliver the conservative Supreme Court the Republicans had promised for decades.) Ad hoc groups proliferated across the country; large spontaneous rallies started taking place on an almost weekly basis; proclamations and manifestos they produced flooded the internet. The Tea Party Movement organized and channeled all the anger and frustration felt by the Base that the Establishment had sneered at for years.

A year after the 2008 election, the Movement was so powerful that it was able to stage an enormous rally of over one million people (that was studiously ignored by the Liberal News Media) in Washington DC. The mood of the attendees could be seen in the fact that every time the name "John McCain" was mentioned, the huge crowd loudly booed; it was an amazing scene: the very people who made up the most active, core contingent of those who voted for McCain, the party's most recent candidate for President, were so fed up with their betrayal at the hands of the RINO Establishment that they booed every mention of his name. Only two Washington Republicans even bothered… or had the courage… to show up: conservatives Senator Jim DeMint and Rep. (later Vice President) Mike Pence. The rest stayed in their offices, hiding under their desks, while their consultants scrambled to figure out if this was just a momentary outburst or a trend they would have to deal with or perhaps, even feign supporting. The inability of the Republican Party to be able to summon the guts to face their own Base without their paid gunslingers from K Street having something ready for them to say was hardly a profile in courage and it perfectly captured how far the Party had drifted from a rank and file that was outraged with their myriad failures to deliver. Following its usual pattern, the media at first ignored, then ridiculed, then slandered, then, in an increasing panic as they realized the movement was growing at a tremendous rate despite their tactics, went into full scale fear-mongering mode. The Establishment Enemedia was quick to join the attack: the Tea Party was extremist, they were reactionaries, they were violent, they were anti-democratic, they were ignorant, they hated women, they were gun nuts, they were cultists who worshiped "cranks" like Ayn Rand, they were being used by talk radio demagogues, they were being used by millionaires and billionaires, they were being used to raise money for conservative groups and, of course, *they were racists who couldn't bear the thought that a Black man had been elected President.*

Of course, when it looked at the Tea Party Movement, America saw something that looked nothing like the monster movie being described by the media. They saw moms and dads, youthful Libertarians and aged grandparents, police and military veterans… average Americans. Frightened out of its wits that a large anti-Establishment, *anti-Duopoly* Liberty Movement had popped into existence right in front of their eyes, the RINOS in control of the Party initially tried to ignore it. Once they realized this was impossible, they tried to co-opt them. Soon they were selling GOP toy elephants carrying tea pots and other Tea Party related merchandize on their official website which, according to the Country Club mindset, should have satisfied the Base as much as colored beads and mirrors dazzled the natives that sold Manhattan Island to the Dutch; and besides, what's more important than raising money for the Party so it can… raise more money? The attempt to co-opt it failed miserably and by the time the 2010 election occurred, the fervor of the Conservative Base not only swept the Democrats out of the House of Representatives and gained seats in the Senate, but it also caused a wave that flooded Republican candidates into office in State and Local races across the country. With only 2 years to the Presidential elections, the RINO Establishment now had two obstacles to returning to power: President Obama, as well as an angry intra-party revolt that wanted no part of them. For them, there was only one answer to this conundrum: deceive the Base by running a RINO in conservative clothing.

MITT ROMNEY: THE CONSERVATIVELY CONSERVATIVE WHO WAS ALWAYS CONSERVATIVE

2010 proved that Collin Powell was *totally* wrong when he said that the conservative orientation of the Republican Party was out of touch with the American people and needed to turn Left to remain viable. To the RINO wing, the answer was clear: Powell was correct, but the problem was how to execute a left-hand turn *into* the Duopoly while claiming to the majority of the Party it was really turning Right, *away* from the Duopoly. In 2012, the RINOs thought they found the person to execute that deception in the former RINO Republican Governor of the most Liberal state in the Union, Mitt Romney. Running against a field brimming with candidates anxious to please the newly Tea Party fueled Base, the Establishment made the decision to run Romney's campaign as part of a long-term marathon to the nomination, during which they would, via the power of their Chamber of Commerce and Wall St. fundraising efforts, debilitate the opposition one by one. Each "Base" candidate would start out hot, get lots of attention, make some minor gaffe that was seized upon by the press as "disqualifying" for a presidential candidate and drop behind the next candidate, who would be forced into repeating the process. First Michelle Bachman, then Rick Perry, then Herman Cain, then Newt Gingrich then Rick Santorum… they all traveled the road from hot pick to dead duck while Romney, never anyone's favorite, plodded along. In the end, only he was left. Of course, along the way, Romney moved heaven and earth to mask his lifelong career as a moderate Republican who was so squishy on the issues that he was able to get elected governor of one of the most Liberal states in the Union. Along the way he had to explain and spin and obfuscate his clearly moderate RINO record and often went to almost ridiculous lengths to do. Such was the case during his speech at the February 2012 Conservative Political Action Conference (CPAC) when he used the word conservative or conservatives 25 times in a 26-minute speech:

> "I was a conservative governor. I fought against long odds in a deep blue state, but I was a *severely* conservative Republican governor," he said. "I understand the battles that we, as conservatives, must fight because I have been on the front-lines."

One can only conclude that the reason he felt it necessary to claim he was a conservative virtually once a minute during his speech was because he knew that his record made the claim preposterous. At a conference where Obama's Health Care Plan mandate was being excoriated by speaker after speaker, Romney and his RINO handlers apparently felt the only way to disguise the fact that the president's plan was, in fact, based on a very similar plan pushed and passed by Romney himself while he was governor in Massachusetts was to drown it out by inserting the word "conservative" into practically every single sentence of his CPAC speech. The result looked and sounded as ridiculous as was, but it allowed Romney to maintain the fiction that he was a conservative while the true (or at least much ideologically stronger) conservatives in the field fell by the wayside. Worse, due to Romney's enactment of an "Obamacare" type government health care system in Massachusetts, his nomination undercut and defused one of the Republican's biggest issues against Obama; how bad, Democrats asked, can government health care be when the Republican nominee more or less created the idea in his own state when he was governor? Through a combination of Establishment organization and money, campaign mistakes on the part of his rivals, a media anxious to see the most moderate Republican win the nomination and the constant pressing of the lie that he was a conservative, Romney won the nomination. Sticking it to the Base at the 2012 convention, rather than picking a conservative to give the important Keynote Address praising his nomination, Romney chose Chris Christie, a RINO rising star who promptly proved he was a New Jersey politician by spending the entire speech praising himself and barely mentioning Romney. Also seeking to throw a dart at the Libertarians, the RINOs made sure that Ron Paul, who received millions of votes in the primaries, not only wasn't given the Keynote Address, *he wasn't even given a speaking position* (thus angering huge numbers of Libertarians whose anger against the Republicans might have at least been mitigated a bit by such an small olive branch proffered to them.) As a result of the RINO strategy, Conservative turnout for Romney was cut by a significant degree and many disgusted Libertarians stayed away from the polls.

True to form, the RINOs had taken a Party that ran the table in 2010 and delivered it into a devastating defeat just two years later in an election where their opposition was reeling from the multiple failures of Obama's economic and health care policies. This sclerotic wing of corrupt hacks was so out of touch that on election night, head RINO cheerleader Karl Rove, who assured Republicans that Romney was the only candidate who could win, who could capture the moderates, who was an adult that could reach across the aisle and all the rest of the tired, false clichés, practically had to be dragged away from his "analyst" desk at FOX News because he refused to give up the ghost and concede Romney had lost the election long after it was a foregone conclusion. His performance was an embarrassment; the RINO failure was an embarrassment; the election was an embarrassment. But it did serve the interests of maintaining the stable rotations of the Duopoly for those who own it. The inevitable denouement came when, after the election, the Establishment, which had forced their fake conservative candidate down the Party's throat, now whined that the reason for the loss was… *THE TEA PARTY!!* Of course, the opposite was true; it was the Tea Party Movement that owned the heart and soul of the Constitutional Conservative Base of the Republican Party.

THE FOREVER DEFEATED

The incredibly weak and incompetent Obama Administration foreign policy produced disasters in Gaza, Syria, Iran, North Korea, Libya, Iraq, Afghanistan and Iran while proclaiming through its compliant Enemedia tools that the world was actually "more tranquil than it has ever been."

Further, Obama was caught up in a kaleidoscope of Administration scandals in the IRS, Benghazi, the reckless release of Taliban terrorist commanders, a misbegotten Fast and Furious Federal gun-running operation gone bad, the Veteran Affairs scandals, the targeting of journalists unfriendly to the Administration and so many others that they tended to almost blur into one another from day to day even as they grew in intensity to the threat they presented to the very soul of American Liberty.

Despite all of Obama's missteps and mistakes, one should never underestimate the RINO ability to snatch defeat from the jaws of victory. Rather than embracing the new vigor brought to it by the Constitutional Conservatives in the Base and welcoming in the fresh ideas and youthful enthusiasm of the Libertarians, the RINOs were busy trying to undercut their most potent contingents. A cohort of RINOs has formed whose sole purpose in life seems to be to defeat the candidates preferred by its own Party Base. According to the AP…

"Groups such as American Crossroads [run by Karl Rove] and the U.S. Chamber of Commerce no longer are willing to risk major investments on hardline conservatives who embarrassed GOP leaders last fall and rattled the confidence of party donors. Many remain concerned after last month's government shutdown highlighted Republican divisions."

This is pure RINO spin—the big business-oriented Republican establishment Super PACs didn't support "hardline" conservatives in the 2012 election cycle; they mostly supported the losing establishment Republican candidates in the GOP primaries. The electoral loss suffered by lifelong Republican "moderate" Mitt Romney in 2012 was proof the claim that principled, limited government constitutional conservative candidates were more likely to be "unelectable" than Establishment RINOs; in fact, the multiple losing records of RINO can-didates such as Dole, Bush 1, McCain and Romney indicate that nominating them is a recipe for disaster at the polls. As with Mitt Romney in 2012, there's no evidence that running as a principled limited government constitutional conservative automatically made a candidate "unelectable" as the RINO "mod-erates" claimed and a whole lot of evidence that running as a Bush/McCain/Romney-type establishment Republican was a recipe for disaster. Despite the fact that as strong a political movement as the Tea Party won massive electoral victories running against Obamacare, the RINO establishment nominated the very man who invented the concept when he was governor of Massachusetts: Mitt Romney. The electoral disaster of 2012 was the direct result of obviating the most important issue the Right had against Obama and… given the RINO propensity to prefer losing elections to losing the support of their corporate donor class... was probably the result they secretly desired.

On February 13, 2013, Phyllis Schlafly, a longtime Movement Conservative leader, debunked the idea that only candidates approved by the RINO Establishment have a chance of winning at the polls in her *Eagle Forum* column stating: "There are two reasons why Rove and his rich donors don't like grass-root Republicans and tea partiers. The Establishment can't order them how to vote, and the Establishment wants candidates to talk only about economic issues, never about social, moral, or national - security issues... Rove's big-money spending last year, which was similarly designed to help only Establishment candidates, especially if they had defeated a real conser-vative in the primary, was notoriously unsuccessful. Of the 31 races in which Rove aired TV ads, Republicans won only 9, so his donors got little return on their investment. https://eagleforum.org/publications/column/battle-for-con-trol-of-the-republican-party-begins.html

By 2016, the Duopoly was clearly in increasing trouble.

THE DUOPOLY DEFLATES

The 2014 Mid-terms proved to once again underscore the fact that it is the Conservative Base that is not only capable of winning elections, but is capable of breaking with the Republican side of the Duopoly and win on its own. Running against the failure of President Obama's programs from the Affordable Health Care Plan to exploding illegal immigration and the general trend toward ever bigger government, the 2014 Mid-terms saw the motivation and organizing efforts of the Tea Party Republican Party retain control of the House of Representatives and win back control of the Senate, taking 9 Senate seats (the largest gain since 1980.)

2014 also saw a net gain of 13 Republican seats in the House, giving them the largest majority in that chamber since the early 1930s. Further, Republicans won State, Local and territorial elections across the country, leaving Republicans holding 31 governorships to 18 for the Democrats. On the State legislature level, Republicans won 68 State Houses, leaving them in control of the most state legislatures since 1928 and the Democrats with their smallest amount of the same *since 1860!*

This second Tea Party victory confirmed a more devastating rejection of Colin Powell's "move to the moderate center" advice than could hardly have been conceived. The Tea Party Movement created activist Constitutional candidates that moved out of the streets and into State and Federal political seats. Two years later, businessman force-of-nature Donald Trump not only rode the iconoclastic, anti-Washington wave that was created by the Tea Party Movement, but added to it by appealing to groups that were formerly firmly in the Democrat camp: manufacturing workers, miners, those concerned with the burdens of illegal immigration and cultural traditionalists. He was able to convince the manufacturing workers that the Democrats cared more about making their transnational corporate donors happy by outsourcing the jobs of American workers overseas and closing their mines in the name of the Gaia worshipping environmental pseudo-religion.

He demonstrated how Democrats gave preference to open borders and the interests of illegal immigrants, rather than to strong borders and concern for American citizens first. He illuminated as well, how they enacted the anti-American cultural demands of progressive elitists into law, and thus undermined as many American traditions and beliefs as possible… which all would contribute to emasculating the ability of the average citizen to fight and overcome the Seventh Crisis.

Despite everything thrown against him by the RINOS, the Left and the Enemedia; despite his own many faux pas and embarrassing mis-statements; despite the over the top rhetoric and despite all the polls that indicated that even an opponent as utterly unlikable as Hillary Clinton would win right up to election day, Trump prevailed. But in doing so, he pushed the Democrat Base into a state of derangement over his election, which they saw as somehow "rigged" and thus "illegitimate."

The vehemence to which both sides of the Duopoly reacted to Trump's election ranged from those who became hysterical among the Establishment RINO Republicans over their loss of control of the agenda (who formed into "Never Trump" cadres, which even contained former Republican presidential nominees like Mitt Romney who voted to convict Trump during the failed 2020 impeachment process and presidential "wanna-bees" such as John Kasich, who endorsed the Democrat nominee Joe Biden at the 2020 DNC Convention) to screeching Liberals howling in frustration in the streets at the loss of their Feminist goddess, Hillary Clinton. This frustration rapidly degenerated into Far Leftwing violence and riots against Trump on a host of issues across the county.

Nothing spoke as strongly to the fact that the Duopoly, apoplectic over the loss of control over its respective Party Bases of support, was in its death throes as did these expressions of frustrated, irrational, violent rage.

This not only caused the Conservative Base to chafe under the constraints of the RINO wing of the Duopoly; the election of Donald Trump also produced a similar political revolt on the Left against their own Corporate wing. Like the Tea Party revolt against Corporate Republican RINOs on the Right, the revolt on the Left also had an ideological origin based on a case of betrayed principles (albeit, *Transnational Progressive / Socialist* principles!) as well as a similar disgust with the transparently phony machinations of Democrat "Party Leaders" working for the same Corporate owners as the RINO Party Leaders. Both were rightly fearful of losing their lucrative berth on a Duopoly gravy train that was rapidly going off the rails.

The nature of the Duopoly, which requires both parties to basically act as two sides of the same coin, ensures that the RINOs have no real interest in a Republican victory anchored in the conservative principles of its Base. Its interests lie in serving, *as do the interests of the Corporate Democrats,* whatever fits the needs of the corporate masters for whom they both work. This fact will never be acknowledged, by either RINOs or Corporate Democrats who cannot survive in a party without the "contributions" provided by rich corporate donors.

As with the Corporate Democrats and their own Base, the entire record of the RINOs is one of disloyalty, subversion, apostasy, contempt, of disrespect and of insult directed toward the Base of the Republican Party. Their record is one of betrayal and ideological treason. It has demanded that Republicans construct a "Big Tent" and then directed it to pursue policies and take actions that ensure it will be ever emptier. They worked to undercut a Conservative Base that was demanding that Republicans act to support traditional values, support a strong national defense, support for the Right to Life movement and oppose "Trade Deals" that result in shipping American jobs overseas while putting manufacturing workers out of their jobs. All that the Tea Party Movement stood for remains anathema to the RINO Establishment which, as their counterparts among the Corporate Democrats do with their own ideologically dissatisfied Base, thinks that paying lip service to their "aspirational ideals" was all that was necessary to keep them in line.

But the Conservative Base was sick of the false neo-Con justifications for endless wars fought in the name of "democracy" and "nation-building" and supported a foreign policy dedicated to preserving American interests before the interests of ungrateful and unreliable "allies," dangerous enemies and transnational corporate interests. RINOs continue to traduce all efforts to lower taxes, curb spending and create a domestic economic policy based on small government Capitalism. They also continue to try to exclude from Leadership positions all those who make up the *overwhelming majority* of the Republican Party. And now, with an outsider in the White House in the form of Donald Trump, they often take the opportunity to exploit every misstatement and mistake this blunt talking, non-politician makes so that they can to subvert his agenda.

RINOS are either opposed to, or at best agnostic, on all the issues which motivate the principles that are at one with those who support Ordered Liberty and who are responsible for any of the electoral success the Republican Party has had. RINOs represent the values of those in the Plutocratic country club that own and support both themselves and their Duopoly partners among the Corporate Democrats.

If the Seventh Crisis is to be faced with a chance to overcome its impact, then Constitutional Conservatives and Trump Nationalist Populists must shun RINO support and spurn their so-called help. They must let them know that they don't need their tainted campaign bribe money and that they don't want their bad advice. They have won election to high office in spite of them, not because of them. RINOS bring nothing to the table except disloyalty and dissention and subversion and betrayal. Millennials and Gen-Xers will not be won over by those who represent the tired and failed components of the Duopoly; while they may be searching for answers now… and will certainly be searching for answers when the Crisis boils over… they will not look toward these archaic failures to provide it.

But the answers offered by the Democrat Socialist Base are not solutions; they are the chains the Big Government Leviathan proffers as a narcotic to a Crisis that seems inevitable. Democrats want to exploit it so as to increase their political power. The critical thinking and spiritual virtues that Gen-Xers, Millennials and Gen-Z will require to fight the Crisis will find those abilities weakened by an educational system polluted by multiculturalism and politically correct orthodoxy. Such a deficit in critical thinking may cause them to look Left and take false solace in the stale Socialist bromides that have brought nothing but catastrophe to those who have implemented them. These non- and indeed, *anti-solutions*, may have been given a new coat of propaganda by the cultural institutions, by the schools, the social media network and the entertainment industry that dominate so much of their modern lives, but they still don't work.

Socialism will not save them because Big Government is bad government—and government is bad when the principle from which it draws strength (in our case, Ordered Liberty) is corrupted and ceases to be as healthy and vigorous in protecting freedom as it should be. When this principle is debilitated and the traditions that are its foundation are ridiculed and abandoned, antagonism is stirred up between the classes and the races and the myriad cultural groups that formerly found common ground in both. Thus, if society loses its moral, economic, military and political values as well as its confidence in the principles that made it strong, it will be unlikely to be able to face the rapidly accelerating Crisis, in whatever form it takes, because it has been suffering its own Crisis of the Spirit for too long.

The deflation of the power of the Duopoly has resulted in a revolt in both of its Left and Right flanks; it has lost the trust of those who are supposed to be its most devoted supporters in the ideologically motivated, activist Base of both.

But an ideological disconnect between the "leadership" in both parties and their respective Bases is a political crisis of the State; when the common values held together by tradition and a devotion to a common national spirit are lost, it is a Crisis of Civilization itself. It is for that reason that those generations who find themselves in the Seventh Crisis must be given an alternative political / spiritual value that is not based in the Collectivist Orthodoxy of the Duopoly, *but in Ordered Liberty.*

- Contrary to popular belief, we do not live in a society where those holding different views of government… between those who want a powerful, centralized government demanding collective subservience to its control struggle with those who want a decentralized, limited government that protects individualism and the Ordered Liberty that makes it possible.. contend.
- In fact, over the last century and a quarter, both parties have more or less been dominated by those who *openly* reject individualism, tradition, religion, Ordered Liberty and National Sovereignty and those who, while mouthing empty platitudes in support for them, *clandestinely reject them as well.*
- Thus, those who rule over us consist of a Duopoly, whose differences are neither profound nor even significant in that both merely grapple for who has power over the people rather than who serves their interests.
- Both Corporate Democrats and Establishment Republicans are the common enemy of those seeking Limited Government, Traditional Values, Free Markets and Ordered Liberty.
- They are, despite all their populist or even socialist rhetoric, the operatives and instruments of a neo-Fascistic Plutocratic Elite that owns them and, through them the government they run, regardless of which party is in power.
- While the activist Base of the Democrat Party desires its leadership to be even more extreme in its support of centralized government power and collectivist solutions, the Base of the Republican party desires its leadership to reject the "me too-ism that its moderate, Eastern Establishment all but openly embraces in virtual partnership with those the Base fears as dangerous subversives in a Democrat Party that is hostile to the American traditions of Ordered Liberty, Capitalism and Judeo-Christian values.
- The history reviewed in this chapter indicates that the plutocratic elites prefer a powerful central government, putatively acting in the name of "fairness", "egalitarianism" and "sharing the wealth" but that in reality serves them and their interests. Their only political "principle" is *the principle of controlling power,* hidden behind the mask of an altruistic policy that seeks to help the "average person" who for which in reality, they have only contempt.

- Those who seek to overcome the Seventh Crisis must understand how it historically developed and why the only real difference between the two Duopoly Parties is how fast the collectivization of society should take place: for the Republican In Name Only (RINO) Establishment, slowly and surely; for the NSDAP Democrats, as rapidly and as radically as possible.
- History teaches that Establishment RINO candidates rarely win and even when they do, they perform in the service of the Duopoly, not the rank and file of the Republican Party, let alone its Constitutional Conservative Base.
- The Generational Cohorts facing the Crisis must reject the false Duopoly idea that Statist intervention in both economic and social policy is the key to a stable and prosperous society, regardless of whether that view is expressed openly and fervently by Democrats or secretly and quietly by Establishment Republicans.
- To overcome the Seventh Crisis, Establishment Republicans must be rejected because they are part of the problem, not part of the solution.
- Instead, those Constitutional Conservatives in the Republican Base must be in alliance with those found among the Trump Nationalist Populists, which includes new voters in the form of manufacturing workers, minorities tired of empty Democrat promises and voters who are pro-Israel

– 3 –

The Tea Party Lights the Way

T he Tea Party served as the *tip of the spear* of the modern Liberty Movement. The movement arose initially as a result of the bank bailouts in late 2008 and gathered steam with the massive stimulus spending bill enacted in the first month of Barack Obama's presidency. The reason it arose spontaneously across the landscape is that patriotic-minded Americans could see that a financial Rubicon had been crossed. There was now so much federal debt that its interest carrying costs could not be financed by the federal budget if interest rates were to appreciably rise. Contrary to political fairy tales, the debt finally mattered.

The Tea Party was largely composed of aging Boomers, or what Strauss & Howe called the Elder Prophets. As Strauss & Howe illustrate in their cyclical analysis of history, as the Fourth Turning enters the Crisis, the aging elders of the Prophet generation step up for their final role. The elder Boomers in the Tea Party stood up to lead, guide and coach the young Hero generation, the Millennials - who must do the heavy lifting in bringing the Crisis to resolution. It is up to the Gen-Xers, Millennials and Gen-Z to chart the path out of the Crisis.

The Tea Party has regenerated interest in limited, constitutional government, free market economics and traditional values that find their champion in *Ordered Liberty* for Millennials to embrace as its Animating Spirit to bring the Crisis to successful resolution.

The Tea Party movement was probably first burned into the American psyche when Rick Santelli, financial reporter for CNBC, first suggested it was time for a "good old fashioned tea party" to the roars of approval in the pits in the Chicago Exchange. Specifically, he asked if those working in the pits "wanted to be paying everyone else's mortgages." At the time in February 2009 an $800 billion so-called Economic Stimulus bill was under consideration. As the public became aware of its provisions it was rapidly becoming perceived as the biggest ever government coerced transfer of wealth from the taxpayers to all the loyal interest groups long toiling on behalf of the Democrat Party.

Santelli's "rant" struck a chord of truth, and cries of support and approval rang from all quarters of the country. The video was replayed hundreds of times across the networks and cable for several days following, but after the initial splash, was never to be seen again on an NBC-owned outlet. The idea of a modern version of the famous Boston Tea Party had taken hold of the imagination of a segment of the American body politic. From such propitious circumstances are historic movements born.

The label "Tea Party" had already been adopted by at least one obscure grassroots organization formed the prior year. Conservative grassroots organizing picked it up during the financial crisis in the fall of 2008. Because a critical mass of both commercial and investment banks was so heavily leveraged with sub-prime and politically driven Community Investment Act, mortgages, many had driven themselves to a literal point of meltdown. All eyes fixed on Washington. Federal officials huddled in the White House where the government's financial leaders, virtually all alumni of the major banks, met to devise a "rescue plan".

The plan they birthed was titled the Troubled Asset Relief Program or TARP. But just who were they rescuing, the average American small business and individual depositor? TARP was a massive $700-billion infusion into the banks via insurance and asset purchases. No executive resignations were required and there were no visible firings. There was nothing surgical about the cash infusion—it was agreed to in one-page letters signed by the major bank CEOs in the White House. They were literally given an offer they couldn't refuse. The result was the banks were saved, but equally as important, so were the bankers—all friends of the officials crafting the deal, Messrs. Paulson, Bernanke, and Geithner.

Conservatives and Libertarians were incensed with what they characterized as a crony bank bailout orchestrated by Bush Administration and Federal Reserve leaders. All this played out simultaneously with the final weeks of the presidential campaign. John McCain mishandled his reaction to the events by dramatically suspending his campaign just a couple weeks after very publicly insisting the state of the economy was good. While McCain appeared out of sync with the crisis, Barack Obama said nothing of substance and went along with the bailout. The press never challenged him, as he clearly was their favorite and he glided comfortably toward the election.

Once elected, Obama vowed to administer TARP as passed and in Rahm Emanuel's infamous phrasing "not letting a crisis go to waste," he immediately began calling for a massive trillion-dollar-sized spending package ostensibly to stimulate economic activity. This, on top of the bank bailout, ignited a detonation across fiscal conservatives and constitutionalists of all political stripes. Blogs overheated, as grassroots organizing and 501c(4) filings spiked before Obama was even inaugurated.

One of those prolific bloggers was Mark Meckler, who was part of an e-mail string of former Ron Paul supporters. They had been keeping the dream alive online long after Mr. Paul's presidential candidacy ended. Others on that string included Jenny Beth Martin and Amy Kremer. With keyboards at the ready on the fateful day of the Santelli rant, this group of bloggers jumped out in front, claiming the Tea Party name for their own. A couple months and one name iteration later, "Tea Party Patriots" (TPP) was born and quickly became the premier Tea Party group.

The leadership of Meckler, Martin and Kremer quickly energized their prior blogging correspondents across the country and suddenly there was a Tea Party leader in every state. Their initial focus was a nationwide rally on April 15th. At the time in the pre-Facebook days of early 2009, many activists found each other by using Meetup.com with its search app for like-minded groups. As activists emerged in virtually every county in the country, a TPP state leader was available for coordination and advice. This movement was truly "organic" in every sense of the word. Independent activists spontaneously launched it into being across the nation. These self-starters instinctively knew what to do to organize for impact.

April 15, 2009 was a spectacular success. Best estimates are there were Tea Party rallies in some 250 cities across the country drawing well over a million people. We'll never know for sure, because mainstream media generally refused to cover the events honestly and began an insidious tactic they'd employ for the next couple years. They refused to publish accurate crowd estimates and many outlets flat out lied about the numbers attending tea party rallies.

The mainstream media coverage of the April 15th rallies featured many of the pure propaganda techniques the Enemedia would deploy over the ensuing years of coverage. They termed the movement "astro-turf" to imply it was staged to reflect numbers far greater than actual. They claimed it was populated by kooks, anarchists and especially racists who despised Obama's rise to the presidency. Reporters would comb through the crowds of senior citizens and average Americans to find someone carrying an odious sign. Such people and their signs were featured in video and newspaper still shots to support many reporters' narrative that the Tea Party was a nativist, racist movement of people who resented a changing and evolving America. TV reporters' on-location voiceovers were dripping with racist innuendo and general ridicule.

But the Tea Parties kept springing up weekly, and contrary to media implications, with no direction from any central organizing entity. Reporters kept asking, "who is your leader," seeking an individual name. The purpose was simple: destroy the movement's leader and deflate and marginalize the movement. The nationally visible organizations, such as Tea Party Patriots, realized the power of a leaderless movement and none of them claimed the mantle of leader. A book titled "The Starfish and the Spider: The Unstoppable Power of Leaderless Organizations" began circulating among Tea Party groups. Everyone involved recognized the power of the leaderless structure and even leaders of massive national rallies such as Dick Army and Glenn Beck demurred to being labeled the national leader of the movement.

Events staged by elected federal officials soon became the preferred location for the rallies and protests. *Federal* officials became the target of Tea Party ire because that's where the big damage was being inflicted on the nation's finances, individual liberties and the inalienable rights of the citizenry.

The major catalysts were the rapidly rising national debt, which had surpassed $10 trillion with the passage of Obama's stimulus legislation. Tea Partiers saw it as largely fraudulent. Hundreds of billions were merely federal to state government transfers designed to keep state and federal workers employed, thereby strengthening the public service unions that funded exclusively Democrat campaigns across the country. The vicious, corrupt campaign funding cycle was on steroids and being funded by the taxpayer.

The country's economic Rubicon had been crossed: at $10 trillion and counting, any honest observer knew that the national debt could not only never be repaid, but at higher, normalized interest rates it could not even be *financed* within any sized national federal budget currently being contemplated. Tea Partiers were infuriated knowing the American middle class was not going to escape the eventual financial reckoning without enduring a world of hurt.

In addition to drowning the people in debt, the Obama Administration was proposing a massive takeover of the health insurance industry under the guise of health care reform. ObamaCare represented the cornerstone of American socialism and the organized Left was intent on sliding it into place in his first term. A first draft of ObamaCare was released in July '09 just in time for the discussion at the representatives' in-district town halls during the August recess.

A third major socialist-styled program was teed up at the same time in an attempt to "flood the zone." Cap and Trade was the brainchild of the environmentalist, global-warming crowd. The idea was to cap carbon usage but allow the developed world the opportunity to purchase "carbon credits" from third world countries to enable the developed world to keep burning fossil fuels - but at a price. Investment banks such as Goldman Sachs actually prepared for a bonanza by building exchanges to trade carbon credits. The whole scheme was designed to facilitate a massive wealth transfer from the developed to the undeveloped world, enriching the financial elites in the process, and all to be underwritten again by the American taxpayer. A Cap and Trade bill passed the House but fortunately was smothered in Senate procedures and never saw the light of day again.

As the aims and legislative agenda of the Democrat-led ruling elite became clear to those unphased by the overwhelming media propaganda effort, their patience boiled over in the summer of '09. Tea Partiers saw an opportunity with the summer congressional recess and rushed into the representatives' town halls in August. They were in no mood to play their part for their congressman's efforts to deliver platitudes and get photo-ops mixing with their constituents. They fired real questions on the budget, the national debt, healthcare and the constitutionality of it all, interrupting many a representative from their prepared script. Cable TV covered these town hall eruptions springing up across the country in the first week of August, and the energy fed on itself and amplified as the month wore on. It became the biggest story in American politics for the rest of the summer and into the fall, off-year election season.

Of course, the media wouldn't cover the phenomenon honestly as a middle-America grassroots uprising ala Network's Howard Beale's "I'm sick and tired and not gonna take it anymore." They recognized this could endanger theirs and Obama's grand progressive agenda. The Tea Party had to be marginalized and crushed in its infancy. They needed to discredit it as anything but spontaneous. They needed to show the whole movement was organized by the Republican party leadership—that it was not organic, that it was not rooted in communities throughout the nation. They needed some kind of cabal or fall guy to vilify and slander, and on which the entire grassroots uprising could be blamed.

Amazingly, this co-author, Bob MacGuffie, served to fit the bill. After a town hall with new Democrat congressman, Jim Himes, in Southport, Connecticut, he wrote what he termed a political action memo advising other Tea Party groups how they might attend and "rock the town halls" to get their representatives to answer some real questions. He wrote up the *best practices* of how with fellow Tea Partiers, we were able to literally set Mr. Himes back on his heals to address our agenda items. He circulated the memo to other regional Tea Party group leaders in addition to forwarding it to the Tea Party Patriots leadership team, where they posted it on their public messaging and resource board.

Within a month, leftist media had downloaded the memo and it went viral throughout the media. Media reports ridiculed what was a local grassroots leader, as a national Republican operative organizing the Tea Party movement from coast to coast. For a week the story was in the white-hot leftist media spotlight being ridiculed as a "disruptor" of the democratic process. It was a case study in leftist, Alinksy-style intimidation: freeze, polarize and attack the target. Mary Katherine Ham of *The Weekly Standard* wrote a very effective article debunking the smear, illustrating precisely how the Left takes a useful incident, misrepresents the facts developing an article with their narrative, then circulates the propaganda package throughout the media. In the United States this happens on a regular basis, each time with a new person and incident in the Left's cross-hairs. As only about half the American public realizes, we are quite literally living in a propaganda state.

By the fall of '09 the Tea Party Movement (TPM) was on the political map but the dimensions of its potential impact were still unknown, even to those of us within the movement. While the movement was being smeared, disparaged, marginalized and defined by the media and the Democrats, the Tea Party activists recognized the imperative of getting into the media and defining themselves and their movement. Like the great leaderless movement that it was, students of history and politics within the movement stepped to the microphones and op-ed pages across the country to set the record straight.

For those willing to listen, Tea Partiers schooled the American public on the country's founding principles, the benefits of capitalism and free market economics, the rights and responsibilities of individual freedom, the guarantees and limits of the U.S. Constitution, and how our system of *Ordered Liberty* spurred a new nation to undisputed world dominance in just 169 years. The TPM publicly decried the attitudes and actions of both major parties. Big government power and spending were self-defining orthodoxy for the Democrats. But the TPM equally called out the Republicans for betraying its century-old principles of limited, constitutional, and conservative government. Many Tea Partiers held the Republican leadership in even more contempt because they squandered so many electoral victories, and betrayed their voters and the conservative principles to which they pledged.

Another effort in which these co-authors played a leading drafting role was the issuance of the "Declaration of Tea Party Independence". In February of 2010, after a year of being smeared and disparaged by the left and fending off attempts at co-option by the Republican party, Tea Party activists were organized in over a dozen states to engage in a collaborative correspondence. The purpose was to declare the Tea Party as an independent and distinct entity - particularly distinct from the two major parties.

The document read in part: "We declare ourselves INDEPENDENT of the Democrat Party and its power drunk junta in Washington, DC, which is currently seeking to impose a socialist agenda on our Republic. We reject a Democrat Party which refuses to give credence to our demands for just redress of grievances and which insults and seeks to demonize our legal right to peacefully protest the unjust laws it inflicts upon us……..We declare ourselves INDEPENDENT of the Republican Party, which has in the past manipulated its Conservative Base to win election after election and which then betrays everything that Base fought for and believed. We reject the idea that the electoral goals of the Republican Party are identical to the goals of the Tea Party Movement or that this Movement is an adjunct to the Republican Party. We reject the Republican Party professionals who now seek to use the Tea Party Movement for their corrupt and narrow political purposes."

The Declaration was simultaneously released to local media by dozens of Tea Party groups across the country to illustrate the movement's breadth and independence. No individual took authorship credit, but every group distributing it implicitly signed on to the Declaration.

Reporters everywhere awakened to the Declaration in their inboxes. It received a fair amount of coverage in the conservative press. Several mainstream outlets such as the *WSJ, NYT* and *WP* made reference to it, while the nationally syndicated program, *The McLaughlin Group* engaged in a long discussion regarding its political impact on TV. But the media dropped it at that. We then recognized that any conservative message that would not provide an opportunity to ridicule or disparage the TPM, would quickly lose the interest of the mainstream media and be sent down the memory hole and treated as if it never existed.

As evidenced by the Declaration effort and others, the TPM was a demonstration of organic power, meaning that the movement was coalescing simultaneously in communities across the nation. Freedom of association is in our DNA as Americans. Tea Partiers immediately recognized national policies that were clearly contrary to the country's founding principles. We were set into motion like cells in a chemical reaction within the body politic to defend the body and confront the leftwing infection. We, who sprang into action spreading the word organizing and protesting, put our regular lives on hold while we assumed new roles on the internet, in the media and in the streets. We materialized simultaneously; we often acted anonymously; we confronted officials or our opponents lawfully but directly. The decentralized nature of the phenomenon itself was the proof that we were not being directed by commands issued through hierarchical channels.

This was a new power model, unfamiliar to a ruling class that relied on command and control. They didn't understand it, they couldn't explain it, and most assuredly they couldn't control it. All they could do was disparage it, ridicule it, misrepresent it, and make excuses for it. The complicit, liberal mainstream press proceeded to weave a narrative that depicted the TPM as a fringe element organized and financed by either the Republican Party, corporate lobbying interests or both. But make no mistake about it, the ruling class, both political and media knew exactly what we were and they were rightly horrified by the TPM. The TPM's homemade signs and incredible self-motivation, which exposed the "Big Lie" charade that the federal government had become, bespoke the truth and touched a raw nerve among the ruling elite and their protectors. The Democrat leadership surely recognized, but couldn't believe, that in their hubris they had pushed their big government agenda too hard, and had unleashed a ferocious unprecedented grassroots backlash incapable of being quelled without in-fact rolling back their agenda. As halting their agenda was not an option, in full fury the leadership and their protectors in the media resorted to their favorite plan B—shoot the messengers!

But the Tea Party had stepped onto the political playing field and already tolled the bell. The movement's purpose was to awaken the American people to the dangers of an all pervasive federal government, over-regulating our lives and plunging us into debt at the rate of $3 billion a day—the equivalent of about 80 new Yankee Stadiums a month! We were being ground up between debt, taxes and regulations. At its essence, the TPM was about devolving usurped federal power back to the states, where our founders intended most issues to be resolved—closest to the people. Tea Partiers took issue with many federal laws and Supreme Court rulings but they didn't want new federal laws reversing them. They want the decisions to revert back to the states where they could be debated and constitutionally decided in state legislatures. Tenth Amendment rallying cries could be heard across the movement.

At the time, a particularly insidious legislative practice was gaining favor with the congress. Bills being written were increasingly deferring the specific rules of implementation to the office of the cabinet secretary and agency heads having jurisdiction over the subject matter. The practical effect of this was to empower federal bureaucrats to write, enforce and adjudicate the law and punish its transgressors. ObamaCare was the poster child for the practice.

In addition, the 2008 campaign of Barack Obama featured a continual drumbeat of calls for higher taxes, usually qualified as taxes on the rich, the definition of which was never provided. Tea Partiers knew the government had a spending problem—not a revenue problem. Enough had been published by individuals who previously had held government finance or operating positions outlining with an insider's perspective, the policies and practices which demonstrated the federal government squandered hundreds of billions of dollars annually. Every creative taxing gambit imaginable was floated into public discussion: a mileage tax, wealth tax, inventory tax, hunter's tax, hoarder's tax. It made our parents' old joke about taxing the air we breathe no longer a comical exaggeration.

As the election year of 2010 progressed, the TPM was turbo-charged in March by the passage of ObamaCare, which incensed a major sector of the electorate. The TPM harnessed that issue and drove it into the mid-term elections, overturning the Democrat House majority with a reversal of historic proportions. The TPM was an historical electoral backlash against the establishment.

Tea Partiers ran for office and flooded into the system in the '10, '12, and '14 elections—all to the absolute horror of the establishment and ruling political elite. The '10 and '14 mid-term elections were huge victories for the TPM, with the senate finally being returned to a Republican majority along with the House. However, the TPM fell short of capturing the leadership in either chamber. This would prove to be a significant failure of the movement. While both chambers, including leadership, were singing from the Tea Party hymnal, conservative ideas and recommended courses of action were not getting traction. But, the TPM had permanently injected itself into the political system on every level - local, state, and national.

Suddenly, the RINOs could no longer play their kabuki dance with the Democrats. As John Boehner play-acted opposition to the outrageous Democrat spending plans, elected congressional "Freedom Caucus" members put the bayonet in his back and made him actually fight for TPM principles. The days of easy breezy "compromise" with the Democrats were over. Boehner knew it, publicly expressed his misery over it, and after 5 years as Speaker of the House, resigned because of it. The TPM had massive success in state legislatures as well. Nearly a thousand state seats flipped to the Republicans. Many of these new legislators were on the streets among the Tea Partiers only a year before. A couple, such as Matt Bevans of Kentucky, became governors; others powered into Congress.

The Tea Party was much more than a comet streaking across the political sky. It was a patriotic movement which took the political playing field with classic can-do American style. It went to the public square to awaken the American citizenry to the dangers of the soft tyranny being perpetrated upon the people by its ruling political class. It illuminated the peaceful, legal path to effecting liberty enhancing legislative changes through the electoral process. Many of its members successfully entered the process, effected change and motivated many more to enter the process to continue the effort. After the movement had run its course, the rest of the Tea Partiers went back home to resume their lives. As a coda to the era and credit to the movement— no Tea Partier was ever arrested after thousands of rallies over the course of about 7 years.

The TPM illuminated the critical issues of its time and showed a constructive way forward. We didn't quite realize it at the time but the Baby Boom generation driving the TPM was commencing an historical effort that they could not see through to conclusion; they would have to pass the baton to those generations on the front lines of the Crisis, so that they could successfully complete the transition as America passed through a momentous gate of history.

The unlikely Boomer "Prophets" had spoken and now the Millennials bear the heavy burden of leading the country to a new era of renewed liberty.

- The Tea Party Movement, which basically lasted from 2009— 20015, was a Constitutional Conservative and Populist reaction against an expansion of government in terms of power, spending and social control under the Obama Administration that was far more aggressive, openly socialistic and antithetical to Ordered Liberty on every level than even the worst of its Big Government predecessors.
- Since the majority of those who gravitated to the Tea party Movement knew their history and maintained a simmering anger over the Duopoly's leadership of the country since the Reagan years, they formed the core of those that had set themselves up to fulfill the Strauss-Howe role of "Prophets"; viz. those who were required to provide guidance to the Millennial and Gen-X generations…essentially by warning them not to follow the anti-liberty example that far too many of their fellow Baby Boomers deluded themselves into accepting in the 1960s.

- The Movement was initially motivated by the grotesque increases in deficit spending and mountainous debt created by economically suicidal Liberal economic programs, but soon morphed into a general Constitutional Conservative / Libertarian / Populist critique of Progressive policies in general, from a trade policy that devastated American manufacturing workers, to attacks on religious groups who opposed governmental attacks on their rights and privileges that the Government justified in the name of "inclusion," to attacks on the traditional culture, its holidays, its History, its heroes and its myths, all in the name of "multiculturalism." It saw high ranking American officials, from President Obama on down, apologizing for American History to foreign leaders and a subsequent diminishing of the U.S. military while at the same time increasing involvement in pointless foreign wars such as in Afghanistan. Slow economic growth and burgeoning tax hikes combined to produce economic stagnation and a hollowing out of the American manufacturing Base, which the Obama Administration relentlessly pushed so as to serve the Transnational Progressive corporate groups that owed Obama as much as it did the previous RINO Republican administration of George W. Bush.
- Riding the wave of massive increases in governmental spending and strangulating "Cap & Trade" environmental regulations, the government moved to take over 1/6 of the American economy with a budget-busting version of socialized medicine called "Obamacare."
- The Tea Party Movement against it all exploded across the country in the form of loud but peaceful demonstrations and raucous but non-violent Town Hall Meetings where Congressional Representatives were shocked to find out that many of their constituents came to demand answers to specific questions regarding policy and not to watch yet another staged campaign event, where long serving political hacks were served up softball questions posed by their political cronies in the audience.
- Party affiliation was no defense against TPM anger; Establishment Republicans were subjected to the same tough questioning as Progressive Democrats. Many TPM groups declared themselves Independent of Democrats, Republicans and the biased Enemedia. It was a Movement dedicated to Liberty and remained free from all Establishment attempts to either (on the Democrat side) replicate it or (on the RINO Republican side) to co-opt and control it.

- TPM policy demands regarding debt, taxes and regulations swept Republican candidates into office in the 2010 mid-terms and increased TPM representation in congress in 2012. It scored huge victories in the 2014 mid-term elections, with the senate finally being returned to a Republican majority along with the House.
- Despite the TPM's energizing of the Base to deliver Republican Leadership into power, it failed in many of its attempts to get that "leadership" to take their issues seriously. Time and again, their TPM representatives on Capitol Hill were marginalized, ignored and in the end betrayed by a RINO Establishment that was, like the Corporate Wing of the Democrat Party, also serving the interests of big banks, big tech, big pharma, multinational industry giants and powerful international finance firms.
- By 2015 members of the Tea Party movement either pursued elective office at all levels, particularly local, went back to revive their neglected small businesses, or charged into the Trump campaign, becoming a key block in the Constitutional Conservative / Trumpist Alliance that was key to his election in 2016. Many channeled their enthusiasm into the social media battles raging outside the formal 2016 campaign, and exercised significant pressure on more Establishment Republicans to adjust their views to reflect a perspective more in sync with the Tea Party Movement or risk losing their next election.

– 4 –

Counter-Punch of the Deep State Feds

"Deep State" had definitely been a below-the-radar term for decades until 2016 when it surfaced on conservative cable TV and was repeatedly used by on-air commentators. A more widely used term up to that point was the "Administrative State", but that referred more narrowly to government organs. The Deep State refers to the permanent federal government—its clique of embedded and intractable bureaucratic officials, plus selected influencers in non-government organizations (NGO), and the critical mega financial individual resources and outside conduits. It includes selected mass media company owners deploying their public-facing print and electronic "reporters" to control the "narrative" presented to the public justifying their actions. Significant swaths of the federal judiciary serve as backstop and enforcer to deep state rule. In addition, the spawning grounds of the entire elitist mindset - university administration and professors within most "citadels of academia" round out the organs of power propelling Deep State rule.

This is not to imply some hidden ring of leaders. No, unfortunately each of these interested entities all navigate by the same collectivist stars. Being instinctive elitists, controllers, and professional self-preservationists, they usually know exactly what to do about most any of the major public issues in play at any given time in America. These entities, bureaucracies, judiciary, media and academia were authorized, designed or launched for the express purpose to benefit the citizenry. But there should be no mistake—gravity has been upended, and these institutions persistently and tenaciously act in their own self-interest and that of the ruling class, virtually all the time.

Together they have "weaponized" many of the bureaucratic organs of the federal government against the American people. In so doing, they have affected the course of events contrary to the will of the American people, as expressed in congressional and presidential elections, countless times in the past 70 years.

JUDICIAL "SOFT TYRANNY"

This is most obvious, notable, and codified when a federal judge under judicial review, issues a ruling minting new national law, such as Anthony Kennedy's SCOTUS ruling legalizing homosexual "marriage" in all 50 states. At the time of his ruling, in only 3 states, Maine, Maryland and Washington, had the citizens actually voted for homosexual marriage. Eight legislatures had voted for it and fully half, 26 states, had homosexual marriage imposed by state court decisions. But one federal judicial official deemed it the "law of the land", as our ruling political class likes to phrase it.

We actually saw a one-two Deep State punch in the spring of 2012. A case challenging the constitutionality of ObamaCare had made its way to the Supreme Court. The justices had heard the arguments in March and were due to rule in June. Knowing full well that Justice Roberts follows media coverage and is close to obsessed with the Court's image, the progressive mainstream media commenced a continual release of press articles and cable TV discussions warning that the Court's and the Chief Justice's reputations would be damaged should the Court strike down Obama's crowning "achievement" as unconstitutional.

In the SCOTUS ruling, John Roberts took it on himself to in effect re-write the legislation to deem the mandate to purchase insurance coverage a *tax,* (directly contradicting Obama's own words saying it was not a tax) which is a constitutional power, rather than a federal requirement that a citizen make a private purchase, which is generally deemed unconstitutional. So, all wrapped into one issue we have the congress over-reach with unconstitutional legislation, then upon legal challenge the media publicly intimidated the Chief Justice into fabricating a rationale to secure a ruling of constitutionality. This episode illustrates the daunting power of deep state organs to impose a law controlling 17 percent of the economy, on the entire citizenry. And that citizenry when polled has *never* indicated that a majority desire ObamaCare coverage.

The Tea Party organized and protested mightily against ObamaCare and all the taxes and regulations within it. Despite the unconstitutionality of the law, the deep state had to teach the citizens who was boss. And three years later SCOTUS had to once again re-write ObamaCare to allow subsidies to those purchasing coverage on a *federally* operated exchange, which had been omitted from the legislation. An unprecedented and embarrassing exclamation point placed on an abominable piece of congressional despotism!

Our country's founders designed three branches of government and although equal, the judiciary was specifically expected to be the least powerful. The legislature was expected to be the most powerful. It was comprised of elected representatives and as such it was designed to be the driving force in the creation of law and imposition of taxes. But the political dynamics of the Millennial saeculum have been so skewed, that multiple congresses averse to facing tough decisions too often defer to court decrees, from which legislative responsibility can easily be dodged. As a result, the federal legislative process has ground to a virtual halt.

From a limited government perspective, this could be viewed as a favorable development. But from a fiscal responsibility perspective this has proven to be nothing less than catastrophic. Specific appropriation bills cannot pass for lack of sufficient votes. So, both House and Senate have resorted to "comprehensive" spending bills which have ballooned in size in order to achieve the necessary consensus to pass. The result is over $23 trillion in federal debt, presently increasing by $3 billion every day in which the sun rises.

ADMINISTRATIVE SOFT TYRANNY

Another dynamic resulting from a gridlocked congress reduced to passing overly comprehensive bills, is that they are indeed all encompassing, resulting in massive unable to comprehend behemoths tabled on the floor for a vote. A typical highly publicized example was ObamaCare coming in at about 3,000 pages. This is all intentional by the bill's authors in their effort to affect every area and activity throughout the industry they intend to regulate. They cannot describe in words every permutation and eventuality of impact - so the language inevitably delegates authority for the endless amount of interim decisions back to the cabinet secretary or agency head's office.

This is where the Agency bureaucrats get to make the rules and regulations with the effect of law. The Agency is also authorized to investigate violations of those rules, issue complaints, adjudicate the complaints, and yes—dole out the fine and punishment. Anyone who has been audited by the IRS or crossed the EPA can vouch for the efficacy of this system. The term currently in use for this experience is "soft tyranny" and if anything the "soft" part is too generous. For some who have become entangled with a federal agency resulting in a fine of some manageable amount, the penalty may indeed be soft. But if you ask Vernon Hershberger, a dairy farmer in Loganville, Wisconsin, he would likely term his experience with the federal government just plain tyranny.

Hershberger produces *raw milk*, milk not pasteurized, for a private raw milk club. Because the FDA insists you market *pasteurized* milk, they sent federal marshals several times to raid Hershberger's farm, confiscating his computers and destroying his milk and cheese. He was conducting a private service and in some cases the buyers actually owned the cows in his barn. He got the SWAT experience several times because he would not *comply*. The Feds want compliance and yes here in the 21st century America, they will do whatever's necessary to obtain it. The Feds couldn't have cared less that he produced the raw milk products exclusively for private citizens specifically seeking the raw milk products or that he did not sell any raw milk products through public distribution channels.

Neither would the Gibson Guitar Corporation term its federal marshal experience as anything other than straight-up tyranny. The company had been importing ebony wood from Madagascar, but ceased in 2009 as a result of a ban on such imports. But on a hot August morning in 2011, over a dozen black SUVs carrying federal marshals decked out in full SWAT gear raided the Nashville Tennessee guitar fabrication plant. As Gibson's CEO described it, "We had a raid with federal marshals that were armed, that came in, evacuated our factory, shut down production, sent our employees home and confiscated wood."

The justification for the raid: the Environmental Investigation Agency deemed the imported wood a violation of the Lacey act, which required the end-user document that it obtained the wood legally. The EIA claimed Gibson knowingly imported tainted wood. The entire episode cost the company millions. As it turned out the seized wood was legally purchased from India, not Madagascar. But when faced with a mountain of prospective legal costs to obtain justice, Gibson did what so many others caught in this trap have been intimidated into - they settled. They paid a $250,000 settlement, a $50,000 environmental fine and over $2 million in legal fees. And casting a pall over the entire episode was speculation that the Obama Administration pursued Gibson because the CEO was a contributor to Republican campaigns. Because it's near impossible to prove specific motivation, this factoid remains as speculation.

THE IRS HARASSMENT SCANDAL

One agency of the federal government which has stricken fear in the hearts of most Americans for decades is the Internal Revenue Service. For most it is the dreaded letter advising of an upcoming tax audit. Horror stories of the handling of ordinary Americans by IRS agents are legend. We are supposed to retain our Constitutional rights during the audit process, and congress has passed specific legislation addressing and safeguarding those rights. But to many who have experienced an extensive audit it seems their constitutional rights were checked outside the door of the IRS office.

The IRS is ground-zero for a federal agency that gets to write the rules, interpret them, summon and interrogate citizens they deem to have violated them, pass judgement on those citizens, determine and impose the penalty, and *enforce* said penalty, including jail time. The experience doesn't exactly have the ring of "government of the people, by the people and for the people." But beyond the collection of tax revenue, the IRS has been exercising an increasingly partisan influence within the political system.

The right of "free association" is one cherished and exercised by genera-tions of Americans going back to our founding. But in the modern era, things have naturally become more complicated. If you, with other like-minded citi-zens, decide to form a formal group or association to advocate for public issues or create discussion forums, you are likely to need to collect money to support the activity. In order to facilitate the money handling you go to a bank, seek-ing to open an account in the group's name. But the bank will require you to present government-approved filing documents including an IRS tax number in order to open a bank account.

From 2009 through 2012 thousands of Tea Party styled, conservative grassroots groups formed and sought to file with the IRS, to secure the nec-essary paperwork and tax number to enable the opening of bank accounts. The appropriate filing for political advocacy groups is a 501(c)(4). Over the years this was a rather perfunctory exercise for political advocacy groups of all stripes, resulting in provision of the appropriate paperwork in a few weeks. The group could then open a bank account, fund itself and become opera-tional. But under the Obama Administration rather than facilitate group for-mation, the 501(c)(4) filing process became a "choke point" on the free speech of the Administration's political opponents.

As we noted, the Obama Administration and its acolytes in government were highly concerned with the building wave of opposition in the form of Tea Party protests across the country. So, during this time period, Obama began publicly criticizing the formation of "shadowy groups with harmless sound-ing names." Max Baucus, Democrat chair of the Senate Finance Committee, asked the IRS to investigate newly formed 501(c)(4)s. This was soon followed by a letter from 7 Democrat senators asking the IRS to investigate conser-vative 501(c)(4) organizations, while Senator Sheldon Whitehouse publicly berated the deputy chief of Criminal Investigation at the IRS for not prose-cuting conservative nonprofits.

To understand the code of the Deep State we do not need to follow up to see if any of these "requests" were formally acted upon. No, the purpose of these public pronouncements was to signal to all two million federal workers to use their federal positions to impair the formation and activities of conser-vative nonprofit groups—regardless of the results of the formal requests. This way the orders to impede and deny conservatives' rights immediately, are in plain sight. Any willing sympathetic federal worker with their antenna up and in a position to help, now felt empowered to do the necessary thing from their roost to suppress conservative speech and action. No future "smoking gun" memo of instruction need ever be written.

One such federal employee was Lois Lerner, director of the IRS's Exempt Organizations unit. The Exempt Organizations Unit is the engine room for approving or denying 501(c)(4) applications. And judging from the time-lines of her e-mails which emerged when her scandal broke, Lerner was well underway impeding Tea Party applications by the time Obama and company publicly voiced alarm. Impossible for the Deep State powers to contain, her Tea Party targeting scandal broke across both the mainstream and alternative press in May of 2013. It was a major story for weeks and intermittently for months, resulting in a faux apology and denunciation from Obama, and two appearances by Lerner before the House Oversight and Government Reform Committee, in which she publicly and arrogantly pled the fifth.

The simple, yet insidious technique employed by Lerner's minions was to engage Tea Party applicants in an endless series of questions and clarifications regarding the applications, thereby extending the application process for months and ultimately years. Once fully up to speed in 2010, the strategy effectively ground to a halt new Tea Party and conservative group formation—mission accomplished. By hardly flexing a muscle, Tea Party group formation was stopped in its tracks by the administrative state's simple abuse of a legitimate power entrusted to it. Of course, Lerner was never prosecuted. She resigned, refused to speak to the press, sat home quietly and was protected by the administrative state and continues to receive her government pension.

The IRS Commissioner during Lerner's subterfuge was Doug Shulman. He received no scrutiny over the scandal. He visited the White House 118 times over the period, generating much speculation that Obama was well aware of and may have been directing the operation. He was allowed to finish his term that fall with no repercussions whatsoever. His replacement, John Koskinen, however, was left to do the necessary cover-up work to contain the scandal and put it to bed. In a practice that was becoming contagious in Washington, Koskinen learned that 30,000 of Lois Lerner's e-mails had been "lost" following the first exposure of the scandal in April 2013. But he said nothing to Congress for two months, until a court case forced the information into the public. After Obama's Justice Dept. stonewalled calls for an investigation, filing no charges against anyone in government, the House Government and Oversight Committee filed a resolution to impeach Koskinen. The impeachment resolution died in the House Judiciary Committee after Trump's election.

KINETIC IGNITION AVOIDED AT THE BUNDY RANCH

The episode at the Bundy Ranch in Nevada in the spring of 2014 is notable for at least two reasons: a classic illustration of the intrusive and destructive reach of the federal government into the lives and livelihoods of rural Americans, it was also a definitive point to date in the Seventh Crisis where a true *ignition point* was reached that threatened to turn our cold civil war, *hot*.

Decades before the confrontation, rancher Cliven Bundy paid Clark County, Nevada for water and foraging rights to graze his cattle on government-owned land. He also made improvements to the land at his expense. Then in the '90s the federal government's Bureau of Land Management (BLM) began to exert control over the area and began charging grazing fees to all the ranchers in the county. Bundy refused to pay fees to graze the land his family had been working for 100 years or more. The ranchers who paid saw the fees continually increase until they faced an economic crisis. One after another some 40 ranchers were forced out of business by the Feds. Bundy was adamant about not being the next one.

BLM insisted that the reasoning for the fees was to provide an alternative habitat for the endangered desert tortoise inhabiting the area. But many contended it was housing development which really destroyed the tortoise habitats. Meanwhile, Nevada senator and majority leader Harry Reid was pressing the BLM director to expand the tortoise boundaries to get control, all for the benefit of none other than his top donor, a major land developer.

Against this backdrop BLM threw the national spotlight on itself by confiscating 25 percent of Bundy's cattle, herding them into a canyon and fencing them off from Bundy. Bundy alerted the press that he estimated over a 100 BLM and FBI agents were heavily armed and encircling his ranch. Cameras appeared and Bundy demanded his cattle returned. Nevada Governor Brian Sandoval issued a statement in support of the Bundy Ranch and decried "BLM's establishment of a 'First Amendment Area' that tramples upon Nevadans' fundamental rights under the U.S. Constitution." BLM was actually trying to pen-in Bundy as well as the cattle, by designating a specific area for him to speak publicly. It was a national story within hours and the public was siding with Bundy.

Within a couple days, militia members opposed to federal government encroachment on citizens' rights were arriving at the ranch from across the country. They brought their arms and vowed to defend the Bundy Ranch. The incident was but a few days old and the temperature was rapidly rising. By week's end the scene resembled an Alamo-styled standoff between the Bundy family with armed militiamen vs. the armed Feds. Public sentiment was overwhelmingly in favor of the rancher. The TV feed on Saturday April 12th pictured a line of armed ranchers and militia, including a couple on horseback and a Gadsden 'Don't Tread on Me' flag lined up along a ridge facing the gully leading to the fenced cattle. On the other side, BLM guards were milling around a group of black SUVs parked on a dirt path just above the fence holding back the cattle. It all appeared as a movie scene, and it didn't look like it was going to end well.

Certainly, Barak Obama was viewing the scene from the White House. Did he really want to ignite a violent confrontation with the ranchers and risk it metastasizing into a full-blown armed confrontation with the rising patriot movement in the country? Could this actually have been a modern Fort Sumpter incident? We will never know for sure but in mid-afternoon the Feds got into their SUVs placed them in reverse and backed out of the canyon. They never even turned around. The word must have come down from on high. About 20 minutes later the TV images showed a cattle rush—the confiscated cattle were charging back through the gully to the Bundy Ranch.

Although not reported as such by the Enemedia, the entire episode was a humiliation for BLM and the Obama Administration. BLM may have been doing Harry Reid's bidding or it may have sought the land for another purported federal purpose—the Dry Lake Solar Energy Zone. But the incident clearly got out of hand. And if the Feds and Enemedia were able to maneuver public opinion to see the Bundy family as the bad guys, maybe Obama would have been bold enough to ignite the match without realizing the consequences. The incident at the Bundy Ranch illustrates the literally "out-of-control" mindset of the Deep State when it seeks to demonstrate its control and intimidate the average citizen. It remains a cautionary tale for both sides.

These are not isolated incidents. They are referenced here to illustrate how the federal government, through regulation and enforcement, is regularly tyrannizing the American people every day. Many more examples of both judicial and bureaucratic oppression of ordinary citizens could be put forward. For a thorough accounting, analyzing dozens of similar actions see attorney Harvey Silverglate's book, *Three Felonies a Day: How the Feds Target the Innocent*. The purpose of this recounting is to illustrate the potency and capability of the judiciary and bureaucracy of the Administrative State to make its citizens cower before them. These are the *enforcers*. And if to date they haven't found an issue directly affecting your community or your life, be assured, in time they will.

The other arms in the service of the broader Deep State are the media, academia and the NGOs. These function as the *influencers*. They serve to shape events both visibly and out of public view, exerting impact in both the short and longer term. It would take another book to examine and assess exactly when a majority of mainstream U.S. newspapers and network news outlets slipped from generally reporting on news events, to structuring their coverage to advance political agendas. We cover the subversive media elsewhere, but for purposes here it can be confidently said that since the Reagan years of the '80s, a majority of mainstream media executives have been directing press coverage through a decidedly liberal lens, pursuing a decidedly progressive agenda.

But tragically for the interests of a free citizenry, since the turn of this century and the election of George W. Bush, the mainstream political press has largely served as a quite visible propaganda arm of the Democrat party, and in more opaque ways, advancing the interests of the ruling political class.

THE SUBVERSION OF AMERICAN ACADEMIA

Perhaps the most corrosive and reprehensible arm of the deep state is the current U.S. academic system. Over the past couple of decades, stories emanating from academia portray college campuses to average Americans as an insular world detached from reality. Though too many of the system's product, the graduates, do indeed emerge with an apparent reverse-polarity view of society and country, tragically it is by design. The path and direction were laid down by the cultural Marxists in the mid-20th century.

Over the past couple decades, college administrators have promulgated repressive speech and harassment codes all designed to quash speech with which they disagree. Conservative guest speakers, or simply controversial anti-liberal speakers, are either disinvited after college administrators learn of their scheduled appearance, heckled from the stage, or otherwise thwarted from delivering their presentations. Important and influential Conservative voices such as Ann Coulter, Ben Shapiro and Candace Owens have all faced aggressive and sometimes violent opposition when seeking to speak to campus audiences they have been invited to address. When such unconstitutional

COUNTER-PUNCH OF THE DEEP STATE FEDS

actions occur, University Administrations simply hide behind the bromide that such speakers are engaging in "hate speech", which serves as a derivative of Orwell's *thought crimes*. Or, if leftist agitators raise enough hell at conservative speaker appearances, administrators can refuse the next request for a conservative speaker claiming the college can't afford security for the speaker. Leftist violence not only thwarts the speaker at hand, it assures no more can be afforded.

When it is their own students voicing dissent with anti-liberal speech, college administrators, professors and students employ smear and humiliation tactics to ostracize the offenders, often college conservatives. Administrators have instituted "speech codes" and "free speech zones" all designed to ban free speech. Violators are investigated by campus "diversity and tolerance offices." It seems any speech deviating from the leftist world view, administrators deem offensive and is banned through the use of campus speech codes.

"Bias" is another current major category of affront to today's progressive sensibilities. Either conscious or unconscious, students' motivations are under constant scrutiny to assure any and all aggrieved minorities receive justice. To enforce university standards, "Bias Response Teams" have been launched on campuses across the country. Their purported purpose is to respond to "acts of intolerance." As with most everything on campus, it is the Left that gets to decide what is and what is not to be tolerated. Any student *perceiving* an offense is encouraged to report said malicious *incident* to college administration. And the way this reporting regime has been developing, not surprisingly, has been quite detrimental to conservative and independent thought. One offense or "microaggression" has ruined academic careers. The chilling, self-censoring impact on the balance of faculty and student body cannot be over-stated. And self-censorship is precisely the tactical objective of today's academic overlords. Students today are literally trapped in an Orwellian propagandized world of spying, informing, and undercutting other students, faculty or even administrators who stray from the politically correct program. In a real sense, they are eating themselves alive—but that should be no surprise to those who have studied the history of Marxist societies in the 20th century.

Another gambit deployed by college administrators, aimed at stifling independent thought and words, is the defunding of disapproved college newspapers. At this point, most, though not all papers are under the spell of leftist editors. At the University of California San Diego the student government, acting at the behest of the administration, defunded the student newspaper, *The Koala*. In 2016 *The Koala* made the fateful mistake of sati-rizing "safe spaces" and "trigger warnings". The defunding appeared to be a straight-up violation of the paper's freedom of speech, so the paper sued the college administration. But a judge in the infamous ninth circuit, itself an activist arm of the deep state, bent himself into a pretzel to rule against the free speech rights of the student newspaper. So here we have yet another example of the deep state's reach of intimidation and power of enforcement, enacted by one of its judicial instrumentalities.

Using transgenders as the spear tip, college administrators have been intimidating those on campus who refuse to use certain proscribed pronouns, thereby quashing independent thought, the free speech rights of both stu-dents and faculty as well as definitional reality all at the same time. In 2017 at Shawnee State University, rather than call a professed transgender student by the requested female pronoun, a professor decided to instead call the student by his name. University officials came down on the professor, threatening to fire him for creating a "hostile environment". The professor sued the univer-sity and as of this writing the case remains unresolved. During the same time period, a teacher in West Point HS in Virginia was fired for refusing to refer to a student by that student's preferred pronoun. It is clear that the entire gender identification paradigm is clearly being used as a weapon against free speech, free thought, and indeed, biological reality.

Since the turn of the 21st century it's been becoming clear to a growing number of Americans that in too many of our universities the main objective has shifted from learning to politically correct indoctrination. Meanwhile, tui-tion inflation has raged along over the past 20 years at an annual rate averaging 7 percent, year after year. This is being driven by lavish expansion of cam-puses and a geometric rise in administrators in relation to student population growth. Just to provide an astounding supporting factoid, the University of Michigan employs 93 full-time "diversity officers", including diversity admin-istrators, directors, vice-provosts, deans, consultants, managers, analysts, and specialists—all minding the diversity count. The salary and benefit cost of this abominable waste of money is $11 million per year, plus with the estimated office and personal tech equipment cost, the total financial drain on the uni-versity is some $15 million. Just think of all the professors that could fund, or the reduction in tuition for that one line item. This one made the news, but rest assured most every university in America is loaded with such significant line items which have absolutely nothing to do with educating students.

The idea that U.S. higher education has transformed from centers of learning to leftist indoctrination mills is regularly ridiculed and poo-pooed by the current progressive mouthpieces. But mid-20th century Marxist proponents publicly advocated for just such a transformation. Antonio Gramsci, the early 20th century Italian Communist theorist, elaborated that "within the school system you can begin to rewrite key components of curricula such as history, economics, social studies, and introduce new concepts like sociology and psychology. Curricula that demonized a country's historic values and inserted Marxist values in their place are critical to destroying a country's culture."

American public figures were so concerned in the 1950s and '60s that in the U.S. House of Representatives A.S. Herlong read into the Congressional Record on January 10, 1963, Gramsci-inspired, Marxist goals for education as enumerated in Cleon Skousen's book "The Naked Communist" as follows: "Get control of the schools. Use them as transmission belts for socialism and current Communist propaganda. Soften the curriculum. Get control of teachers' associations. Put the party line in textbooks. Gain control of all student newspapers. Use student riots to foment public protests against programs or organizations which are under Communist attack." Sounds like *mission accomplished* to a large swath of normal America.

OUTSIZED INFLUENCE BY THE NGOS

The acronym NGO is often referenced in the press and by talking heads, but not everyone knows it stands for a "non-governmental organization". And fewer realize that an NGO is a non-profit, citizen-run group that functions independently and outside the official government structure...but can be *funded* by the government, provided no government representatives are members of the organization. Their names are invariably designed to convey they serve a specific political or social purpose. They do, but make no mistake, for many NGOs their larger purposes are distinctly different from that declared on their mastheads. If this describes a murky, deceptive and off the radar domain - it does, and NGO world seems to be designed for exactly such shady activity.

Despite there being many high-profile NGOs like Doctors Without Borders, pursuing worthy endeavors, there are far too many using their status and infrastructure to pursue subversive political aims rather than the societal development goals in their charters. There are 1.5 million NGOs in the U.S. and from incidents which have surfaced over the past couple decades, far too many function as water-carriers for the deep state, acting as conduits for left wing politics. Most all carry 501(c)3 designation, categorizing all donations as tax-deductible.

Few NGOs operate as completely subversive as ACORN, the Association of Community Organizations for Reform Now, which was completely exposed, by investigative reporter James O'Keefe, as abetting vote fraud, discussing illegal activities, providing illegal advice, and ultimately losing its government grants in addition to its private funding. It was forced to cease operations as a result of the scandal. Most NGOs provide a modicum of genuine community services, which serve as effective cover for their more subversive and propagandistic activities.

George Soros's Open Society Foundations are notorious for channeling billions of dollars to dual purpose NGOs which often surface as involved in headline stories of violent protests, political corruption, illegal alien trafficking, voter fraud, etc. The Open Society website, www.opensocietyfoundations.org lists over 7,000 recipients. Over 200 of them are known to have operations or stated objectives contrary to what normal America would consider to be in the interests of the United States. Many, such as the infamous Gamaliel Foundation of Chicago are organized on the Saul Alinsky subversion model, i.e., their stated purpose is to assist residents in accessing government welfare programs, while their practice is to aggressively recruit new claimants with the objective of overwhelming the system with dependents. This strategy of overwhelming and imploding the welfare system under its own weight is another specific collectivist strategy first articulated by Richard Cloward and Frances Piven in the mid 1960s. The objective is to crash the current system so that they can rebuild it according to their Socialist outlines. Following the Cloward-Piven blueprint, Barack Obama conducted his infamous "community organizing" work agitating for the Gamaliel Foundation in the 1980s. Also, while in Chicago he was a guest lecturer at the University of Chicago Law School, and the only picture of him at a blackboard there shows him illustrating an Alinsky concept/diagram of the "oppressive" interrelated power of corporations, banks and utilities.

Name any issue about which we see the organized Left agitating for media coverage and approbation and you will find numerous NGOs channeling money, organizing and other "resources" to further the Leftist agenda. If the issue is amnesty for illegal aliens, you will see the American Immigration Law Foundation agitating, advocating and actually *litigating* against the federal government on behalf of the illegals.

If the issue is racial agitation and division, for decades the Malcolm X Grassroots Movement has been advocation for "reparations" in its magazine *BAMN* (By Any Means Necessary), whose masthead alone telegraphs its intentions.

The Center for Community Change, another Alinsky-style agitation outfit, proclaims its goals of "fundamental transformation" right on its website.

If you seek to access every conceivable government welfare program, the American Institute for Social Justice will "hook you up."

One organization rivaling Soros's Open Society in funds raised and influence is the San Francisco-based Tides Foundation. Tides is an entire world of related groups which incubate numerous front groups functioning as "pass through funders," channeling hundreds of millions through the vast "Tides Network."

Another in the same league is the Ford Foundation, currently endowed with some $12 billion. Originally seeded by Edsel and Henry Ford II, this outfit has strayed far from its original charter. It has become notorious for donating to subversives such as the Labor Community Strategy Center, which promotes the Communist ideology of "the destruction of free markets." Other recipients of funding are the FALN, a U.S. government declared terrorist group, and the discredited Leftist group, Occupy Wall Street.

Between the Open Society, the Tides Network and the Ford Foundation, the subversive Left has not wanted for funding over the past two decades. Today's most visible recipients of funds funneled through this triumvirate are Black Lives Matter and Antifa. Leftist groups such as these have never been so flush as they are today, and the urban destruction wreaked by these outfits has never been so pronounced as has been exhibited across the country in 2020.

The enormous funding streams from these NGOs serve to amplify both the message and power of the organized, subversive American Left. They fund the naïve army of what V.I. Lenin termed "useful idiots" of volunteers agitating in communities across the country. There is now more money funding violence on American streets than ever before, and its origins are easily traceable to tax exempt organizations chartered with the federal government. The background and activities of a seemingly endless network of these 501(c)3 tax advantaged organizations of the Left can be further investigated by visiting www.DiscoverTheNetworks.org.

Working with political allies in governments around the world who are, for all intents and purposes, serving the interests of the transnational NGOs who own them and control their ideological direction, this deadly combination of entrenched Big Government power and transnational plutocratic interests has become far more open about their ultimate goals for world order than they have in the past.

The Transnational Progressive elites have announced that they intend to seize control of the planet's historical momentum with something they call "The Great Reset." The term has been popularized by Klaus Schwab, a German professor of business at the University of Geneva, who in 1987 founded the World Economic Forum, another not-for-profit foundation that claims to be committed to improving world society.

Writing against the traditional limited government, Free Market Capitalist order (which he terms "neoliberalist") in Time Magazine, https://time.com/collection/great-reset/5900748/klaus-schwab-capitalism/ he states:

> *"For the past 30 to 50 years, the neoliberalist ideology has increasingly prevailed in large parts of the world. This approach centers on the notion that the market knows best, that the "business of business is business," and that government should refrain from setting clear rules for the functioning of markets. Those dogmatic beliefs have proved wrong. But fortunately, we are not destined to follow them."*

Schwab and his fellow Transnationalists want to "re-imagine" the current world order along different lines. Former President Barak Obama called this an attempt to "fundamentally transform America." Of course, the question arises why one would seek to "fundamentally transform" something they liked, let alone revered and loved. To avoid this uncomfortable question, the Elites embraced the new, more nebulous word "re-imagine."

Unfortunately, regardless of the phrase they use, it is all said in the same manner as those on the Left and in the Enemedia utilize it; that is, as a popular phrase used by those who want to refer to something that they wish "destroy" but are reticent about stating that truth outright lest it provoke a counter-response.

Be it the police or the education or healthcare systems or any other system that is essentially seen as successful (and that has engendered no mass outcry among the population to change them) such systems are nonetheless seen as posing a threat to the transnational progressive agenda. In order to seduce populations into a sense of false security, Tranzi elites falsely mis-use the "new" word "re-imagine" where they formerly mis-used the by now tired word "reform." In this case, it is the Capitalist System and Traditional Society, with its emphasis on Individuality, Ordered Liberty, Critical Thinking and Political Freedom under the Rule of Law that Schwab and his fellow elitists want to "re-imagine" out of existence.

In the Time Magazine article, Schwab goes on to write:

"Free markets, trade and competition create so much wealth that in theory they could make everyone better off if there was the will to do so. But that is not the reality we live in today.

Technological advances often take place in a monopolized economy and are used to prioritize one company's profits over societal progress. The same economic system that created so much prosperity in the golden age of American capitalism in the 1950s and 1960s is now creating inequality and climate change. And the same political system that enabled our global progress and democracy after World War II now contributes to societal discord and discontent...

...Yet there are reasons to believe that a better economic system is possible—and that it could be just around the corner. As the initial shock of the COVID crisis receded, we saw a glimpse of what is possible, when stakeholders act for the public good and the well-being of all, instead of just a few....

...Building such a virtuous economic system is not a utopian ideal. Most people, including business leaders, investors and community leaders, have a similar attitude about their role in the world and the lives of others. Most people want to do good, and believe that doing so will ultimately benefit everyone, including a company's shareholders. But what's been missing in recent decades is a clear compass to guide those in leading positions in our society and economy."

Everything that is essential to the Transnational Progressive effort to undo society as we have known it and replace it with an authoritarian, spiritually sterile, techno-collectivist order is encapsulated in Schwab's confessional:

The claim that Capitalism is outdated and needs to be "re-imagined" (i.e. destroyed) and replaced with a not-so-crypto neo-fascist regime run by elites ("those in leading positions") who control large, powerful governments that will *not* "refrain from setting clear rules for the functioning of markets."

The claim that Free Markets "create so much wealth that in theory they could make everyone better off" is unrealistic, but that destroying that wealth creating mechanism and replacing it with an elite-run form of collectivism *that historically produces nothing but poverty* is the only thing capable of altering that negative "unreality."

The claim that Capitalism is at odds with the tenets of Gaia Worship and is guilty of promoting "climate change"; that Capitalism is moving the world toward greater inequality; that Capitalism creates "societal discord and dis-content" and that "building such a virtuous economic system is not a utopian ideal"—which, of course, all Socialism irrationally rests on—are all claims made by Schwab in his elitist Time Magazine manifesto.

In fact, the 2020 Biden Campaign slogan, "Build Back Better" is also the slogan of the Great Reset, coined by none other than Klaus Schwab himself, which indicates just how tightly tethered puppets like Joe Biden and Kamala Harris are to the strings pulled by globalists such as Schwab and Soros.

"Every country," insists Schwab, "from the United States to China, must participate, and every industry, from oil and gas to tech, must be transformed."

Prince Charles is a key advocate for the Great Reset, as is International Monetary Fund chief economist Gina Gopinath, U.N. Secretary General António Guterres, as well as heads of many major corporations, including Microsoft.

Former U.S. Secretary of State John Kerry is all in, recently exclaiming: "The notion of a reset is more important than ever before. I personally believe … we're at the dawn of an extremely exciting time." And Canadian Prime Minister Justin Trudeau is remarkably frank about the subterfuge under which the global reset elites are operating: "This pandemic has provided an oppor-tunity for a reset. This is our chance to accelerate our pre-pandemic efforts to reimagine our economic systems that actually address global challenges like extreme poverty, inequality and climate change." (https://dailyangle.com/articles/the-great-reset-is-here)

All must participate.
All must be transformed.

Schwab and his fellow Tranzi elitists define the Great Reset as a massive transformation of all major social systems, be they economic, environmental, military, technological, financial, governing or health systems.

As it is in sync with the globalist outlook of the transnational progressive elites, the idea of "The Great Reset" is to be an effort undertaken on a global level. More, to be successful, it must utilize a crisis or a series of crises that will be international in scope, such as the COVID-19 pandemic; in this way, the "crisis" is not allowed to go to "waste," but rather be used to advance and implement the goals of the Great Reset to destroy and replace the traditional nation-state system with a transnational progressive world order.

Schwab has openly stated this in his book "COVID-19: The Great Reset" that COVID-19, which has caused so much pain, misery and death on a planetary scale, is actually an *"opportunity [to be] seized to make the kind of institutional changes and policy choices that will put economies on the path toward a fairer, greener future..."*

In effect, they seek to "re-imagine" the planet as a transnational, neo-Fascist, plutocracy hiding behind a Potemkin Village consisting of empty Socialist slogans and propagandistic, collectivist bromides about fairness, egalitarianism and "social justice," endlessly vomited out by its Fake News outlets in the Enemedia… and all designed to drown the individual soul in a tidal wave of massive, authoritarian government that *is* the corporate state to be created by the Great Reset.

- The Deep State is that part of the federal government that is permanent and basically impervious to democratic, electoral change.
- It is a clique consisting of embedded and intractable bureaucrats, the representatives of influential multi-national corporations, non-government organizations (NGOs) mega-rich financiers and bankers, selected mass media companies and lifetime members of the federal judiciary.
- This group uses the Deep State to employ the various Federal departments that comprise the Investigative, Police, Legal, Tax, Financial and Bureaucratic agencies to serve as their enforcement arm.

- They are all ready to weaponize any law or flout any Constitutional protection in order to run roughshod over the Liberty of the common citizen. This is done so they are better able to protect that which is their first concern: the interests of the Corporate Elites, which provides the Deep State with a reason for its existence, just as the Roman Emperors once provided a *raison d'etre* to its Praetorian Guard.
- Beyond this inner circle, the spawning grounds of the entire elitist mindset can be found among the Think Tanks and University Administrations, whose professors within Academia collect their lucrative government grants by grinding out propagandized drones who are designed to lack the type of critical thinking that could pose any threat to the Deep State or its corporate owners.
- Academic institutions do not only provide pseudo-intellectual justification for ever-increasing expansion of the power of the Deep State, but also serve as incubators for the production of its most fervent supporters through their effective and constant propaganda assaults on the students in their charge.
- The mind-rape committed by Academia has left far too many of those in the generations who will face the Seventh Crisis without the ability to think critically and who have been frightened, shamed, coerced and bullied into accepting all the Transnational, Progressive, Multicultural, Politically Correct dogma that serves Deep State interests.
- Since they are closest to it and are in its most direct line of fire, *it is against Academia that the Millennial and Gen-Z generations must strike first.*

– 5 –

False Alternatives of the Radical Left

I f Gen-Xers and Millennials prepare to face the Seventh Crisis through the strengthening of Ordered Liberty, they must also be aware that their ability to overcome it is not only being hobbled by the political power of the Left operating inside government, but that its power to resist Big Government itself is being subverted by the Left operating *outside* of government. Not only are institutional government allies in Academia, the Enemedia and the Social Media undercutting the Gen-X / Millennial / Gen-Z ability to think critically and weaken its resolve to overcome the coming Crisis, they are also the targets of an "Outside Left" that is totally committed to insuring that an alternative…albeit a false one… to Ordered Liberty appears to be available, but which serves an entirely different purpose.

This alternative is not dedicated to overcoming the Seventh Crisis but to turn a resistance to the Crisis based on Ordered Liberty into a failure by inject-

147

ing a radical socialist virus into the bloodstream of the body politic. By doing so, the Outside Left will be able to exacerbate the Crisis and allow it to be used as a rationale to take "emergency action," which can only be effective if the Left is granted more and more and more instrumentalities of governmental power. Such an exacerbation of the problem caused by increased governmental power will be used as an excuse to demand *even more power* in order to rectify a situation made worse by increased governmental interference in the first place.

This strategy is very familiar to the so-called "Machtergreifung" or "seizure of power" that took place in Germany in the early 1930s, where a political, social and economic crisis opened the way for a radical fringe movement that used violence, intolerance, bullying, a fanatic cadre of "Youth" cultivated by radical voices in Academia and, of course, anti-Semitism to demand that government be made powerful enough to "deal" with the Crisis. Unfortunately, we see similar actions being undertaken today in advance of the developing Crisis by the "Outside Left," which embraces the strategy and tactics of a fascistic "Machtergreifung" in its entirety, while at the same time posing as its opposite. These subversive organizations and movements, some of which are highly organized and controlled and others which are decentralized and ad hoc, are already laying the groundwork to further confuse and co-opt the very Gen-Xers / Millennials / Gen-Zs they seek to use to advance their political interests and power.

To understand what is at the heart of how those on the Left wish to carry out their "seizure of power," one must understand the inverted, "mirror universe" relationship that exists between their rhetoric and their reality.

The Left doesn't wish to "occupy" Wall St. but to formalize its role as a Corporate functionary in the service of a gigantic, Leviathan State run *by* the Left! When such a corporate relationship exists between Business Elites favored by the Elites who control the Government exists, it is the very definition of the Fascist "Corporate State" beyond which, as the founder of Fascism, Benito Mussolini noted, totally encompasses society: "Everything within the state, nothing outside the state, nothing against the state."

Therefore, no matter what names are chosen or policies are advocated by those who support the Left, they have adopted the tactic of identifying themselves in terms that are strictly the opposite of what they really are or what they really want.

That is, Antifa is not "anti-Fascist," but is instead *existentially fascist* in its theory and especially in its practice. As is demonstrated by their utter lack of concern for Black people who are routinely murdered in vast numbers every day in cities run by those Democrat politicians with whom they are politically aligned, Black Lives Matter treats Black life as if it doesn't matter at all, except to serve the revolutionary interests of the admitted Marxists who run BLM. Support for Alexandra Ocasio-Cortez and her Socialist Squad consists of a largely anti-Semitic, violent cadre of fanatical "Red Guard" cultural nihilists, who operate as the coercive Storm Troops seeking to impose an authoritarian, repressive, neo-Fascist agenda that is to be inflicted on the United States. Further, the Left's dishonest facade is made even more grotesque as it is fueled by the Elitist acceptance of the utterly kook and grotesquely anti-White racial determinism found in the pseudo-intellectual claptrap of "Critical Race Theory" - which is, of course, thoroughly racist.

Let us examine some of these organizations, what their goals are, and the people that control them.

OCCUPY WALL ST.

The Movement known as "Occupy Wall St." formed in the wake of the so-called Arab Spring in 2011. It found its impetus in a Canadian-based media organization known as "Adbusters" that initially was focused on environmental issues and describes itself as "a global network of artists, activists, writers, prankster, students, educators and entrepreneurs who want to advance the social activist movement of the information age."

An Adbusters editor, Micah White was instrumental in organizing Occupy and sought to exploit the "revolutionary potential of (student) struggle." In September 2011, the international hacker group "Anonymous" used the internet to encourage Leftist protestors to "flood lower Manhattan, set up tents (and) barricades and Occupy Wall St." Claiming to represent the "99%" of earners whose interests were being hurt by the corrupt, ultra-wealthy "1%", the protestors represented a large swath of the more radical elements of the far Left including anarchist groups that saw no alternative to changing what they saw as the social injustice of Capitalism through a violent overthrow of the entire system that Capitalism rested upon. While initially proclaiming that they were non-violent, they rapidly descended into the type of violence and riot advocated by their most radical, anarchist members. Destroying property and setting fires, Occupy protests spread across the country. Hundreds of documented violent crimes were committed by Occupy protestors, as can be easily verified by a quick perusal of the internet, including:

NY: 10/1/2011 — Police Arrest More Than 700 Protesters on Brooklyn Bridge

Phoenix: 10/28/2011 — Flier at Occupy Phoenix Asks, "When Should You Shoot a Cop?"

NY: 10/18/2011 — Thieves Preying on Fellow Protesters

NY: 10/9/2011 — Stinking up Wall Street: Protesters Accused of Living in Filth as Shocking Pictures Show One Demonstrator Defecating on a POLICE CAR

NY: 10/7/2011 — Occupiers Rush Police … More

Cleveland: 10/18/2011 — 'Occupy Cleveland' Protester Alleges She Was Raped

NY: 10/10/2011 — 'Increasingly Debauched': Are Sex, Drugs & Poor Sanitation Eclipsing Occupy Wall Street?

Seattle: 10/18/2011 — Man Accused of Exposing Self to Children Arrested

10/12/2011 — Iran Supports 'Occupy Wall Street'

Portland: 10/16/2011 —#OccupyPortland Protester Desecrates Memorial To U.S. War Dead

Portland: 10/15/2011 — #OccupyPortland Protesters Sing "F*** The USA"

Chicago: 10/17/2011 — COMMUNIST LEADER Cheered at Occupy Chicago

10/15/2011 — American Nazi Party Endorses Occupy Wall Street's 'Courage,' Tells Members to Support Protests and Fight 'Judeo-Capitalist Banksters'

Boston: 10/11/2011 — Boston Police Arrest Over 100 from Occupy Boston

New York: 10/15/2011 — Harassing Police with Accusations of Phony Injuries

New York: 10/9/2011 — 'Occupy Wallstreet' Protesters Steal from Local Businesses

New York: 10/25/2011 — Three Men Threatened to Kill 24-Year-Old Occupy Wall Street Protester for Reporting Rape

Baltimore: 10/18/2011 — #OccupyBaltimore Discourages Sexual Assault Victims from Contacting Police

Portland: 10/27/2011 — Occupy Portland's Attempt At Wealth Redistribution Ends In Theft

Los Angeles: 10/14/2011—Anti-Semitic Protester at Occupy Wall Street

10/27/2011 — A Death Threat From an Occupy Wall Street Protester

Boston: 10/20/2011 — Occupy Boston Doesn't Want Police Involved in Rape

New York: 10/2011 — Occupier Tries to Steal Police Officer's Gun

New York: 10/27/2011 — Occupiers Block Traffic, Get Arrested

Oakland: 10/27/2011 — Occupiers Throw Garbage at Police

Oakland: 10/19/2011 — Abusive #OccupyOakland Protesters Ban Media from Tent City

NY: 10/20/2011 — #OccupyWallStreet Threatens Businesses, Patrons

NY: 10/14/2011 — Violence Breaks Out During #OccupyWallStreet March Toward Stock Exchange

NY: 10/14/2011 — Protesters March On Wall Street, Scuffle With Cops

Oakland: 10/19/2011 — #OccupyOakland Protesters Threaten Reporter

Oakland: 10/26/2011 — Occupiers Scuffle with Police

Oakland: 10/24/2011 — Protesters Storm, Vandalize, Shut Down Chase Bank

Chicago: 10/26/2011 — Occupiers Under Investigation by FBI for Links to Terrorism

Cleveland: 10/29/2011 — Rape Reported at Occupy Cleveland

Dallas: 10/24/2011 — Police Investigating Possible Sexual Assault Of Teen At Occupy Dallas

Bloomington, IN: 10/26/2011 — Man Claims Occupy Bloomington Protesters Drugged, Handcuffed Him

NY: 10/10/2011 — Sex, Drugs and Hiding from the Law at Wall Street Protests

Glasgow: 10/26/2011 — Woman Gang-Raped

...the list of violent assault, rape, drug use, hate-America rhetoric, riot, vandalism, arson and anti-police activity goes on and on; it is as endless as it is under-reported or even unreported by Anti-Fa's apologists and sympathizers in the Enemedia.

However, the supposedly "leaderless" grassroots, ad hoc nature of these OWS protests as well as their independence from neo-Fascistic corporate control by the very people they purport to despise, is a complete sham. In October 2011, Reuters ran an article which indicated the connections between the billionaire George Soros and the Occupy Movement which was supposedly opposed to everything a piratical, shadowy, manipulating plutocratic financier like Soros ever was, is or will ever be. Reuters reported that "Soros is No. 7 on the *Forbes 400* list with a fortune of $22 billion, which has ballooned in recent years as he deftly responded to financial market turmoil... 'I can understand their sentiment,' Soros told reporters... at the United Nations about Occupy Wall Street demonstrations, which are expected to spur solidarity marches globally... He declined to comment further." Carefully placing buffers between him and a series of shell operations carrying out his directives, Soros provided money that was critical to initiating the Occupy Movement by funneling it from the "Open Society Institute" that he runs through a $3.5-million grant, to the Tides Foundation which, according to Reuters is "...a San Francisco-based group that acts almost like a clearing house for other donors, directing their contributions to liberal non-profit groups." Part of this money was then doled out to Adbusters, the radical, anti-Capitalist youth-oriented magazine that Reuters indicates "...wants to 'change the way corporations wield power' and its goal is 'to topple existing power structures'".

Again, it was Adbusters that kicked off Occupy. Of course, Adbusters denies that Soros ever directly gave them any money which, of course he didn't. Per Reuters "Adbusters co-founder Kalle Lasn, said the group is 95 percent funded by subscribers paying for the magazine. 'George Soros's ideas are quite good, many of them. I wish he would give Adbusters some money, we sorely need it...' he said. 'He's never given us a penny.'" Soros is much too canny to ever directly give money to any of his instrumentalities; that's what the shell organizations are for. But why would a billionaire financial manipulator want to support a far-Left movement like Occupy, which loudly voices its hatred for mega-rich financial operators like Soros? In fact however, Soros is not a "Capitalist" at all; he is something those at Occupy (and, as we shall see, at even more far-Left movements that popped up later) should despise above all else. Soros is, in essence, a Fascist.

To understand the seeming contradiction of a Fascist financially supporting a supposedly militantly anti-Fascist movement, we need to understand what, at a macro level, it means to be a Fascist.

Soros is an advocate of what former President Bill Clinton and others have called "The Third Way"—viz. between Capitalism and Socialism. Capitalism is defined as a system based on individual liberty, the sanctity of private property and its disposal as well as the right to make profits free of overly intrusive governmental interference. Socialism is a collectivist system without private property or profits, which instead vests the ownership, production and distribution of all goods and services in the hands of the Collective, which is defined by its governmental enforcement arm, the State. Fascism is also a collectivist system with a strong central government that permits no opposition or criticism of the State.

Both Socialism and Fascism view property rights as belonging not to the individual but to the State; however, while Socialism negates both private property and profits altogether, Fascism allows for private ownership and profits, *but transfers control of property to the State.* The idea of "ownership" without the right to use or dispose of property is a contradiction in terms; there can be no "ownership" without ability to control or dispose of what is supposedly "owned." The differences between the supposedly contradictory systems are only a matter of superficialities. In Fascism, you only "own" property or make "profits" to the extent that it *serves* the interests of the State. Both Socialism and Fascism are anti-Individual and pro-Collective; both negate individual liberty and subordinate all human rights to the power of the State. Both enslave the poor and expropriate the middle class; Socialism obliterates the rich and Fascism imprisons them under the yoke of its total control. Or as "Third Way" neo-Fascist theory would have it, Big Business would own the economy in conjunction with the Big Government that would run it; corporations would either comply with the rules, directives, regulations, subsidies, special privileges set by the Government and the Big Business Cartels that support it or face expropriation of their property, or worse. This is the "Third Way" that Soros-type Plutocrats seek to utilize to supplant Capitalism and thereby eliminate the traditional concepts of Ordered Liberty that are not only essential to a free society but also will also serve as a bulwark against the oncoming Seventh Crisis.

By perverting young minds to accept the "Third Way" that exists behind the false front of a Potemkin Village consisting of empty and impossible Socialist nostrums and lies, he gives strength to the ability of himself and other Plutocrats… as well as those employees on their payroll that are found in both parties in Government… to exploit the inevitable Crisis as a means to achieve power. In this manner, Soros and his fellow Plutocrats are able to control not only the power of the State but also to control and direct those who would supposedly form the most violent opposition to their machinations; it is the ultimate in co-optation. This is not to say that Soros directly controls or directs the group's day to day activities… protests, demonstrations, violent or otherwise, propaganda and media access… but then again, the whole idea is to set radical operations like Occupy into motion and then fall back into the shadows where plausible deniability can be claimed and responsibility can be disparaged as "conspiracy theory." This continues to be the modus operandi with the newer and even more radical groups that have come into being since Occupy began.

ANTIFA

One such successor to Occupy is "Antifa," a loose confederation of Communist Anarchist groups whose name stands for "Anti-Fascist Action" or "Anti-Fascist"; their flags are the red and black banner of Communist Anarchism. The name itself is intriguing because there are few things that have more sinister similarities to Fascism than Antifa. It models itself on militant Anti-Fascist organizations that engaged in street fighting with their equally anti-democratic, anti-Capitalist Fascist counterparts dating back to the chaotic post-WWI era of 1920s Europe. Such groups were often haphazardly organized as "Workers Brigades" or "Frei Korps" paramilitary units, and passed through various phases of popularity with disaffected youth groups across the decades. In the 1950s they identified as "beatniks" who rejected the "uptight" "homogenized" culture of post-war America. In the 1960s, they manifested themselves as "Yippies" (the "Youth International Party") which engaged in riotous post-adolescent street theater that advocated Utopian Socialism and embraced the idea of abandoning corporate, materialistic, bourgeois lifestyles for a more natural, pacifistic, communal way of life. This approach rapidly lost advocates once those who were initially attracted to it eventually realized the naive futility of it all and drifted back to more traditional lifestyles.

However, the 1970s saw the Yippies morph into a movement that was far less squeamish about using violence to achieve utopian ends: The Weathermen, who committed numerous acts of violence, murder, riot and carried out deadly bombings, all done in the name of fighting the "Fascist" American system, which they saw as war-mongering, imperialistic, racist, religiously intolerant and oppressive to the poor. This version saw no value in debate or discussion or compromise with their enemies because there can be no debate, discussion or compromise with those deemed "Fascist" or "Nazi"; there can only be violent confrontation. In his book, "Antifa: The Anti-Fascist Handbook" author Mark Bray charts the alliance of Anti-Fascist street violence and the anarchist and nihilist strains found in the Punk Movements of the 1980s and 1990s.

By the late 1970s, this attitude swept the country and later settled down onto college campuses where former activists now taught and spread their message to at least 2 generations of college students, always disguised as a social justice movement against Capitalism and the oppressive and greedy culture it represented. Knowing that the message would resonate better with youth if it were cast in anti-Racist rather than anti-Fascist terms, the 1980s saw college groups like Anti-Racist action come to prominence.

As their predecessors did in earlier generations, Antifa started out targeting White Supremacist groups as their targets for street violence, doling out "righteous beatings" on the objects of their rage. But it rapidly moved on to a larger audience; anyone who didn't support them were *all* considered to be "Nazis," with whom there was no moral obligation to recognize as having any value at all, let alone any right to their own equally abhorrent views. By 2018, anyone who disagreed with Antifa became an open target, including controversial conservative speakers on campus as well as all sorts of conservative activists advocating positions Antifa considers "Fascist." To Antifa, Nazis and Fascists have no rights that they are bound to respect, and violence is therefore the only way to deal with them. They shut down their opponents with campus riots and online threats; they violently breakup conservative rallies (as they did during a "Rally For Trump And Freedom" in Portland in April 2017); they organize boycotts and threaten those who don't go along; they commandeer city streets and direct traffic away from areas they "control" as "no-go" precincts; they publish the private information of individuals whose political contributions they disapprove of, and brutally attack journalists who investigate their violent activities. But Antifa is against more than certain aspects of American life; they are against America's very existence.

On August 17, 2017, Antifa contingents in Berkley California openly voiced their desire to wipe out the USA at a rally protesting Trump's border wall to prevent illegal immigration. Antifa's response was the slogan "No Trump, No Wall, *NO USA AT ALL!*" The implication is in line with Antifa's views on the inherent immorality of any that oppose them; that is, since the USA is evil, anyone or anything that seeks to protect or preserve the USA is evil as well. Violence, therefore, is a legitimate, "necessary evil" required to win the Social Justice war against "Fascism." Again, masked, uniformed terrorists who engage in violence, riot, arson, attacks on private property and free speech, as well as brutal bullying and assault against all who disagree with them is not emblematic of anti-Fascism. Justifying the violent repression of the political and civil rights of one's opponents in the name of advancing what they believe is a superior moral position that trumps all other considerations regarding the rights and liberties of others is not at all "Anti-Fascist"; *it is the essence of Fascism.*

From the Nazi Storm Troopers of the 1930s to the Ku Klux Klan of the 1960s to the violent Alt-Right of today, Antifa is of a piece with all of them. "As noted by the conservative watchdog website Discover the Networks, "Upstate Antifa has also promoted violence against "fascism" via posters bearing slogans like: "Fighting fascism is a social duty, not an antisocial crime," and "Fascism is not to be debated. It is to be smashed." Such positive characterizations of the use of violence are taught and encouraged, in part, through pro-Antifa publications like *Repress This*, *The Invention of the White Race*, Our Enemies in Blue, and *Whatever You Do, Don't Talk to the Police*." https://www.discoverthe-networks.org/organizations/antifa/

However, the danger this group represents goes beyond even the violent threat they pose to social order and Liberty; via their advocates and supporters among the leftwing intelligentsia in Academia, they represent a direct threat to the ability of the Gen-X and Millennial generations to fight the Seventh Crisis. Antifa opposes everything that will be needed to overcome the Crisis.

They are opposed to all Western tradition as being racist, sexist and homophobic; they have no tolerance for individual rights and liberties; they espouse collectivist *group*-rights and champion identity politics; they insist on the extirpation of the civil society and see traditional concepts of law and order as a Capitalist fraud designed to oppress minority groups; they call for the establishment of a State powerful enough to overthrow the Free Market (or what's left of it) and replace it with a forcible Marxist re-allocation of wealth to groups they consider "historically oppressed."

Once again, the reality behind these supposedly anti-Plutocrat radicals is quite the opposite of what they pretend to advocate. Due to Antifa's decentralized nature it consists of loosely affiliated groups and as such it is difficult to identify its funding sources. However, the links to George Soros and his Open Society Foundation are present, albeit deliberately far from clear.

Discover the Networks goes on to indicate that while money from financiers such as Soros "wash" their contributions many times before they find their circuitous way to Antifa, a key organization behind Antifa's corporate sugar-daddies is the Alliance For Global Justice (AfGJ.) According to Discover, AfGJ is an offshoot of the "Nicaragua Network," which supported the tyrannical, pro-Castro, Sandinista regime in Nicaragua. The AfGJ also gives financial assistance to the group known as "Refuse Fascism," whose tentacles reach into many of the disparate groups that make up Antifa. It is AfGJ that serves as the money laundering service for Soros and his band of Plutocrats, which includes organizations such as the Tides Foundation, The New World Foundation, the Brightwater Foundation, the Aetna Foundation, the Bank of America Charitable Foundation, the Fidelity Investments Charitable Gift Fund, the Schwab Foundation and even the leftwing ice cream makers at Ben & Jerry's.

One might ask how the relationship between these multi-billion dollar entities propping up Antifa differs from the relationship German Industrialists such as Krupp and Thyssen had with the Nazi Party in Germany? It seems apparent that Plutocrats see the value in violent street thugs who can be used as stooges to advance their own agenda. That agenda is to create chaos and offer false alternatives to the Ordered Liberty required to meet the Seventh Crisis in order to exacerbate it and use it to seize power for themselves. It is a dangerous game, but one that Plutocrats such as Soros have no problem playing, especially when those who suffer are either their stooges or those their stooges' target. Hiding behind a thick smokescreen of money-launderers, they keep their hands clean while their puppets stupidly think they are fighting Fascism instead of serving it.

However, while violent and dangerously anarchistic, the false alternatives proffered by radical groups like Antifa and OWS are not used by the Elites simply as a tool to spread nihilism; they are to serve the purpose of the Elites to undermine a lawful response to the Crisis. That is, by undermining the forces of order, they ensure that there is no order; *and if there is no order, there can be no Ordered Liberty to rely on to defend freedom and to thwart the dangers of the Seventh Crisis.* Antifa is relentless in its violent hatred for the police as encapsulated by Michael Isaacson, an adjunct professor at the John Jay College of Criminal Justice, who used his academic perch to co-found the Antifa group "Smash Racism DC." Issacson claims that "Nazis" have "infiltrated" police departments across the United States and in 2017 tweeted: "Some of y'all might think it sucks being an anti-fascist teaching at John Jay College but I think it's a privilege to teach future dead cops."

BLACK LIVES MATTER

Black Lives Matter is an anti-police group that, in actuality, opposes all organizations (FBI, ICE, DEA) designed to maintain Law and Order. BLM sees the very phrase "Law and Order" as a lie designed to cover up the fact that all such organizations are merely arms of an oppressive "Fascist" (or even "Nazi") AmeriKKKan government that targets Blacks, Hispanics, Immigrants and sexual minorities. To this mindset, Police are not peace-keepers but an oppressive GESTAPO, out to murder and oppress the poor and the non-White; therefore, they not only *don't* deserve respect, they deserve to be violently confronted. BLM works tirelessly to exploit any and all incidents that can possibly be used to inflame passions against the police as being an "Occupying Power" in poor neighborhoods and seek to undermine all aspects of police work in minority communities. Any criticism of them is immediately deemed "Racist"; if they are criticized by non-Whites who realize the danger of separating police from poor, crime-prone areas, those non-Whites are castigated as "Race Traitors." The very concept of Law and Order is deemed to be an assault on minority Civil Rights; once this attitude takes hold, anti-police violence soars while police morale plummets.

The Marxist revolutionary political orientation of BLM was confirmed by co-founder Patrice Cullors in a video interview with Jared Ball of The Real News Network (https://www.youtube.com/watch?v=kCghDx5qN4s&-feature=youtu.be) where she stated "We are trained Marxists. We are super-versed on, sort of, ideological theories. And I think that what we really tried to do is build a movement that could be utilized by many, many black folk..." In fact, her mentor, Eric Mann was "an avowed communist revolutionary, was the New England coordinator for Students for a Democratic Society (SDS) in 1968. The following year, a more radical wing splintered from the SDS, led by Bill Ayers and Bernadine Dohrn, calling for violent "direct action" over civil disobedience." (https://www.breitbart.com/politics/2020/06/24/black-lives-matter-founder-mentored-by-ex-domestic-terrorist-who-worked-with-bill-ayers/)

Meanwhile, cowardly, pandering local politicians cast the law and those who uphold it into the waste bin as they scurry like rats to side with those "activists" they need to provide the votes required to continue their lucrative ride on the Government Gravy Train. With neighborhoods awash in the blood of young people mass murdered on a weekly basis in violent inner cities, BLM calls for defunding the very police departments that are needed to prevent such violence. They demand voting rights for illegal immigrants who are a threat to the employment prospects of poor Black citizens. They call for the end of successful Charter Schools in areas where Public Schools have produced nothing but failure and ignorance… while calling for free college for black students who Public Education has left unable to read on grade level or demonstrate the most basic of math skills. BLM is not just an attack on the idea of Ordered Liberty; it is an attack on the idea of "Order" itself.

Once again, covering their tracks through a series of front organizations and shell corporations, the usual bunch of Plutocrats is at work. Despite posing as street revolutionaries, BLM takes in more than $100 million in grants from elitist Progressive groups including the Ford Foundation, the Borealis Philanthropy, The Center For American Progress and, of course, George Soros' Open Society Foundation which, as it does with all its money grants, covers its tracks with a series of layers through which it launders its contributions. Borealis euphemizes the hate-police philosophy of BLM by announcing that it "provides grants, movement building resources and technical assistance to organizations working to advance the leadership and vision of young black, queer, feminists and immigrant leaders who are shaping and leading a national conversation about criminalization, policing and race in America."

Liberal politicians, anxious to pander to a Black Community that is already solidly in their grasp, join in the anti-Police rhetoric. Democrat Presidential candidates continue to refer to one such police shooting in Ferguson, Missouri as a "murder" even though the Obama Justice Department declined, after a full investigation, to prosecute the case because it deemed to be a justifiable use of force. BLM is always anxious to describe all such shootings as unwarranted acts of racist police brutality… even in majority Black Police Departments! They seek to garner votes by disempowering and disenfranchising of police and thereby produce a collapse of respect for law enforcement that will lay the groundwork for the Elites to benefit from exploiting the explosion of anarchy that may result during the general turmoil brought on by the Seventh Crisis.

THE SOCIALIST SQUAD

While Liberal politicians have more and more come out as the "Democratic Socialists" they have always clandestinely been, others on the Collectivist Left have moved into far more radical precincts. We now see developing in the Democrat Party a group that has moved beyond even "Democratic Socialism" to the outright advocacy of what can only be called a form of blatantly Fascistic "Third World Authoritarianism." Four freshman Congresswomen (Alexandria Ocasio-Cortez, Ilhan Omar, Rashida Talib and Ayanna Pressley) have formed the "Squad," which is designed to lead the most far-Left elements in the ever more increasingly radical Democrat Party Base; that they do not represent a majority of Democrats is unimportant. What is important is that they have great sway with the most activist elements of the Party Base, viz. those that vote in primary elections, that take part in retail politics and that always respond to pleas for donations, votes and in-the-street activism, including violent activism.

They appeal to the most ideologically committed part of the Base and much of the rest of the Party quietly follows lest it incur the wrath of the Squad condemning them as being "sellouts" or "racists." It is instructive that no matter how ludicrous a Squad proposal is (such as their impossibly expensive and ignorantly utopian "Green New Deal"), or how incendiary their rhetoric (calling holding centers for illegal immigrants "concentrations camps" and ICE officers "Nazi guards"), or how politically radical their policy proposals (open borders, massive welfare spending programs, "free" college, "guaranteed" national income to those who refuse to work, reparations for the descendants of slaves and a form of forced collectivist egalitarianism that will supposedly be paid for by confiscatory taxation on the rich and the middle class), the Base will be wildly supportive of it.

Bucking the control of the old Corporate Donor Class hacks in the Democrat Party "leadership" who they see as weak pawns of "the rich," the Squad seeks to replace their corrupt rule with the type of "revenge" politics that has been popular on the Left since Franz Fanon wrote his violently anti-Western, anti-White, pro-Socialist screed "The Wretched of the Earth," which demanded the extermination of the rich and middle classes that he claimed were irredeemably evil, greedy, racist and exploitative hypocrites. The Squad is at one with Fanon. The not-so-crypto Fascism of all this is best exemplified by the Squad's virulent hate for America's strongest and most reliable ally, the State of Israel. Blatantly pro-Islamist (Rashid is proudly pro-Hamas and Omar is on record offering apologias for the Al Qaeda) the Squad, with the Democrat Party Base in tow, presses the button that is most associated with debased Fascistic politics: *anti-Semitism in all its myriad, poisonous forms.* The pervasive themes running through all "false alternative" groups can be summed up as follows:

All are anti-Democracy, anti-Capitalist, anti-Order, anti-police, anti-Liberty, anti-Free Speech, anti-National Sovereignty, anti-Constitutional, anti-Individual Rights, anti-Israel and anti-American.

All claim to be anti-Fascist while fully embracing Fascist ideology, rhetoric, methods and policies. All claim to be grassroots "street organizations" fighting for Communist Anarchism when in fact all are funded and covertly controlled by rich elitist Plutocrats who use them to promote their own agenda of increasing their power. All are detrimental to the ability of the Gen-X and Millennial generations to understand the developing Seventh Crisis as well as what actions they need to take to overcome it. Regardless of the hot, juvenile and ignorant rhetoric they spew and violently dangerous actions of these so-called "alternatives" undertake, they will not only fail to overcome the Crisis, they will be used by their Plutocratic controllers to insure it serves their ability to exploit it in the pursuit of expanding and solidifying their control of society.

In the end, they are less revolutionaries than they are pawns and dupes of the very elitists they supposedly despise.

- The power to resist Big Government is also being subverted by the Left operating *outside* of government. Beyond the institutional functionaries of the Deep State in Academia, the Enemedia and the Social Media who seek to continue and constantly re-enforce the intellectual and spiritual emasculation of the Gen-X / Millennial ability to think critically and weaken its resolve to overcome the Crisis. That is, the front line generations are also the targets of an "Outside Left" that seeks to provide a false alternative to *the only thing that can prevent the front line generations from being destroyed* by the Seventh Crisis: *Ordered Liberty.*

- Like those found among the Transnational inner circles, the Outside Left doesn't seek to overcome the Seventh Crisis, but to exacerbate it so that it can be used as a rationale for Big Government to take "emergency action," which they claim can only be effective if the Left is granted more and more and more control of the instrumentalities of governmental power. They seek to destroy any attempts to use Ordered Liberty to fight the Crisis because Ordered Liberty is the greatest threat to their power and control.
- Those in the Millennial and Gen-Z generations must realize that while such "Outside Left" groups pretend to stand for tolerance and egalitarian socialism, they really represent repression of free thought and a form, albeit re-packaged for modern consumption, of brute neo-Fascism not seen since the 1930s in Europe.
- The Millennial and Gen-Z cohorts must learn to recognize and reject the false and often violent alternatives proffered by these groups, which include, Occupy Wall St., Antifa, Black Lives Matter and the increasingly openly Marxist members of Congress who style themselves as a socialist "Squad" operating within the current Democrat Party.
- This will be difficult as the front line generations are terribly encumbered with the mental handcuffs and chains slapped upon them throughout their lives by all the disastrous ideas of the Baby Boom generation: a false religion (Gaia Worship) a false, failed ideology (Socialism), a false community (Trans-national Globalism) and a false anti-morality that attacks all the foundational and traditional underpinnings required to maintain a society based on the only thing that can confront and overcome the Seventh Crisis: Ordered Liberty.
- Only Ordered Liberty, which depends on the maintenance of Freedom through a democratically arrived at Constitution that limits the power of government, can prevent systemic oppression from being managed from the center by a self-appointed elite that seeks to be permanently maintained in power by exempting themselves from the oppressive, poverty creating rules they seek to enforce on everyone else.

- The front line generations must resist the subversive strategy of the Marxist Antonio Gramsci, which seeks to control the semi-official ideologically those institutions that support the state apparatus—that is, Academia, Mass Communications, Religion, the Legal System, the Arts and the Entertainment Industry, which Gramsci has correctly understood as being *the best way to win the revolution is to eliminate the need for it by delivering its goals via cultural subversion.*

– 6 –

The Fault Lines of Engagement

The forces that have been unleashed and put into play, as outlined above in The Seventh Crisis, have inevitably created what might be termed *fault lines* through our body politic and indeed our entire culture. What used to be recognized as mere "differences of opinion", easily brushed off as banter between friends, have now taken on a far more antagonistic tone begetting hardened and intransigent positions that often preclude any hope, or even desire, to compromise. Our differences are now amplified, resulting in private gatherings being more antagonistic and hostile than enriching or connecting. In too many cases now "differences in opinion" have caused permanent fallings-out between family members and friends.

The unfortunate reality is that the sowing of dissent among us is the intent of the agenda-setters of the Ruling Elite. Those in our political class are masters at the techniques of "wedge-issue" politics. Political leaders and their minions in the consulting class that feed off them have been honing these strategies on the American public for over half a century, and have continually deployed them to their advantage. Since WWII, Senate incumbents have a re-election rate of 84 percent, while House incumbents have an incredible 94 percent re-election rate, and this is across both parties. Is it any wonder that such probabilities have engendered our ruling class with a hubris that is constantly on display in their *pronouncements* and *dictats* that they issue in both Washington and back in their districts.

Our ruling political class, with whole-hearted reinforcement from mainstream media, have persuaded the overwhelming majority of voters to show fealty to a limited number of "principles" or "identities". We are told to vote for the candidate most likely to deliver on our favorite issue or group of issues. And the Democrats in recent election cycles have completely aligned themselves with "identity politics" which fractures society into various interest groups by race, gender, sexual preference or ethnicity. They then promote the practice of voting for a candidate of the same race, gender or ethnicity as you.

Democrats incessantly broadcast to us that your race or gender is the most important determinant in casting your vote while at the same time disparaging racism and sexism. Conversely, Republicans relentlessly spread the fear that Democrats are scheming to eviscerate the Bill of Rights around the next corner, while never indicating they are often scheming to do the same along with them behind the scenes..

While we watch this roundup play out cycle after cycle, its "validity" is reinforced with relentless political polling, analyzing the electorate's votes along the lines of these identities and issues. Each voting group to varying degrees seems to predictably align itself with either the Democrats or Republicans. The entire American population has been conditioned to view itself in these terms. And just in case you're wavering you are told in no uncertain terms to vote for the candidate most likely to benefit you personally and your little world, wherever that may be, i.e., the mid-west, the south, the cities, the suburbs, rural areas, colleges, farms, coal country, silicon valley and on.

The elections are run and the candidates take office, or most likely remain in office. The electorate goes back to their lives and the ruling political class pursues its agenda of appropriating our tax dollars in such fashion as to improve its chances of being re-elected when the next roundup comes two years hence. The issues intentionally and purposefully do not get resolved, and in fact get recycled and used again to stir up the electorate in the next cycle.

Sadly, the American public who build, maintain and operate our amazing modern society are ignored, taken for granted and consistently plundered by the ruling political class. The American public, often cynically referred to as cattle, are viewed as exactly that by our ruling elite. The elite metaphorically stand on top of a ridge looking down at all the identity issue cattle pens they've constructed in the valley, and every two years they conduct a cynical game among themselves to see who can round up and corral enough of us into specific pens, as they've aligned them, in order to prevail in any given election. To them it's a simple contest of polemics, cynicism and deception.

For us it is a tragedy.

Instead of amicably resolving them, many of the same "wedge issues" have percolated over the past several decades as new ones have emerged, all driven with the same intent—to separate us from each other. In division there is weakness. There had always been comfort for the elite in knowing the public was largely split, facing off against each other. That way they would not be unified and face off against the elite. It has always been in the interest of the elite to have the citizenry split along ideological and party lines. But in recent years pressure has been applied back upon the ruling political class, and their disdain for those they rule has increasingly been on public display.

As the agenda of the organized Left has been relentlessly pressed upon the American people over the past three decades, the organs of the Deep State loudly proclaim that opposition to its agenda is evil, racist, homophobic, Islamophobic, xenophobic… Those who hold the opposing view today are not merely wrong, but "deplorable"; more, they are simply *evil*. The complete intolerance of the Left has clearly increased the temperature of what is regularly referred to in the alternative media as a *cold civil war*. However, while the elite see only the fault lines they have constructed between the contentious issues of the day, they fail to acknowledge the *real* fault lines their autocratic and totalitarian actions have created between themselves and those they deign to rule. As an increasing number of Americans recognize the real fault lines between the "rulers" and "the ruled", society's tectonic plates are shifting below the surface.

While our political class continues to pursue its cynical bi-annual roundup over the perennial surface issues, a growing portion of the citizenry are reacting to the more fundamental cleaving of society. This pressuring and threatening of the establishment's grip on the levers of power has forced the ruling class to expose itself as it has fought back against us. In the process, a rapidly developing two-tiered society has come into clearer focus. First and foremost is our completely exposed two-tiered system of justice.

A TWO-TIERED JUSTICE SYSTEM

One of the most recent egregious examples that the laws which apply to us no longer apply to protected members of the ruling class was on full display as FBI Director James Comey stepped to the microphones on July 5, 2016.

The subject was Hillary Clinton's infamous unofficial e-mail channel managed on her home-brewed server. Comey proceeded to enumerate a stunning list of federal offenses, but then concluded that no prosecutor would pursue a case against her based on the evidence in hand. But his litany amounted to a virtual indictment under 18 U.S. Code 793(f). According to his investigators, they reported her handling of State Department related e-mails, both classified and otherwise, as an act of "gross negligence". However, "gross negligence" is named as a specific violation in the code's wording as follows:

> "Whoever, being entrusted with or having lawful possession or control of any document, writing, code book, signal book, sketch, photograph, photographic negative, blueprint, plan, map, model, instrument, appliance, note, or information, relating to the national defense, (1) through *gross negligence* permits the same to be removed from its proper place of custody or delivered to anyone in violation of his trust, or to be lost, stolen, abstracted, or destroyed, or (2) having knowledge that the same has been illegally removed from its proper place of custody or delivered to anyone in violation of its trust, or lost, or stolen, abstracted, or destroyed, and fails to make prompt report of such loss, theft, abstraction, or destruction to his superior officer…"

Knowing a finding of "gross negligence" would require an indictment recommendation, Director Comey decided to change the phrasing in the report to "extremely reckless". Problem solved—she was naughty, but not indictable. And he repeated the term "extremely reckless" several times throughout the statement. He also focused on "lack of intent" as exculpatory, but alas, a requirement of "intent" is not to be found in the statute. Additionally, to put an exclamation point on it all, Comey absconded with the Attorney General's power to himself and declared that Clinton would not be indicted. His explanation was that the Attorney General, Loretta Lynch, had already been compromised when her completely unethical secret meeting with Bill Clinton on the Phoenix airport tarmac was exposed to the public by a *real* reporter for a local news outlet.

This truly was a breathtaking performance. Several decades ago the assembled press would have rhetorically thrown rotten tomatoes at the Director. The press would have ripped the statement apart and publicly ridiculed Comey for days, precipitating further official action. Putting despicable acts by public officials in a white-hot press spotlight has historically forced action. The subject has nowhere to turn and is almost always forced to address the issue. For these reasons the press's value to a constitutional republic cannot be overstated. But we are increasingly presented with illustrations that the press no longer holds "the protected" class accountable for their actions. As we have observed and illustrated, the media has transformed itself into an enabler of the ruling class which endeavors to solidify its hold on the levers of power of the permanent government, and thus the lives of the "unprotected" citizenry.

Also in the summer of 2016 our ruling class provided the perfect corollary illustration of two-tier justice. Kristian Saucier, a 22-year old sailor on the nuclear submarine USS Alexandria, took six photos in classified areas of the sub, as mementos, before being reassigned. He did not share the photos with any unauthorized recipient, but when discovered he was arrested. His defense team even raised the Clinton precedent, fresh in the public's mind, with the prosecutors in a plea for equal treatment.

Facing the threat of six years in prison, he pleaded guilty to "unauthorized detention of defense information" and received a one-year prison sentence, six months of home confinement and 100 hours of community service. At his sentencing his lawyers said it was "unjust and unfair for Mr. Saucier to receive any sentence other than probation for a crime those more powerful than him will likely avoid. It could be argued here that depending on what your name is, that's the type of justice you get in the United States."

Since the election of Donald Trump, the exposure of actions taken by an entire array of deep state actors has forced the justice and enforcement arms of the state, the courts, DOJ, and FBI to show their hands in administering outsized favorable treatment of its own. Examples abound that Trump allies get indicted, while Resistance actors walk free. Government officials who have been caught lying, with their efforts documented in the furtherance of impairing, damaging or subverting the Trump Administration are rewarded with book deals, TV contracts, and when necessary immunity from prosecution—

see McCabe, Andrew, Deputy FBI Director; Comey, James, FBI Director, and Brennan, John CIA Director. Supporters of President Trump get rounded up at 5 a.m. at gunpoint, placed in solitary confinement, and prosecuted and sentenced to the maximum possible extent—see Manafort, Paul; Stone, Roger, and Lt. General Flynn, Michael. Or they are simply threatened, harassed and have their reputations ruined—see Page, Carter and Papadopoulos, George.

The FBI has quite visibly declined to prosecute any of its agents who lied, tampered with, or mishandled evidence. McCabe lied to Congress and was fired from the FBI on the day he became vested for his pension; he went on to become a "news analyst" on CNN. Comey lied and admitted he leaked classified information to the press; he went on to write a book heaping praise on the *morality* of his actions. The foreign activities of the Clintons' pay-to-play money laundering syndicate, otherwise known as the Clinton Global Initiative, never raised an investigative eyebrow in the DOJ; the Clintons retired to Millionaire Acres in Chappaqua, New York.

The list extends to James Clapper, Lisa Page, Peter Strzok, James Baker, Bruce and Nelie Ohr, Dana Boente, and Sally Yates, who each had a hand in either the handling of the Steele dossier or otherwise perpetuating the fraudulent Russia investigation. Each of these are unelected elite career operatives who have skated free and clear of any legal repercussions, really should be considered fugitives from justice. To quote Kim Strassel of the *WSJ*, these people are "an unelected mandarin class that believes itself exempt from democratic accountability."

If the Millennial generation seeks to age in security and raise their children as free citizens in America, they must send their best Constitution-loving legal minds into the justice system to dismantle the corrupt network of sentries protecting the ruling class from facing "equal justice under the law." They will need to engineer a return to the system where those enacting the laws are subject to every provision of those laws without exception.

THE FINANCIAL DIVIDE

While the political elite assure that the ruling class remain "protected" within the justice system, the financial elite arrange the financial system to benefit themselves and the chosen among the "protected" class. Though the fundamental elements began being assembled a century ago (with the authorization of the Federal Reserve and Federal income tax) additional pieces have been emplaced over the last several decades. The objective is to present the appearance and general functionality of free markets, while retaining sufficient leverage to generally control financial events at critical times to the benefit of the ruling elite.

The financial levers are engaged both in full public view, such as Federal Reserve monetary policy and interest rate decrees, as well as other levers being pulled away from public scrutiny. Though the major equities markets and investment banks are either publicly traded or owned by groups of private individuals, public shareholders have little to no influence upon how they are managed and administered. By definition, the financial elite run and administer the machinery of the United States financial markets. Very little happens in the financial marketplace that is unknown to those whose perspective emanates from the crow's nest.

Although many observers over the decades, in both the public and private sphere, have questioned the Fed's motives for its market interventions, it always seems to proceed with ample authorization (aka, cover) for its actions, whether taken in the stock market crash of October 1987 or the dot-com bubble burst of 2000. However, the financial crisis of 2008 was so severe that every available governmental lever was employed in conjunction with The Fed to grapple with the ensuing catastrophe it engendered. The roots of the '08 crisis were entirely the making of the financial and political elite. Each working hand in hand with the other to pursue both their joint and disparate interests, they distorted the marketplace to the point that the credit markets seized up forcing the crisis to spread to virtually every other financial market…across the globe.

Doing justice to the roots of the entire affair is beyond the purview of this book. But for those watching with independent eyes, the actions taken to "resolve" the crisis revealed that the financial elite were forced to expose their interests and machinations to public scrutiny. The *last* thing they wanted to do was go public and arrange a bailout of the banks, requiring votes in congress. Regardless, their incompetence and *criminality* was laid bare for the American public to see. Any questioning or challenging voices were stilled by conjuring images of another Great Depression, with the wealth of the great American middle class washed down the tubes with falling stocks and failing banks. The system was about to collapse, we were told, the banks had to be saved. And oh yes—the *bankers* too.

There was no doubt that abuse of the mortgage underwriting process, mortgage-backed securities market, and derivatives market had the credit markets reeling. The cry went up: "consumer deposits have to be guaranteed - the ATMs have to be funded", but behind the cries on behalf of the little guy, the elite were of course, endeavoring to save themselves. The Troubled Asset Relief Program (TARP) was hatched and touted as the bold plan to bailout the banks, save the financial system and assure Americans their savings were safe. Through all the public mea culpas about maintaining a free-market system came the cry, "we have to let the government bail out the system in order to save it."

In a nutshell and at its core, the following captures what transpired in the fall of 2008. Developing through the prior decade, in order to accelerate and expand lending activity, banks made increasing use of Collateral Debt Obligations (CDO). CDOs are bundles or packages of asset-backed securities consisting of auto loans, credit card debt, corporate debt, or the *infamous* mortgage-backed securities. Banks would originate the loans, quickly bundle and classify them and sell them off to financial companies, pension funds, mutual funds, investment banks and other commercial banks. The idea was to quickly open up the opportunity to expand the writing of primary loans/mortgages and spread the risk across a wide spectrum of financial institutions. It is an effective business expansion technique, but wide open to abuse by its very nature.

Contributing to the debt expansion was Fannie Mae's (the federal government underwriter) entrance into the subprime loan securitization process and then issuing *guarantees* for the bundled securities. This was all a part of extending credit into the low-income housing sector further to the infamous Community Reinvestment Act (CRA). None other than Clinton "fixer" Jamie Gorelick made the announcement that Fannie Mae would be guaranteeing the bundled mortgages, to the bankers attending the American Bankers Association's 2000 annual convention. Fannie Mae's purchase of CRA loans is considered by many, ground-zero for the '08 financial meltdown. It literally turbo-charged the entire malfeasant scheme.

Jamie Gorelick is a marquee example of how the administrative state makes millionaires of its loyal operatives. After doing her yeoman's share of Clinton dirty work as Assistant Attorney General in the mid-90s, she was awarded a perch as vice chair of Fannie Mae in 1998. When she left in 2003, she had collected some $26 million in salary, bonuses, and options. She had no banking experience going in, she lit the financial meltdown fuse while there, and exited a rich woman, who remains an infamous untouchable today.

The financial institutions buying the mortgage-backed securities sought to protect or hedge the risk—enter Credit Default Swaps (CDS). The CDS is said to have been developed by a banker at JP Morgan. Put simply, the CDS "insures" against the default of the mortgages in a package of mortgage-backed securities. If the mortgages in the bundle go belly-up, the CDS pays the financial institution holding the bundle. Purchasing CDSs on its books of collateralized assets gave the banks a sense of security, albeit as it turned out—a false sense.

The writers of the CDS/insurance were largely specialized insurers in the financial guarantee business, e.g. AIG, Ambac, MBIA, Swiss Re. They justified the assumption of risk by spreading their underwriting across a broad classification of asset classifications, e.g. mortgages, auto loans, credit cards etc. This classic underwriting technique gave them comfort because all classifications of risk couldn't crater at once…could it? But tragically there was *moral hazard* riddled throughout this chain of commerce, i.e. these transactions, by nature of their structure, failed to motivate the players to control risk.

In order to increase their volume, the underwriting standards of mortgage originators became increasingly loose and in some documented cases, non-existent. After all, they were bundling the mortgages and passing them out the back door and off their books almost as soon as they wrote them. And to maximize the leverage, the banks were rapidly expanding the sub-prime market of higher risk loans. The buyers of the asset-backed packages didn't care all that much about their quality since they were buying CDS to hedge and *insure* their risks. The insurers issuing the CDS took comfort in a broad spread of risk and a continually rising housing market.

The rising housing market was key to the entire scheme—it covered all errors, over-leveraging and outright fraud…until it didn't. The housing market hit the wall in 2006 and the financial statements of the banks and insurers began to rapidly deteriorate. As events accelerated from '07 to '08 the entire scheme engulfed the personal finances of millions of Americans and was laid bare before the entire country.

Faced with this literal "meltdown" of the financial system, congress quickly passed the $700 billion TARP, and Treasury Secretary Hank Paulson called the CEOs of the country's eight biggest banks to the White House and reports indicate, *forced* them to take the capital infusions—regardless of whether they needed them. In the same time period, AIG was meeting with Goldman Sachs at the New York Federal Reserve, ostensibly to discuss locating funding sources for AIG's tanking book of CDS business. TARP had already been done, but there was another massive shoe to drop.

Most of the banks were deep into the cratering mortgage-back securities business, but they had bought CDS to insure large portions of their portfolios. Unfortunately, AIG was very aggressive and imprudent in writing CDS for the banks and clearly couldn't make good on the avalanche of claims flowing in. Meanwhile, there wasn't a prayer of finding a private funding source for AIG and Goldman knew it. They were at the New York Fed quietly making the case that AIG needed a bailout too. And Goldman had a vested interest in making it happen—AIG owed Goldman $20 billion in CDS claims. They wanted to get paid and "coincidently" Hank Paulson was the prior CEO of Goldman. Is the picture coming into focus?

AIG's CDS book was so big that if it was unable to make good with the banks, they'd probably need another bailout! AIG was virtually sitting with torpedoes loaded, ready to fire financial broadsides into many of the leading banks and financial institutions in the country. In all, AIG received $182 billion in TARP and other loans to keep it solvent—more than any of the banks. The upshot was the banks got paid and were kept solvent. The big boys took care of each other: the public elite in government; the private elite in the banks; and the quasi-public elite in the Fed. Most managers even received their annual bonuses, with the proffered justification that it was necessary to retain bank management! No, you just can't make it up. After Lehman Brothers, nothing was allowed to fail. The financial elite raided the public treasury to keep themselves ensconced at the levers of financial power after perpetrating a massive financial fraud upon the American public and bringing the economy to its knees. Not a one of them was convicted of any financial wrongdoing.

The handling of the financial crisis set up the biggest business moral hazard in history. By bailing out the banks and leaving the managerial elite in place, future bankers will not be constrained by conscience, precedent, or fear of the downside because they'll know that if they cook up a big enough mess the government will again come to their rescue. They were now "too big to fail." There were honest solutions, complicated but with teeth, that would have kept future bankers honest and preserved a semblance of the free market. They would have been structured along the lines of letting banks fail but providing federal guarantees for the deposits, firing and prosecuting management where appropriate, selling remaining good assets, and bringing in new management to rebuild the banks. The myth that the banks had to be bailed out in toto is just that—a myth!

The banks repaid all the TARP-related loans within three years, but the government gained unprecedented and lasting influence upon the banks' management, and regulatory control, going forward. The financial elite preserved both their wealth and their hold upon the nation's biggest financial institutions. But the casualties of the entire episode were the millions of financially ruined American lives strewn across the landscape. Average Americans not only lost their homes, but half the value of their investments in the stock market. And with unemployment approaching 10 percent, millions were now out of work. There was no longer any question about who in society was "protected" and who was not. Right in front of our noses, the ruling financial elite saved themselves at our expense. The financial divide was never so wide and deep.

But the financial "solution" activated in late '08 wasn't a solution at all. It was, and continues to be, a *financial narcotic*. The Federal Reserve's infusion of liquidity into the financial markets when the credit markets seized up was prudent and an appropriate action. However, since the financial elite refused to let any of their brethren and their crippled institutions fail and let the economy reset on sound footing, they were compelled to utilize the Federal Reserve in unprecedented ways. Without continued infusions of *cheap money* into the system, many financial institutions were doomed to failure or "zombie" status. In addition, a stock market holding the nation's savings had lost half its value. Under normal growth rates it would take a generation to recover the loss, and there would be a lot of failures along the way.

For the financial elite the only "solution" was continued cheap money. Then Fed Chair, Ben Bernanke, made the decision to launch a series of actions euphemistically termed "quantitative easing." The Fed would step in and buy massive amounts of Treasury bonds direct from the U.S. treasury. Since they would be a big, guaranteed buyer, the interest rates would stay exactly where they were - inordinately low. The Fed had lowered rates precipitously through the depth of the '08 crisis. Now one hand of the federal government would be regularly buying the country's debt from the other hand—and we're not to ask how the Fed conjures the "money" to purchase the bonds. As we noted earlier, this was the type of financial management commonly associated with fascistic banana republics.

Where did all the cheap money go? The stock market, of course. With interest rates at one percent, the cheap money moving through the system made its way into the stock market where it began its rise from a rock bottom DOW of 6,547 in March of 2009. The market had declined about 50 percent in six months. Where did the money go? Though they all know, no one in the financial press and TV talking heads ever really examines that question. They make the presumption that we think we all took a shellacking in the market. But, in fact, that horrendous stock market slide was largely a wealth transfer from the middle class to the financial elite.

This was the third equity market bubble burst in 21 years. The people that work and make this country run for a living and held savings in the market were getting used to the financial professionals' perennial advice to not sell at the first signs of trouble, then don't sell when it's down 10 percent or so because it will bounce, and it's too late to sell when it's down 30 percent, you'll be taking a huge loss! Funny how that works. The middle class is continually counseled to "hang in there" while their savings are looted by the professional traders who know better, cash out *their* accounts and harvest *their* gains before the music stops. Happens every time. Bernanke knew if he didn't do *something* the pitchforks would be out. Therefore, he started re-inflating the bubble with money basically printed out of thin air in the form of the infamous QE-1, QE-2, QE-3 and more.

The great re-inflation began in the spring of '09. It didn't take long to refill everyone's accounts with cheaper money. Just three years later the DOW crossed the 13,000 mark in February 2012, completely retracing it's dramatic collapse. Those fortunate ones who didn't have to sell near the bottom because of lost jobs or balloon mortgage payments, saw their mutual funds and 401Ks float back to prior levels. But too many Americans were caught in the general financial squeeze and had to draw down funds to live on during the bust years, and didn't get to benefit from the re-inflation.

Yes, and in the process, ole Ben drove a wedge into another vulnerable segment of society—the seniors. In the main, seniors relied on interest-bearing financial instruments to provide steady and reliable income from their savings through their retirement years. But forget it - gone was the steady 5, 6 or 7 percent interest common before the crisis. Seniors now had to make do with the less than one percent being offered on bank CDs—their retirement cash flow being stolen right out from under them. But the *system had to be saved* no matter how many innocent casualties piled up across American society. After all, the Banksters who arrogantly see themselves as the gods of finance are too big…and too elite…to fail; to allow them to do so would reveal the breath of their corruption, the depth of their cupidity and the heartless immensity of their guilt.

For the decade following the great recession and beyond, the great reflation has continued, with national debt topping $27 trillion and accelerating from a $3 billion a day expansion to over $8 billion a day in 2020, with no end in sight. Trillion dollar plus annual deficits are now institutionalized into the budgeting process. This monstrous post-pandemic debt is not even news anymore—clearly the Tea Party lost that battle long ago. Does anyone believe congress will ever produce even a balanced budget, not to mention actually pay down some of the debt? And more ominously, does anyone believe that this massive debt bubble will not burst with catastrophic consequences for *most* Americans? Yes, *most* but not *all* Americans. Within two months of the initial 11,000 point pandemic crash, the market recovered some 7,000 points, and within six months was breaking new all-time highs.

Tragically for most of us, as with the prior bubbles, the financial elite will be in the crow's nest as we approach the next iceberg. The financial elite sit all day with their hands on the controls of the markets. And when they're not at their posts, they have their computers programed to buy and sell based on the headlines coming across the wires. After a decade of one percent interest rates, much of middle-income America had little alternative but to put the majority of its savings into the stock market. The markets have had several severe "flash-crashes" since 2008, but in each case, over varying periods lasting up to a year, the markets recovered and pressed on to notch new highs.

Most all the financial press and TV talking heads either ignore the national debt issue or reference it as a manageable phenomenon as they quickly avert their glance. Those few who do address the debt, soberly reference it as a debt bubble or the biggest bubble of them all. Senator Tom Coburn wrote a book and titled it "The Debt Bomb." Citing the progression of severity of bubbles back to the late '90s, the banks bailed out the Long Term Capital financial bust of '98, the government bailed out the banks in '08, but who's going to bail out the government when the public debt bomb explodes?

Answer—we are.

Banks across the globe are quietly writing into their by-laws provisions to allow them to confiscate a percentage of each deposit account in the event of another catastrophic financial industry failure. Such provisions are called "bail-ins" because depositors of the impaired financial institutions will have their savings confiscated, or bailed in, at the direction of management. There is precedent for this in other western nations. Polish pension funds have been halved to cut sovereign debt, bank depositors in Cyprus had 10 percent of their accounts confiscated to save the banks, Canada has written bail-in provisions into law, and in the U.S. several different schemes to confiscate percentages of IRAs and 401Ks have been drafted and discussed. Another proposal would replace the securities in our 401Ks with government bonds. Although no bail-in style legislation has been passed in the United States as of this writing, the rapid drafting of TARP and its enactment into law provides the road test for controversial legislative enactment in the midst of a financial "crisis."

From where the average American sits, we are staring at potential financial meltdowns on three fronts—the stock market, the bond market, and bank deposit accounts. But the fuse is most likely to be lit in the debt market. The financial analysts talk up the new highs in the stock market, but when there's interest rate gyrations in the bond market everything suddenly gets serious and stocks take the immediate hit. The issue is the dreaded "inverted yield curve" when short term (2 year) yields spike above long-term (10-year) yields. Lending money for two years should never pay more than lending for ten years.

Traditionally an inverted yield curve meant that investors lost faith in the stock market run, moving money out of stocks and into longer term bonds as a safety play. The infusion of money into long bonds naturally drives down the interest rates and if the shift was massive, 10-year rates would drop below 2-year rates. Historically the inverted yield curve usually presaged a recession by a few months to a year. But since the crisis began in late '08, the Federal Reserve has kept rates artificially suppressed, allowing for an occasional inverted curve when short term rates spiked due to massive Treasury debt issuance to support historic-sized federal deficits. Such "technical" inversions, and their immediate negative impact on stocks, have proven that in the post '08 crisis era the bond market dictates to the stock market.

The financial elite are well aware of this phenomenon and have consistently run up the stock market at every interest rate cut, hint of a cut, or accommodative public statement by the Fed Chair. Low interest rates dictate both the paltry earnings available from bank deposits and low borrowing costs for funds available for investment in the stock market. Meanwhile, the elite's behavior in the post-'08 environment indicates that the primary driver of stock prices has shifted from corporate earnings to the availability of cheap money. As the elite continue to plow cheap money into stocks, be assured they each keep one eye trained on the exit. Although there have been several flash-crashes with rapid recoveries, the trading class and their *protected* clients intend to be early through the exit when they sense the massive stock bubble of their making is about to burst.

It is at this point, a material and accelerating market sell-off, that the *financial divide* between the financial elite and average Americans will again be tragically apparent to everyone. For the financial elite will have for the third time in recent memory, sold off the market, pocketed a massive share of the wealth of middle America, and left the average American with vastly depleted investment accounts. But this time the re-inflation game will not be an option—because there just won't be enough *credible* money on the planet to reflate every investment account in America. The ruse will truly be over.

Many astute observers, including these authors, thought this final bubble would have burst during the Obama years. But the Federal Reserve has been hyper vigilant on its end-game watch, and has perfected a broad array of both visible and hidden tools and machinations for keeping the bubble inflated. This subterfuge even has a nickname among the astute financial observers. Those who know what's going on, cynically refer to the Fed's efforts as the "plunge protection team" or PPT for short. The term even makes it into the press, particularly when the Treasury Secretary or Fed Chair calls in the nation's largest six to eight banks to coordinate strategy.

Their cover story is always that the banks are being assured of sufficient market liquidity by the Fed. Since the '08 implosion, like financial fire fighters, they have been called into action in January '16, January '18, December '18, and March '20. In each of these cases, equity markets were in apparent free-fall and the Treasury Secretary knew they could tip into the feared and dreaded financial reckoning. In each case they were able to stem the plunge and coax the markets back onto their generally upward trajectory. Each drill is a sophisticated combination of visible and invisible market interventions, coupled with carefully calibrated statements by the Fed Chair and the Treasury Secretary, plus the reassuring words emanating from most, but not all, organs of the financial and political press. But they know, as do we, that this dangerous game cannot go on forever.

When the music stops, the financial catastrophe they will have created will be of such magnitude that literally a "financial reset," of Bretton Woods magnitude, across the entire western world may be required to stabilize the world's financial gyroscope to try to prevent the crisis from engulfing middle class Millennials in a deluge of economic collapse.

THE NEW ARISTOCRACY

When considering the New Aristocracy of Celebrity that is currently on the rise in the United States, it is only with greatest irony that one can recall that the American Constitutional Republic was formed out of a revolt against the pretensions, the arrogant elitism and the favored legal status that the 18th century British Aristocracy exerted over what they viewed as their colonial inferiors in North America. However, the Old British Aristocracy had its origins in the medieval military prowess of those warlords who served the winners of royal power struggles, some of which dated back to centuries in the past. Their distant descendants, most of whom had given up the battlefield for the palace, had long since devolved into a decadent collection of the bored and idle rich. Their lifestyles had absolutely nothing in common with… or sympathy for… the serfs who worked their large landholdings and whose wealth they looted. When they desired personal glory, they pretended to act in the royal interest, using their class influence to take control of military affairs which often resulted in throwing away the lives of the soldiers who suffered under their incompetent command. The bourgeois professionals… the merchants, doctors, lawyers and politicians who served their purposes… were looked upon with as much contempt as their scullery maids and stable boys because they actually had to earn a living. They considered themselves a breed apart; separate, superior, privileged by fate and favored by God. The stuff our New Aristocracy is made of comes out of a very different mold but is made up of much the same material and exhibits the same type of attitude.

The New Aristocracy is not born from the mold of Class but from the mold of Celebrity; it is composed of sections of the population that up until relatively recent times were dismissed by society as irrelevant, trivial, superficial, decadent and even morally reprehensible; however, they are now often raised into the New Aristocracy simply because they have achieved the only criteria for membership: popularity with the masses. For example, we are now almost daily subjected to celebrity "comedians" who apparently believe their job is not to be clowns but to be cultural critics despite the shallow nature of their intellects or the lack of any success in any field beyond standing on a stage telling mostly stolen or recycled "jokes." At one time in the not so distant past, foul-mouthed comedians were only seen in smoky, sleazy burlesque clubs telling dirty jokes to the drunks in between the appearance of the strippers the patrons actually came to see. Now, we are subjected to their commentary on any and all subjects and worse, their condemnation of traditional values and morality as not being as "progressive" (i.e,. as leftwing) as they think it should be. They demand to be taken "seriously" and that their social commentary, badly disguised as "comedy," be credited for making a serious contribution to serious issues.

Yet when their arrogant ignorance inevitably winds up getting them into legal trouble because they have taken an action or made a statement that could get them sued or land them in court or, worst of all, kill their career, they cowardly jump behind their lawyers and publicity firms and demand a pass because, after all, they're just comedians trying to be funny. A similar case can be made for actors, actresses and "pop singers," another group that was once looked upon (as recently as the beginning of the 20th Century) as an unserious and immoral group who wound up in that "profession" because, if they were men, were too incompetent and lazy to work at a "real" job and if they were women, were too immoral to find a decent husband. To this group have been added sports celebrities, who engage in similar social commentary that they demand be taken "seriously" even though it is based only on their prowess on the field of play; in fact, once many of them realize they no longer have (or never actually had) any real prowess on the field to begin with, they try to extend their celebrity by engaging in some outrageous act that demands the attention of a debased Enemedia that is always looking to publicize controversial martyrs to causes they favor.

It would be a waste of the reader's time to go through the near endless list of such pampered New Aristocrats who have gotten favored treatment after committing some criminal infraction, from shoplifting, to drug possession, to drunk driving to sexual harassment to rape to violent assault and in some cases, even to murder. A simple internet search combining any of the above crimes and infractions with the words "comedians, actors, pop singers, sports figures" will result in a long list of those who fit the charge of being rich and influential celebrities who got lenient treatment for actions that regularly send non-celebrities to prison and their reputations sent deep into disgrace. More often than not, trouble with the law can actually increase a celebrity's influence, wealth and power; as long as they are committed to the same "progressive" leftwing social / political agenda as the Enemedia and "Entertainment" Industry that creates and maintains their careers. Their troubles are framed as "martyrdom" for the Cause. More, if it serves the purpose of the Left, it might even result in far more money given by corporate sponsors who desire to be associated with popular celebrities who are "in sync" with some particular segment of the population that represents a new set of potential customers to market to. Of course, should some celebrity go against the prevailing leftwing agenda, they will find their careers stymied, their views smeared and their reputations ruined. In a word—Cancelled!

The New Aristocrats should not simply be dismissed because of the shallow fatuousness with which they approach life and form their empty-headed opinions, which are all shaped by those who control their careers; just the opposite. This is because modern society is increasingly becoming one which is watched on TV, on film, on I-phones and on the Internet, more than it is lived… and it is celebrities who are the people being watched on them. The average child spends far more time interacting with the views and opinions of those who are held up as "celebrity role models" simply because they are famous than they do their own parents, relatives, teachers or mentors, none of which can match the all-important celebrity of those exalted by the cultural rapists in the Enemedia and "entertainment" Industry. "The closest study to Common Sense Media's may be the Kaiser Family Foundation 2010 study, which estimated an average of 5½ of media use for those ages 8-10, 8 hours and 40 minutes for those aged 11-14, and just under 8 hours for 15-18 year-olds." https://www.washingtonpost.com/news/the-switch/wp/2015/11/03/teens-spend-nearly-nine-hours-every-day-consuming-media/

Every single one of those hours is spent, overtly and subtly, absorbing every single political and social view of the Transnational Progressive elites, sublimated through celebrity pop stars, comedians, actors, actresses and sports stars… that is, as long as they tow the Transnational Progressive ("Tranzi") line.

Is it any wonder that most young people all have the exactly the same emotionally driven opinions on issues relating to climate, sex, economic "fairness" and social justice? Is it any wonder that, after 6 hours of the same indoctrination in school and 9 hours of social media propaganda that they are so easily drawn into the anti-traditionalist netherworlds of repressively politically correct campus activism and Gaia Worship or the even darker, more violent fever swamps of the Antifa or Black Lives Matter?

The most dangerous aspect of the New Aristocracy of Celebrity is that, unlike the Old Aristocracy, which was contemptuous of those beneath them and thereby incurred their wrath, the New is obsessed with co-opting the support of those they view as their inferiors and cult followers... or, in the modern parlance, their fans. They are constantly being used to shape the opinions of those who are molded to worship their success, wealth and fame to imitate and emulate their political and social views. Far more importantly, the New Aristocracy contribute to their inability to think critically about the doctrines and dogmas of Progressive Liberalism so that when the Seventh Crisis boils over, they will be helpless before it and therefore desperate to be saved... not by the ignorant, pliable celebrities in the "Entertainment" and Sports Industries, but by the true Aristocrats of Plutocracy, found in the Transnational Progressive corporate elite who own the collective soul of the shallow, drug-addled actors, clowns, troubadours and ball throwers posing as the "New Aristocracy."

MEDIA FAULT LINE

Given Donald Trump's close identification with the phrase "Fake News," it is interesting to remember that it was Hillary Clinton who originally coined the phrase: "On 8 December 2016, Hillary Clinton made a speech in which she mentioned 'the epidemic of malicious fake news and false propaganda that flooded social media over the past year... It's now clear that so-called fake news can have real-world consequences,' she said. 'This isn't about politics or partisanship. Lives are at risk... lives of ordinary people just trying to go about their days, to do their jobs, contribute to their communities.'" It wasn't until a month later that "President-elect Trump took up the phrase in January 2017, a little over a week before taking office. In response to a question, he said 'you're fake news' to CNN reporter Jim Acosta. Around the same time he started repeating the phrase on Twitter." https://www.bbc.com/news/blogs-trending-42724320

However, regardless of who first used the phrase, which is simply another way of calling Enemedia and Social Media fueled personal and political attacks directed your way regardless of political affiliation, the concept of "Fake News" is nothing new. False propaganda being weaponized by one's political opposition is less important than the fact that Clinton is *correct in her assessment* that

Fake News can have real-world consequences. Further, it can have particularly bad consequences when it periodically overflows out of the foggy netherworld of American politics and into the very tangible world of foreign affairs. The record of the so-called "Mainstream" Media and now, the even worse record of the Social Media, (where dishonest memes and false stories are supercharged into the public's consciousness, or where conversely, real stories are either underplayed of completely ignored to serve the political preferences of Big Tech) strongly indicates that its rapid descent into even deeper depths of the propaganda abyss that has occurred since the 2016 election is breathtaking.

The lack of concern regarding facts now runs so rampant that presidential contenders like former Vice President Joe Biden are comfortable publicly stating "We choose truth over facts!" Biden even went on to praise the influential Socialist Congressional Representative Alexandra Ocasio-Cortez, who publicly condemns the idea that "There's a lot of people more concerned about being precisely, factually, and semantically correct than about being morally right..." https://thefederalist.com/2019/08/09/joe-biden-endorses-ocasio-cortezs-support-truth-facts/

The idea that it is more important to be morally right than factually correct may appear ridiculous to anyone with a modicum of common sense (in that if you are being factually incorrect in the service of making a supposedly moral point you are nonetheless *lying*) it is unfortunately true that such thinking is essential for the Elites to use against Gen-Xers, Millennials and Gen-Z to further undermine their ability to think critically in the face of the accelerating Seventh Crisis. Believing that one holds a moral position even if it isn't based on facts is part and parcel of the attack on one's ability to mobilize facts, reason, logic and empirical truth and apply them to deal with whatever form the Crisis threat takes. Bereft of this ability, all that is left is for the helpless masses of fact-deficient people to be corralled into the pens the Elites' desire to segregate us into so that it can achieve the control it justifies as being necessary for them to "resolve" a Crisis the people have no idea how to deal with at all.

Fake News becomes even more insidious when one understands that it is re-enforced by other Leftwing institutions. Once a Fake News meme is established, it is only a matter of time before one begins to see television and film productions apply the meme to some fictional storyline that always casts its opponents as the evil "bad guy" and the character that supports the Enemedia Fake News meme as the hero.

This process is accelerated and multiplied by the internet, where false stories spread around the world long before they can be checked or effectively debunked. Websites in the service of Fake News have effectively been lifted from any serious process of verification. By the time an effective counter-argument can be mustered the lie has become the truth in the eyes of those who seek confirmation of views they already hold, and the counter-narrative is itself cast as the untrue "talking points" of those who have been "exposed."

While it is true that the Left has originated and dominates this Orwellian process, the Right has apparently decided that they must adopt it as well in order for their view to survive against their more powerful media enemies. Neither opponent helps the public to understand and discern the truth, which obviates the entire purpose of an unbiased Free Press…

…and if Truth cannot be discerned or understood, then any narrative can be foisted on a public that doesn't know the difference between fact and fantasy.

As dangerous as Fake News is when applying it to political, social and economic issues, it is mortally dangerous when it is applied to foreign affairs. If past is prologue, we have a lot to worry about regarding a public that has been conditioned to not only be unable to understand the truth but to not even be able to recognize its importance. How will it ever be able to deal with an existential crisis, especially one dealing with war and peace, if it rejects facts in favor of moral memes and narratives of Fake News?

FOREIGN POLICY FAULT LINE

Gen-Xers, Millennials and Gen-Z would do well to remember that there has been more than one full-fledged war that was launched with the help of Fake News. In 1898, the USS Maine sunk in Havana Harbor in Cuba due to what was later determined by most experts to be the result of a coal bunker fire that caused the explosion that sunk the ship. However, at the time, those corporate forces in the United States who were anxious to join the other Great Powers in their imperial ambitions to acquire overseas colonies and control the resources they offered, used the incident as a pretext to go to war with Spain, which was Cuba's colonial master at the time. The Press raged against the Spanish, accusing them of piracy, atrocities and tyrannizing the Cubans. Politicians desirous of obtaining military glory to fuel their ambitions for higher office, such as Teddy Roosevelt, demanded that military action be taken to save the Cubans from the Spanish and establish a "democracy" in Cuba. With the screaming newspapers in tow, the public was maneuvered into supporting what TR later called "a splendid little war," which killed thousands of people and ended not with Cuba becoming a democracy, but rather becoming an American colony that wasn't free from unwanted United States control or interference in its affairs for decades to come. This same play... the "need" to liberate a weak country and establish "democracy" in order to protect vaguely defined or non-existent "American interests"... was put into effect many times over the course of the 20th Century.

It is now clear that Woodrow Wilson was covertly helping the British evade the German sea blockade during WWI in order to provoke the Imperial German submarines to attack U.S. shipping. Getting into a war due to an atrocity committed by a "barbaric" enemy (in this case the sinking of passenger liners that were illegally filled with contraband war material headed for the Allies) was again a perfect excuse to justify saving the Anglophile elite bankers that controlled Wilson and whose loan repayments were predicated on a British victory that was far from certain at the time. The same pattern was followed throughout many U.S. military interventions, both large and small from the Dominican Republic to Panama. It was used by President Johnson in the Tonkin Gulf Incident which, though a complete fraud, was the Fake News sold to the public to justify the start of a U.S. intervention that led to the 10-year nightmare of Vietnam. The Gulf War, which was supposedly about saving Kuwait from an Iraqi invasion, was partly justified by false and incendiary Media accounts of Iraqi atrocities against Kuwaiti babies being thrown out of incubators. Defeating the Iraqi invasion was supposedly also necessary for a far "loftier" goal: bringing about President George H.W. Bush's Globalist desires for what he called a "New World Order." The pattern was again run by Bush's son who followed him into the White House a decade later during the War in Iraq, which was predicated on Iraq illegally having Weapons of Mass Destruction that were later revealed not to exist; thereafter it was justified as "creating democracy" and "nation building" in the Middle East. The pattern is always the same: a false threat, followed by a false attack, followed by false evidence, followed by Media frenzy, followed by public outrage, followed by war and ultimately followed by disillusion, debilitation and disgust when the reality of the False Policy and Fake News was revealed.

However, the pattern has been so successful that it is unlikely to be abandoned. This is because the focus of the Transnational Progressive Elite, who are almost never found among those who do the fighting but who nevertheless dominate the direction of American Foreign Policy. The justifications for the Globalist focus are provided by so-called "experts" who are invariably culled largely from an academic intelligentsia that is dependent on the Elite's financial largess to the institutions in which they work; they are utterly controlled by their need for the sponsorship and media publicity provided by the Tranzi elites to sell their books and provide credibility for their policy prescriptions. Like their controllers, academics are also rarely found on the Front Lines of any conflict or in the foxholes fighting any battle. The idea of America only fighting wars that are in its national interest is considered obsolete by those advancing the idea of Transnationalism, which repudiates the idea of National Sovereignty in the name of global government. The constitutional provisions that require a Declaration of War by Congress have been all but abandoned in favor of executive military actions taken with tacit congressional support (via its funding of the action) but which lack the far more deliberate considerations and unifying justification the Constitutional process that declaring war brings. This allows the military action to take place but, lacking an immediate victory, allows for a premature abandonment of the troops that have been committed to the effort. Of course, to the Elites, a national military is simply another atavistic institution that should be replaced by more Globalist "peace-keeping" forces that are felt to be less "jingoistic" and more conducive to "negotiations" that can more easily facilitate appeasement and surrender of national interests… which, in any event, is viewed in itself as a barbaric leftover from less "enlightened" times.

It must be remembered that the public's concept of Foreign Policy is quite straight-forward: only fight when it is in the national interest, fight to win, totally destroy the enemy's ability to ever again become a threat and then leave the area to its own devices and its own recovery process (that is, reject the ludicrous Collin Powell concept "you break it, you own it.") Once the mission is accomplished, the defeated should be left with nothing more than a stern warning to never again incur our military wrath. This is not the Foreign Policy concept of the Transnational Progressives or the Foreign Policy elites they own.

The key to understanding the fault-line between a Foreign Policy based on protecting and advancing American national interests and the Foreign Policy of the Transnational Elite and its operatives is that the latter have *no interest at all* in furthering American national interests - because American national interests are *the only thing that stands between them and a successful completion of their efforts to take power in such an all-consuming way as to never have to face the prospect of having to give it up.*

American national interests... that is, protection of American citizens, property, military assets, military objectives, diplomatic concerns and support for allies with polities and economic systems America heavily interacts with... *all* stand in the way of their ultimate objective to obtain unassailable, global political power. In fact, *it is America as we have come to know it that is the main thing that blocks the way to that ultimate goal.*

Therefore, it is in the Transnational Progressive interest to follow an aggressive "neo-conservative" policy that seeks to go forth looking for "monsters" to slay supposedly in order to make the world safe for democracy; or create "world peace" by diminishing national sovereignty and subjecting it to Globalist international organizations such as the United Nations or any of the various NGOs. Such organizations and entities refuse to recognize international borders or native customs, traditions and laws regardless of whether or not the so-called "benighted" people who live there desire the "progressive" change the Globalists insist be forced upon them. Tranzi foreign policy often justifies intervention in order to "save" authoritarian regimes from totalitarian regimes which, in fact, can barely be distinguished from each other. It seeks to put American troops on the borders of dozens of countries around the world but maintains that having American troops protect its own borders is somehow... "un-American." As indicated above, it gins up its propaganda network to manufacture fake horror atrocity stories in order to produce sympathy for foreign interventions with the corollary that it is better to "fight them over there rather than over here."

This insane open-ended warmongering has held American Foreign Policy in its grip since the Second World War; it has fought off every attempt to even question it by branding the dissenters as "isolationists" or worse, being in the service of foreign enemies. By corrupting the idea of rejecting the type of appeasement of powerful enemies that led to WWII, they have created a situation where any reckless adventure based on any flimsy or trumped up justification (usually to justify some form of "preventive war") is legitimate and more, serves the "moral purpose" of advancing a global order dominated by the Transnational Progressives that is not to be questioned. In a frighteningly Orwellian fashion, the Tanzis launch a series of wars, all claimed to be preventing something worse that might happen... which always sets the stage for the next war to be launched, *not prevented.* It has resulted in sending the children of the Middle and Working classes off to die in places such as Korea, Vietnam, Kuwait and Iraq… all of which most Americans had never heard of before the propaganda mills began banging the war drums. Worse, once these wars had either been won or at the least, put into a state of Armistice, *they became part of a policy which requires that they never end!* Involvement in the affairs of these countries becomes America's perpetual burden; regardless of the guilt of the leaders of these countries or the lack of strength or courage of the people they led, it was America that had to "fix"… at the cost of hundreds of billions of dollars and the further loss of American life… what America "broke" by engaging in yet another "preventive war."

It is not the purpose of this work to debate the pros and cons of America's involvement in these various wars; rather it is to question why Americans should listen to and follow those who have inflicted such a failed and disastrous policy on its phenomenally brave and patriotic soldiers, their families and tax-paying citizens who love them and appreciate their valor. It is to warn against endlessly open-ended commitments that are made permanent, and which condemns any who call to end such commitments to derision and slander.

This is especially ironic since it is the Transnational Elites who, once they have bogged America down in a foreign war, are inevitably the first to subvert and abandon the effort. The same propaganda organs that called for blood at the start of the war and ran atrocity stories about the enemy turn on a dime and call the war a lost cause, run atrocity stories against its own troops and plead for peace at any price! This process, starting with the Washington-backed stalemate in Korea and perfected in Vietnam, convulsed the American public. They could not understand why the same Elites that demanded war now bemoaned it as a defeat and a quagmire. They could not understand how the intellectuals who had justified the war now justified calling it someone else's mistake; in fact, the intellectuals placed the blame for that mistake on the American people themselves, whose "arrogant, aggressive, racist war-mongering" had caused the blunder the intellectual class now inveighed against. The same Academics who wrote endlessly about the necessity of the war and of keeping commitments and of taking on the role of the world's policeman, were later found leading the college students whose minds they were in charge of deforming in "peace" protests, lest they be cast into the meat-grinder their professors justified and advocated be fed only a short time before.

And it goes on. A recent example of this can be seen with President Trump's removal of a tiny number of troops from a war zone in northern Syria, where they had been stationed to help the local Kurdish people fight the beyond-vicious Islamist terrorist group known as ISIS. The fighting in Syria, in one form or another had been going on for nearly 10 years; it was a combination of a civil war, a religious war and a terrorist war all built upon a rancid form of ethnic tribalism that had gone back centuries. All those involved, the neo-Nazi / Allawi's-Islam regime of Syria's Bashir Assad, the Yazidi / Shafi-Islam Kurds, the Shia-Islam Iranians, the Salafi-Islam ISIS terrorist fanatics, the authoritarian Putin regime in Russia and our supposed NATO ally, "secular" Turkey took a part in the bloodbath, often against each other but primarily against ISIS. The American interest in the war was the defeat of the international threat posed by ISIS and the need to deprive it of the large base of operations they had formed in the area, which was known as "the Caliphate." With American military aid and financial support, as well as military special forces on the ground to insure that the aid provided was put to the most effective use against the ISIS militants that were mass murdering and torturing the Kurdish people on a daily basis, ISIS was soundly defeated and their Caliphate Base was destroyed. Their mission accomplished, President Trump ordered the very few troops remaining in the area to leave, given that he had been elected on the promise to put an end to the endlessly concatenating Middle East wars that America had been involved in since it was attacked by the Al Qaeda terrorist organization on 9/11/2001.

When Trump campaigned on this policy the foreign policy elites, both Republican and Democrat went berserk. Hundreds of them signed protests indicating the Trump would be courting disaster if he removed America from the endless wars in the Middle East as well as from the vampiric grip of the Military Industrial Complex in which many such "experts" had found homes, patrons, jobs and donors. Almost all of Trump's 2016 primary rivals were neo-Cons who had long supported aggressive military action and were almost all surrounded by think tank intellectuals that provided them with convoluted rationales for eternal American intervention in foreign wars, regardless of whether or not it served the U.S. National Interest. But this is not surprising, since the primary interest of such political hacks is not America's national interest but the interests of the Foreign Policy "experts" in organizations such as the Council on Foreign Relations, who in turn provide the intellectual justification for Globalist policies neo-con politicians push at the behest of the Transnational Progressive corporate elite, which fully owns them both. Needless to say, despite the fact that they accused Trump of having no understanding of foreign policy, the American people had had enough of their failures and false rationales, and Trump was elected over and against the hysterical fear-mongering of his opponents.

When Trump announced his plans to finally withdraw the miniscule amount of American troops in the area, the familiar pattern asserted itself again: to leave Syria would "betray our Kurdish allies" despite the fact that without American help and aid ISIS would have exterminated them; we *had* to stay or we would lose our "credibility" and if we were ever "called on" to fight again we would lack allies who could no longer "depend on us." The Turks, who are members of the archaic NATO alliance that was originally designed to protect Europe against a Soviet Union that now no longer even exists, were attacking their ancient Kurdish enemies, over long disputed land rights in a part of the world which, again, most Americans couldn't locate on a map. NATO, whose members have to be strong-armed to even pay their dues to support it, was supposedly the crown jewel of Tranzi foreign policy: an international coalition of "equal partners" (or rather, as one Cold War Soviet official put it, a partnership between "one millionaire and ten beggars.") However, now that it served their purpose for America to be further debilitated by loss of life and treasure by getting involved in yet *another* war where no American national interest was to be found, Turkey… NATO "ally" or no NATO "ally"… was declared to be committing "atrocities" against the Kurds who, after "fighting for us," couldn't be "abandoned." The neo-Conservative foreign policy that clamored for America to stay and engage in a deadly and mega-expensive policy of "nation-building" in Iraq and Afghanistan had resulted in almost 20 years of war; yet Iraq remains a political disaster inching ever closer to its co-religionists in Iran… and Afghanistan continues to be a violent barbarous backwater that is immune to any attempt to civilize it. Thus it is, thus it has always been, and thus it probably always will be as long as we give our foreign policy over to "experts" who serve a master other than the American people.

Regardless of the bloody failure nation-building has been in all the earlier horror stories, the "experts" seek to enact it again by insisting we follow its advice once more in Syria.

The Gen-X / Millennials / Gen-Z must, at long last, free themselves from the grip of those whose purpose is not to conduct a foreign policy that keeps them secure and at peace, but which seeks, in the name of a Transnational Progressive vision of a streamlined, neo-Fascist Globalist corporate world system (or, in George H.W. Bush's words "… a big idea… a New World Order") to undercut and debilitate the only thing that stands in the way of its success: a militarily strong and morally confident United States of America. That is, an America which puts its own national interests before the interests of a Plutocratic transnational elite that thinks nothing of spilling its blood and squandering its wealth on worthless adventures *that are designed to fail in order to create crises it can exploit to expand its power.*

Though some possibilities have been explored, what, where and how a foreign policy incident could manifest itself into triggering the Seventh Crisis is mostly beyond the scope of this work. However, the generations that will be called on to face it have been even more debilitated in their capacity to recognize the true power-expansion goals of the Elites and the lies of their political and Enemedia operatives than were their parents' or grandparents' generations. The danger of them falling into a foreign policy "Crisis Trap" that allows the Elites to justify a power grab on the false basis of needing it to "solve" such a Crisis, will become ever more acute. This is because Gen-Xers, Millennials and Gen-Z will be increasingly incapable of understanding the nature of the threat. Being trained to reject "facts" and emote rather than think, will gull them into blindly accepting the efforts of the foreign policy elites (and the Fake News that serves them) to make them the victims of the next foreign policy disaster that is cooked up in order to direct them into the arms of their "saviors"; that is, the necessity for a Tranzi controlled Big Government to come and "save" them from the very wars and foreign policy crises that Tranzi Big Government created in the first place.

– 7 –

The Endgame of the Left

The Seventh Crisis, however it manifests itself, will be the central issue facing Gen-Xers and Millennials and will be the most important external event in their lives as well as the lives of their younger Gen-Z children and siblings. But it appears that they will likely be forced to face it bereft of the traditional tools with which their predecessors faced their own "Crisis" periods in the past. Worse, once those tools are lost to them, those who are in control will make sure they are never available again.

The Millennial and Gen-Z cohorts will be facing the Crisis saddled with a "Prophet" generation (the 1960s "Baby Boomers") whose reputation for shallow solipsism and morally crippled self-righteousness is only matched by their hypocrisy, dishonesty, cowardice and superficiality. It should not be surprising to anyone, that no one wants to hear even more "progressive" hectoring from the Boomers, who could never quite come to terms with the fact that they will never measure up to the triumphal success of their parents... who overcame the Great Depression, achieved a hard-fought victory in WWII, created massive prosperity, defeated Communist Imperialism and ended the existential threat of the Cold War without firing a shot at their country's main adversary in that struggle.

But there is a second threat the Gen-X / Millennials face from the Boomers: the fact that the Boomers have psychologically castrated their ability to deal with the Seventh Crisis by saddling them with a false religion (Gaia Worship) a false, failed ideology (Socialism), a false community (Trans-national Globalism) and a false anti-morality that attacks all the foundational and traditional underpinnings required to maintain a society based on the only thing that can confront and overcome the Seventh Crisis: Ordered Liberty.

For it is the 1960s Boomers who are the most responsible for the mis-education of the Gen-X / Millennial generation via its control of the institutions primarily responsible for their socialization: Academia, the Information Dissemination Industry (via both the Enemedia and the Social Media) and the so-called Entertainment Industry. All of these elements work to undermine any support structures, be they social values regarding Judeo-Christian morality, sex, abortion, marriage, gender social roles, traditional religious and family values or economic values associated with Capitalism or patriotic devotion to one's "nacio" (or "kindred group") as manifested in their history, the beauty of their land, their heroes, their myths and their many positive accomplishments.

Worse, all these burdens have been exacerbated by the neo-Fascistic Technocracy embodied by Big Tech's social media networks, which have expanded the reach of transnational progressive propaganda, social enforcement, and social banishment through the controlling mechanism of "cancel culture" beyond the wildest dreams of 20th Century totalitarians. Whatever doesn't fit their narrative is either ignored or excoriated; whoever doesn't bend to their will finds their ability to get work, get internet access, be published or even be taken seriously to be "cancelled."

All values are to be replaced with new, Transnational Progressive anti-values, which replace the time-tested and successful traditional values that had previously created a well ordered society, with moral relativism, gender ambiguity, collectivism, atheism (and/or Eco-Paganism,) and "open" family structures that undercut and debilitate the basic man-woman relationship required to establish a truly stable family unit. Further, transnational anti-values replace patriotism and love of country with a borderless, transnational, multicultural "Globalism."

In order to reach the goal of a transnational society, the Left understands that it must not only mobilize a cadre of resistance to the traditional order, but must also prepare a hierarchy into which leaders can be created and put into place so that they, in turn, can order their followers to take action.

Starting at the lowest level of the hierarchy, they seek to infiltrate... and dominate... the K-12 educational system with cadres devoted to carrying out Transnational Progressive ideology, where they can inculcate a sense of distrust in established institutions into the young. These would include undermining family, faith, traditional culture, national sovereignty and limited constitutional government. By undermining faith in such fundamentally essential cultural and political norms, they can sow psychological dissatisfaction and discredit those they oppose as being "racist," "sexist," "homophobic," "greedy," "heartless," "ecologically dangerous" and "exploitative" of the poor and disadvantaged.

Upon this foundation, new cadres are created, propagandized and moved up to the next level so they can correctly absorb the lessons of group organization and training in revolutionary tactics during their college years. While in the grip of Leftwing professors for four years, they are channeled into Leftwing groups both on and off campus, after which they are unleashed on the public in the form of direct actions such as demonstrations, boycotts, shutdowns and strikes against various forms of "oppression" and "institutional racism."

Such groups are funded, often in clandestine fashion, by financial backers working behind the scenes (such as the various Soros front groups) so that they have both the financial and legal means to penetrate as many segments of life as possible, including student organizations (high school as well as college) unions, sympathetic Left-leaning religious organizations, "Social Justice" advocacy groups, local media outlets and corporations (usually though Human Resources programs designed to promote "diversity," where "consultants" browbeat employees into accepting ideologically structured, "progressive" beliefs regarding race, sex roles and gender consciousness.) All such corporate efforts serve the inflexible mandate that demands all employees accept the dictates of those practicing identity politics on pain of attending "sensitivity training" classes and, if all else fails, termination of employment.

The cadres are now ready to move beyond simple infiltration and on to actively subverting the institutions into which they have insinuated themselves. At this level they begin to build a platform of groups designed to take their subversive activities out of the schools, unions, churches and Human Resources departments and into the streets. As this move is undertaken, the national Enemedia intensifies its propaganda cover for them by downplaying their violent activities as "peaceful protests" and casting blame on those groups targeted as "the Enemy": Constitutional Conservatives, Nationalist Populists, traditional religions and middle-class cultural norms, all of which are cast as reactionaries and White Supremacists, no matter how opposed they are to such anti-social racist groups.

Once having gone national, the hierarchy is ready to direct pressure - both overt via violent riot and covert via manufactured crises such as the Russian Hoax, the police "war" on minorities and anthropogenic Climate Change - on all levels of government including placing sympathizers and even their own members into town councils, city halls,(as they already have in several West Coast cities) state governments and the U.S. Congress.

We are now near the top of the Hierarchy of Insurrection, where violent rhetoric intensifies to white-hot levels, underground subversive activity increases, police are forbidden to take action, acts of destructive sabotage become commonplace and violence escalates from street riots to small scale guerrilla war to large scale guerrilla war *to all out civil war.*

At this point the Crisis reaches its crescendo and the Elites will step in to demand the power required to restore the very order they worked so hard to destroy... except there will be no restoration of Order; there will only be oppression and the destruction of Liberty.

The climaxing of the Seventh Crisis will be used to advance the goal of the Elites: viz. the creation of a new, transnational world where faceless, unelected and unaccountable bureaucrats dictate culture, economics and politics from a central corporate governing structure along the lines of the United Nations or the E.U. or some future more powerful combination of both.

Deliberately made incapable to cope with the coming Crisis, the average person will be "managed" from the Center and their wants and desires will be controlled by a distant Elite that will keep them in a permanent state of dependency long after the time the Crisis passes. The collectivist economy advocated by these Elites will result in a permanently shrinking pie, from which the Elites will dole out whatever sub-minimal "needs" it thinks their dull-witted charges require. It will, in effect, create a society of virtual serfs living in the collectively owned, borderless world run by a small neo-aristocratic elite, who will live in luxury all while decrying selfishness and castigating self-interest as morally reprehensible.

The Gen-Xers / Millennials / Gen-Z should fully understand what the elites want to create for them: a modern form of feudalism in which a self-appointed elite is permanently maintained in power by exempting themselves from the oppressive, poverty creating rules they seek to enforce on everyone else. In this modern feudalism, the masses will create the wealth and the Elite will take it… and then watch as the serfs fight amongst themselves for the leftover crumbs that are tossed to them.

Thus, the co-opting of the Gen-X and Millennial generations by the Elite is essential to fulfilling their plans and this can only be accomplished by implanting Leftwing radicalism into society on a cultural level so that change seems "evolutionary" and prevents the kind of shocks to the social system and subsequent backlash against it that violent revolutionary actions often incur. No, the idea is to pollute and undermine the kinds of values that would inoculate the public against Elitist manipulation. Social values long held to be positive are to be slowly replaced through ridicule and moral opprobrium as being outdated, intolerant, mean-spirited, bigoted, exclusionary, greedy, unfair, cruel and jingoistic.

Interestingly, the person most responsible for the idea of slowly radicalizing society is a relatively unknown Italian Communist named Antonio Gramsci, who lived in the early part of the 20th century. Gramsci felt that Marx's call for violent revolution and brute expropriation (if not extermination) of the old Capitalist, Traditionalist order was overly aggressive to the point of being counter-productive to accomplishing the goals of communizing society. For one thing, Gramsci felt the odds were stacked in favor of the existing repressive state apparatuses such as the secret police and military. Europeans were shocked when they saw that the Russian Revolution of 1917 could bring forth a chaotic Socialist, if not Communist, society in their own countries and would tolerate the most stringent forms of oppression to prevent such a thing from happening. Living in a world that was witness to the rise of Fascism in many countries, Gramsci well understood the power of his enemies and sought a more subtle, long-term solution to re-order society and indirectly but effectively challenge not only oppressive Fascist… or powerful Capitalist… regimes, but also question the very worth of open-ended, liberal inquiry itself, which was grounded in Western culture since the Enlightenment. He found the answer in the idea of Cultural Hegemony.

Cultural Hegemony is the domination of societal culture by a revolutionary class that manipulates the nation so that their political, economic, racial, social, religious or anti-religious worldview becomes the norm. Gramsci understood that Marx's all-out class warfare, or "War of Maneuver," might fail in a total war with the forces that could be mustered by the anti-Socialist, traditional societies that opposed them. Instead, he recommended a "War of Position" during which the Leftist revolutionaries would wage underground intellectual and cultural warfare against that which was sanctioned by the Capitalist, Traditionalist, Religious order and, over time, subvert them.

Rather than sending armed workers into the streets to battle the forces of the Ancien Régime as Marx advocated, Gramsci sought to send Leftist revolutionaries into the very cultural institutions that had been created by traditional society and use them, over the course of several decades, to propagate revolutionary ideas and organizations *from within*.

Gramsci saw that, over time, several generations of students would graduate into society at first questioning, then rejecting, then outlawing the very Capitalist / Traditionalist / Religious values they had been taught to despise as unfair, greedy, racist and superstitiously ignorant. Once these generations reached the age to take over positions of power in the cultural institutions, Academia, the Communications Media, the Arts, the Entertainment Industry and ultimately the government itself, there would be no need for a violent War of Maneuver in the streets, except for the repressive actions of Leftist thugs that would be employed whenever enforced compliance was required. At some point, what was once perceived to be natural and inevitable was now to be recognized as an outdated artificial social construct that was designed to perpetuate political, economic and social injustice. Conversely, what was once considered "revolutionary" only one or two generations before would now be seen as "normal." The revolutionary war Marx saw waged by angry workers over economic issues in the streets and on the barricades would be more certainly and safely won in classrooms, in movie theaters, on radio, in newspapers and in other cultural institutions, which would be used to preach politically correct, Leftwing values and multiculturalism. Gramsci wanted to create a "socialist class consciousness" in those who made up the captive audience found in public schools, among the passive readers of the news in their living rooms or amid the avid viewers who are narcotized by films (and later, by TV programs and Social Media) that glamorize Leftwing themes. He understood that the Left had to secure its own Cultural Hegemony in order for society to become Socialist, Transnational and Progressive rather than Capitalist, Sovereign and Traditional.

The need to create a counter-hegemony based on Leftwing revolutionary values required the kind of education that could develop intellectuals sympathetic to Leftwing ideals. Their task was not to start a Marxist revolution, but to alter the existing, traditionalist intellectual viewpoint into one that was more and more congruent with the goals of the Left.

Once this task was completed, there would be no need for a violent revolution because the revolution's goals, after several generations having been exposed to Leftwing cultural indoctrination, would be accepted as *normal* without the need for a violent revolution to put those goals into place.

Of course, Gramsci did not oppose a more direct and confrontational form of revolution; however, he realized that if one broke out, its success would be facilitated if the Left had already set the stage by seizing the commanding heights of the culture. Through the creation of an anti-Civil Society, the previous Civil Society would be seen as too inadequate, incompetent and immoral to be allowed to continue.

Unfortunately for the Gen-X / Millennial / Gen-Z generations, they are exactly the groups who have been most affected by this trans-valuation of values. One sees it reflected in every poll, in every movie, in every song, in every computer app and in every opinion that a wide swath of them hold. One sees it in the ever-growing rejection of the values of the previous order, which created the most successful society in History, in favor of empty Leftwing panaceas that have caused nothing but tyranny, poverty, mass death and failure everywhere they have been implemented. The situation is one in which a *standing army* of Leftwing academics propagandize a *kneeling army* of captive students, who have been deliberately and systematically deprived of the ability to think critically so that they blindly swallow the poisonous, politically correct dogmas excreted by a *crawling army* of ideologically driven collectivist pseudo-intellectuals.

By controlling the ideological state apparatus—that is, Academia, Mass Communications, Religion, the Legal System, the Arts and the Entertainment Industry, Gramsci has correctly seen that *the best way to win the revolution is to eliminate the need for it by delivering its goals via cultural subversion.*

The Gen-Xers / Millennials / Gen-Z should not kid themselves: *they are the target to be subverted* and they need to be clear that the attack on traditional culture is an attack on both them and their future. It is designed to destroy Ordered Liberty by convincing them that they should neither want it nor need it. But what will take its place?

How do we understand the mindset of the crawling army that seeks to capture the hearts and minds of the generations targeted by the Left for a modernized form of serfdom; viz. one where they are ignorant of Liberty, deprived of the capacity for critical thinking that is necessary to it and sent out into the world chained to their keyboards rather than to a plow? To find the answer, it is instructive to look to Thomas Carlyle, a 19th Century philosopher who advocated against Liberty and for a view that held it to be a sham that seduced the dull-witted masses away from their proper role as worker drones for their superiors in the Elite, thus upsetting a hierarchical order of things that he saw as "natural."

Carlyle found the very idea of Liberty to be dangerous in the extreme; he wrote (emphasis added):

> "Liberty, I am told, is a divine thing. Liberty when it becomes the 'liberty to die by starvation' is not so divine!" Lest the *animal-like* "man" starve due his *unnatural affection to be free* of direction from his "betters" he should learn, or to be taught, what work he actually was able for; and then by permission, persuasion, *and even compulsion,* to set about doing of the same!"

Carlyle is not reluctant to state quite boldly how little he thinks of the "common man" and his abilities to run his own life without the interference and control of his supposed intellectual superiors who, by running the state also run the various "plans" that dominate his life. As he states here:

> "You do not allow a palpable madman to leap over precipices; *you violate his liberty, you that are wise*; and keep him, were it in strait-waistcoats, away from the precipices! Every stupid, every cowardly and foolish man is but a less palpable madman: his true liberty were that a wiser man, that any and every wiser man, could, by brass collars, or in whatever milder or sharper way, *lay hold of him when he was going wrong, and order and compel him to go a little righter.* Or, if thou really art my Senior, Seigneur, my Elder, Presbyter or Priest, if thou art in very deed my Wiser, *may a beneficent instinct lead and impel thee to 'conquer' me, to command me! If thou do know better than I what is good and right, I conjure thee in the name of God, force me to do it;* were it by never such brass collars, whips and

200

handcuffs, leave me not to walk over precipices! That I have been called, by all the Newspapers, a 'free man' will avail me little, if my pilgrimage have ended in death and wreck. *Oh that the Newspapers had called me slave, coward, fool, or what it pleased their sweet voices to name me, and I had attained not death, but life!*--Liberty requires new definitions."

Yes, a "new definition." One that will no doubt continue to be provided by the Gramsci cultural subversives that have emptied and raped the minds of the Gen-X, Millennial and Gen-Z generations so that this Orwellian nightmare of a definition is burned into what's left of their capacity to think. Carlyle is very open about the need for an aristocracy (which is identical to the type of "central planners" the Socialists seek to impose on their Gen-X / Millennial / Gen-Z victims) that pretends that their "plans" are the answer to dealing with the Seventh Crisis.

It can be seen here, where Carlyle states (emphasis added):

> "When a world, not yet doomed for death, is rushing down to ever-deeper Baseness and Confusion, it is a dire necessity of Nature's to bring in her Aristocracies, her Best, *even by forcible methods.* When their descendants or representatives cease entirely to be the Best, Nature's poor world will very soon rush down again to Baseness; and it becomes a dire necessity of Nature's to cast them out."

This nakedly ruthless view, which utterly rejects the idea that mankind is capable of existing as a people whose freedom is maintained by a state of Ordered Liberty, is the ugly reality behind the soft phrases, false ideals and dreamy utopianism of the Transnational Progressive project, which seeks to use the developing Crisis as an opportunity to shackle us all to the putrid failure of the Socialist Leviathan government they seek to control.

Of course, there was (and is) a better way and its justification should be consulted in order to refute the neo-Aristocratic view of the modern day Carlyles, who never cease measuring the length and weight of the gold-painted iron chains with which they intend to incapacitate society.

Thomas Babington Macauley, 19th Century English essayist and Whig politician was one of the most successful and respected men of his day.

Writing about the need to resist, even violently, the tyranny of a government controlled by an arrogant Elite that tramples on Ordered Liberty, Macauley wrote (emphasis added):

> "The heads of the church and state reaped only that which they had sown. The government had prohibited free discussion: it had done its best to keep the people unacquainted with their duties and their rights. The retribution was just and natural. *If our rulers suffered from popular ignorance, it was because they had themselves taken away the key of knowledge. If they were assailed with blind fury, it was because they had exacted an equally blind submission.*"

Macauley understood that Ordered Liberty wasn't easy or flawless and in fact was often difficult and messy; he knew that mastering its implementation required enduring the time period people needed to acclimate themselves to making their own decisions, overcoming their own failures and benefiting from their own successes rather than blindly following the dictates and commands of those Elites that Carlyle thought the benighted public needed to run their lives. Macauley wrote (emphasis added):

> "Ariosto tells a pretty story of a fairy, who, by some mysterious law of her nature, was condemned to appear at certain seasons in the form of a foul and poisonous snake. Those who injured her during the period of her disguise were forever excluded from participation in the blessings which she bestowed. But to those who, in spite of her loathsome aspect, pitied and protected her, she afterwards revealed herself in the beautiful and celestial form which was natural to her, accompanied their steps, granted all their wishes, filled their houses with wealth, made them happy in love and victorious in war. *Such a spirit is Liberty.* At times she takes the form of a hateful reptile. She grovels, she hisses, she stings. But woe to those who in disgust shall venture to crush her! *And happy are those who, having dared to receive her in her degraded and frightful shape, shall at length be rewarded by her in the time of her beauty and her glory!*"

Macauley understood that a free society protected by Ordered Liberty would overcome its period of transition from Statism and Tyranny to Limited Government and Liberty; more, he realized that once its time inside the chrysalis was completed, Ordered Liberty's true form would be very much worth the wait. For Macauley:

> "*There is only one cure for the evils which newly acquired freedom produces; and that cure is freedom.*" When a prisoner first leaves his cell, he cannot bear the light of day: he is unable to discriminate colors, or recognize faces. But the remedy is, not to remand him into his dungeon, but to accustom him to the rays of the sun. The blaze of truth and liberty may at first dazzle and bewilder nations which have become half blind in the house of bondage. But let them gaze on, and they will soon be able to bear it. In a few years men learn to reason. The extreme violence of opinions subsides. Hostile theories correct each other. The scattered elements of truth cease to contend, and begin to coalesce. And at length a system of justice and order is educed out of the chaos."

Contrast this with Carlyle's arrogant hatred for the abilities of the common man, whose dreams of Liberty were to him those of an "enchanted ape," who should consider it "merciful" if he were "check(ed)… in his mad path" by Elites who, with "mild persuasion, *or by the severest tyranny* so-called… turn him into a wiser one!

All painful tyranny, in that case again, were but mild 'surgery;' the pain of it cheap, as health and life, instead of galvanism and fixed-idea, are cheap at any price.

Macauley's response to this type of thinking should be deeply pondered by the Gen-X / Millennial / Gen-Z generations, as they are the ones who are being targeted for "the severest tyranny":

> "Many politicians of our time are in the habit of laying it down as a self-evident proposition, that no people ought to be free till they are fit to use their freedom. The maxim is worthy of the fool in the old story, who resolved not to go into the water till he had learnt to swim. *If men are to wait for liberty till they become wise and good in slavery, they may indeed wait forever.*"

When the Seventh Crisis climaxes, there will be no time left "to wait for liberty," for the "severest tyranny" will be ready to chain any Gen-X / Millennial / Gen-Z it considers to be a dangerous "ape," who they fear may be strong enough to resist being "enchanted" by its charms.

Ordered Liberty is not only the way to overcome the Seventh Crisis, *it is the only way to avoid the "severest tyranny" the Transnational Progressive Elite has in store for us.*

And that severe tyranny may not be that far away…

* * *

San Francisco, 2051

After another fruitless day trying to find the occasional gig work that barely keeps him alive, ZeSmith dejectedly walks home. The streets he travels on are covered in the ugly, indecipherable graffiti that he has been told is "art" and are strewn with un-picked up garbage, human waste and discarded drug paraphernalia. As he passes the boarded up and burnt-out stores that were abandoned after some long-forgotten riot, he sees the usual group of dazed, homeless vagrants hovering nearby. He also tries to avoid the even more dangerous bands of violent criminals without conscience who lurk in the shadows as he desperately hopes he can get back to his dwelling place safely without his dirty, reusable canvas bag of weekly Government World food rations and his meager guaranteed minimum wage card being stolen from him. He knows that the prospect of the Social Justice Officers arriving in time to de-escalate any attack and save him from harm are non-existent, as is any sense of public safety since the police were defunded and then disbanded decades ago as being too dangerous to minorities to be trusted with enforcing the law.

ZeSmith is lucky enough to be renting a compartment in a former city bus. He and 3 others "live" in subdivided compartments that are attached to the spotty public power outlet provided several hours each day by Government World so that he can run his computer, his lights and his meager kitchen utilities in between the daily rolling blackouts. Public water, toilet and showering facilities are down the block and always seem to be either broke or under repair due to the rampant public vandalism that always comes with a widespread lack of personal property. Ever since fossil fuel use was criminalized there existed a permanent inadequacy of power. Dependent on the insufficient outputs of solar, wind and the new, untested hydrogen technologies mandated to "protect Gaia," these "ecologically sound" power sources were only available on a consistent basis to the Elites, who could afford the high cost.

ZeSmith reflected on the fact that, between the sketchy and totally inadequate public welfare provided by the state and the occasional "gig" work he procured as a programmer for Tech World, he could barely manage to eke out a living. Even so, as wretched as his situation is compared to his parent's generation, it is still better than that of those who have access to nothing but the scraps passed out by Government World. These types remain on the streets or wind up in jail or find themselves living out their shortened lives inside their own self-incarcerated prisons of drugs and crime and electronic virtual reality.

He doesn't complain about his situation because he fears the repercussions of such an anti-social act. Complaints against Government World would result in his welfare benefits being cancelled, his health benefits cancelled, his travel passes cancelled, his internet access cancelled and his gig work permit cancelled. Social stagnation has been such a part of his life for so long that he doesn't even know what upward mobility means and simply assumes that this is the only possible reality for the vast majority of people who live outside the Corporate, Government, Media and Tech World elites.

As he lies down on the abandoned couch he found where he sleeps, he accesses Media World on his computer, which somehow always makes him feel that he is the one responsible for the poverty and social rot he simply takes for granted as normal.

If only, the beautiful and clean Media World newsreader says, people like him weren't so greedy and selfish they would happily pay more taxes to achieve their "fair share" of the social welfare burden; then those who were worse off could enjoy more of the basics of life. Government World, she reported, was asking so little and yet it had to put up with those who had no social conscience. If only people worked harder to help out the less fortunate, things would be much better. If only they appreciated how hard the leaders of Corporate World, Tech World, Media World and Government World were working for them to have an ever more free and prosperous life, things would improve, soon... soon... soon...

ZeSmith's mind wandered as he quickly tuned out this endlessly repeated meme that was belied by the eternally threadbare existence all around him; but try as he might, he found that he couldn't put his thoughts into words or context that expressed his frustration. He was the product of a public, multicultural, politically correct school system, which stressed that conformity was good and that thinking critically was criminally anti-social. He has few communications or writing skills and has no knowledge of the literature, art or rich culture that his civilization had produced in the past; but he was trained to do the sort of low-level programming that allowed him to procure the type of "gig work" occasionally required by the Tech World elite.

He has no heroes to emulate, no history to refer to, no myths to inspire him, no home to protect, no gender to find solace in, no nation to belong to, no ultimate truth to believe in and no GOD to worship. All were deemed anti-social and extirpated from acceptable society decades ago. He has been taught that there is only *Right Now* and if the future exists at all, it's nature will be revealed to him by those he serves at work and as a digital citizen in one of the four "worlds" that run his life. He has no idea what is past, what is passing or what's to come. He has no say in that matter, nor does he even consider the critical idea that he should.

Too poor to care for anyone but himself, he lives alone. He has no mate, no family and no friends. As it is looked on as dawdling on the job by his employers in Tech World, he hardly ever speaks to anyone face to face either at work or after, and his social interactions are almost all virtual. He plays games and texts with people online who he never meets and his only sexual outlets are the computer gendered fantasies that he programs to his tastes. The very concept of personal interaction strikes him with almost as much revulsion as he and all his contemporaries feel toward children and the elderly.

Although the State aborts and euthanizes as many of these parasites as possible and then profits off the sale of their body parts, ZeSmith knows from his schooling that reproduction without social purpose is a selfish act that serves no Government World need. It is viewed as a waste of resources, of which the transnational progressive elite very much disapproves. It interferes with business. It creates more mouths to feed for a welfare system that is already collapsing under the load. Worst of all, it represents competition and distraction from the goals demanded by the World Elite for the digital serfs that labor for them in their ugly, cyclopean office buildings of glass and steel as well as on their vast, well-manicured Corporate Manor "Campuses."

Like most people in his society, ZeSmith is the product of a single parent unit supplemented by public day care centers. This is because Government World considers Family to be an incubator for anti-social thoughts including many of the prohibited "-isms," and "-phobias,"—including individualism, capitalism, sexism, cis-genderism, private life and "racism" practiced against politically protected groups—which have all been criminalized. Complaining about such laws results in being charged with hate-speech and hate-thought, which are even bigger crimes and which will certainly result in the dreaded penalty of "cancelling."

He wonders if the womyn in the next bus compartment, ZherJones, is also considering the same bleak atomization of her own life and if they might find some comfort by sharing their misery. But he never speaks to her because he is unsure how she gender-identifies. The myriad, intersectional rules concerning social interaction between genders confuses him to no end so he simply avoids any such interaction. In turn, she shuns him as do many of her kind, who have been taught that all men are violent, potential rapists who seek to dominate them.

She has been taught that association with men may lead to children and that would make her life immeasurably more difficult. Her own drives had caused her to dangerously ignore this advice in the past, but she avoided its consequences several times by taking the Sacrament of Abortion at the Government World Womyn's Health Clinic. Seeking to avoid having to exercise her Right to Reproductive Freedom again, she instead simply changed her gender and now finds transitory relief in virtual reality pornography sites. Like ZeSmith, she accesses the same shallow and meaningless "pleasure" it provides. Both ZeSmith and ZherJones have no frame of reference to compare their lives to, and so also simply accept that there is no other way to live.

But what about after life is over?

Corporate, Government, Media and Tech World demand that they must trust in Science, not in a GOD that *Settled Science* says doesn't exist. Instead, there is Gaia and it is the ecology of the Earth itself that should be worshiped… regardless of the fact that Corporate / Government / Media / Tech World has presided over an environment that is as polluted for the masses as it is pristine for the sheltered and privileged World Elites. They, of course, can afford to avoid the consequences of committing crimes against Gaia by purchasing "Carbon Credit" indulgences from Corporate / Government / Media / Tech World.

ZeSmith and ZherJones simply go on as did their ancestors in the 1100s went on, except that they have even been deprived of any spiritual reserves to fall back on or GOD to pray to because they have no spirituality outside of the empty, ludicrous neo-paganism they pretend to believe in to avoid cancellation.

As prisoners in the stasis of the eternal Now, adrift in History without liberty or prosperity or progeny or prospect for improvement or even prayer to GOD for hope and salvation, their lives are spent enriching those who impoverish them and oppress them and spy on them and control them… *and detest them as expendable "inferiors" and "deplorables"* in this new, Digital Dark Age…

* * *

The potential reality of this bleak projection is, unfortunately, based on a very solid foundation and much of its support structure is already clearly in place. It is not only a reality that is plausible but, as we shall see below, it is becoming more and more of an actual reality with each passing day.

For example, the idea that upward mobility and material progress is something that can be seen as ongoing is belied by the worldwide decline of the middle class, where 60% of family incomes either remained flat or declined in the 25 most advanced national economies. - Wolf, Martin (2017, July 19) *Seven charts that show how the developed world is losing its edge* The Financial Times, https://www.ft.com/content/1c7270d2-6ae4-11e7-b9c7-15af748b60d0

In Joel Kotkin's truly frightening book, "The Coming of Neo-Feudalism," (Encounter Books, 2020) he states "In the developing technocratic world view, there's little place for upward mobility, except within the charmed circle at the top. The middle and working classes are expected to become marginal… Everyone else will come to subsist on some combination of part-time entrepreneurial "gig work" and governmental aid" (Kotkin, 2020, p 34—35).

While almost two thirds of all American adults get their news from internet sites like Google and Facebook, the publishing industry is in steep decline (Kotkin, 2020, p 36). Where the print "press barons" once used their power to push conservative views regarding union workers, imperial expansion and the danger of socialism, the modern digital press barons push a progressive agenda stressing issues of race, gender and the environment as well as demanding ever more far-reaching socialist panaceas to force increased economic egalitarianism (Kotkin, 2020, p 37).

In fact, the Enemedia has long ago abandoned any pretense to a lack of bias, as can be seen by the fact that most reporters are extremely liberal and far outnumber conservatives; in 2017, only 7 percent of US reporters claimed to be Republicans and 97 percent of their political donations went to Democrats. - LaTour, A. (2017, August 16) *Fact check: Do 97 percent of journalist donations go to Democrats?* https://ballotpedia.org/Fact_check/Do_97_percent_of_journalist_donations_go_to_Democrats

The effects of this bias on Americans' ability to think critically about what it reads and to understand current events based on a familiarity with the facts and within the context of History is devastating. The rape of free, unbiased journalism by the Social and Enemedia works hand in hand with Academia to produce a society that is geared to accepting one view of life: that of the transnational Left.

Kotkin reveals that "...a study of fifty-one top-rated colleges found that the proportion of liberals to conservatives was 8 to 1, and often as high as 70 to 1. At liberal elite schools... the proportion reaches 120 to 1" (Kotkin, 2020, p 64).

> "This political skewing has the effect of transforming much of academia into something resembling a reeducation camp... Employers report that recent graduates are short on critical thinking skills. Equally worrying is that students in the West are not acquiring familiarity with their own cultural heritage... We are in danger of "mass amnesia," being cut off from knowledge of our own cultural history..." (Kotkin, 2020, p 65).
>
> Reading for pleasure in decline among the Millennial and Gen-z cohorts and their interpersonal skills have atrophied. Employers find that 60% of those applying for jobs "are found to be lacking in basic social skills... social media seem to be creating a generation with little ability to communicate in person" (Kotkin 2020, p 93).

Despite Big Tech's false promise of connecting people so that they could better understand, know and get along with each other, it has instead created an increased sense of isolation among those who regularly use it.

> "Social isolation — which the researchers defined as a lack of a sense of belonging, true engagement with others and fulfilling relationships — has been linked to an increased risk of illness and death according to the study.
>
> Currently, "mental health problems and social isolation are at epidemic levels among young adults," lead study author

Dr. Brian Primack, director of the University of Pittsburgh's Center for Research on Media, Technology and Health, said in a statement." - Miller, Sara G. (2017, March 6) *Too Much Social Media Use Linked to Feelings of Isolation* - https://www.livescience.com/58121-social-media-use-perceived-isolation.html#:~:text=A%20little%20more%20than%20a,isolation%2C%20according%20to%20the%20study.

A form of "mass amnesia" regarding the Millennial / Gen-Z cohorts has also resulted in a flight from traditional religion, which forms the basis of much of Western Civilization.

"Today, nearly four in ten (39%) young adults (ages 18-29) are religiously unaffiliated—three times the unaffiliated rate (13%) among seniors (ages 65 and older). While previous generations were also more likely to be religiously unaffiliated in their twenties, young adults today are nearly four times as likely as young adults a generation ago to identify as religiously unaffiliated. In 1986, for example, only 10% of young adults claimed no religious affiliation.

Among young adults, the religiously unaffiliated dwarf the percentages of other religious identifications: Catholic (15%), white evangelical Protestant (9%), white mainline Protestant (8%), black Protestant (7%), other non-white Protestants (11%), and affiliation with a non-Christian religion (7%)."

Public Religion Research Institute (2016, September 22) https://www.prri.org/research/prri-rns-poll-nones-atheist-leaving-religion/

In place of traditional religion is the neo-pagan pseudo-religion of "Gaia Worship," which centers itself on a worship of an anthropomorphized Nature. Mutilating Science to prove the validity of its dogma, "…the green movement seeks to steer people toward a life in better harmony with Nature. Environmentalism… has become 'the religion of choice for urban atheists'" (Kotkin, 2020, p 69).

Similarly, the idea of a traditional family unit is also under attack.

"The 'Brahmin Left essentially employ a concern for global ecology to force the middle and working classes to absorb the costs of centrally imposed scarcity under the pretext of 'human survival'" (Kotkin, 2020, p 90).

Meanwhile, the traditional family is in sharp decline. "What is emerging is a post-familial society, in which marriage and family no longer play a central role. In the United States, the rate of single parenthood has grown from 10 percent in 1960 to over 40 percent today... more than a quarter of households in 2015 were single-person households. In places like New York city, that figure is estimated at nearly half." (Kotkin 2020, p 96 - 97). This situation "appears to incubate not only an aversion to having children, but also difficulty in relations with the opposite sex (Kotkin 2020, p 141).

Such atomization of life is mandated by an economy where short-term, inconsistently available "gig work" has created a work force that exists on subsistence wages, without benefits and without any hope of long-term employment. - Standing, Guy (2016, November 9) *Meet the Precariat, the new global class fueling the rise of populism* https://www.weforum.org/agenda/2016/11/precariat-global-class-rise-of-populism/

Gig workers "barely make ends meet. Almost two-thirds of American gig workers in California live under the poverty line... Workers without representation, or even set hours, do not have the tools needed to protect their own position; they are essentially fungible, like day workers anywhere... gig work for many has turned out to be something closer to serfdom." (Kotkin, 2020, p 111).

Of course, all this is to be presided over and controlled by the mega-wealthy New Robber Barons that control Big Tech, who lord it over the gig-worker serfs who toil on their enormous Manor-Campuses around the country.

"With traditional family-friendly housing out of reach for all but the wealthiest people, most tech employees will live in something like dormitories, perhaps into their thirties... housing costs have soared too high for most to have a chance to break out of renting... executives... are not expecting their employees to aspire to buy a house to raise children. Instead, they prefer workaholic employees who embrace a modern form of 'monasticism'" (Kotkin, 2020, p 146—147).

With the cost of housing out of reach, gig workers will have been reduced to living at the homes of friends or in their cars or in homeless shelters (Kotkin 2020, p 133).

But complaint is out of the question; Big Tech's increasing monitoring of individual life will provide the control necessary to enforce compliance and prevent revolt. Such control, through the granting and revocation of "social credits," will be severe.

With its ability to monitor all one's transactions—purchases, sales, friends, emails, phone calls, travel destinations, banking transactions, criminal records regarding transgressions both major and minor, tastes (sexual or otherwise) and public comments criticizing those in authority—Big Tech is capable of an intrusion into and control of one's life that makes Orwell's nightmare vision of "1984" look tame. Ubiquitous cameras empowered with facial recognition software will eviscerate privacy to such an extent that one will not even be able to hide in a crowd.

But all this is not science fiction; *it is science fact* and it is going on *right now* in the border to border prison that is the People's Republic of China.

> "All because the government has declared you untrustworthy. Perhaps you defaulted on a loan, made the mistake of criticizing some government policy online or just spent too much time playing video games on the internet. All of these actions, and many more, can cause your score to plummet, forcing citizens onto the most dreaded rung on China's deadbeat caste system, the *laolai*.
>
> And the punishments are shocking. The government algorithm will go as far as to install an "embarrassing" ring tone on the phones of *laolai*, shaming them every time they get a call in public. But an embarrassing ring tone, flight bans and slow trains are just the beginning of the dystopian nightmare that is now daily life in China for tens of millions of people.
>
> A low social credit score will exclude you from well-paid jobs, make it impossible for you to get a house or a car loan or even book a hotel room. The government will slow down

your internet connection, ban your children from attending private schools and even post your profile on a public blacklist for all to see…

…Tapping on a person marked on the map reveals their personal information, including their full name, court-case number and the reason they have been labeled untrustworthy. Identity-card numbers and home addresses are also partially shown," ABC reported.

There are reports that those whose social credit score falls too low are preemptively arrested and sent to re-education camps. Not because they have actually committed a crime, but because they are likely to.

Elements of the system are in place throughout China, as the government refines its algorithm, and the final rollout is scheduled to be in place nationwide by 2020."

Mosher, Steve W. (2019, May 18) *China's new 'social credit system' is a dystopian nightmare* https://nypost.com/2019/05/18/chinas-new-social-credit-system-turns-orwells-1984-into-reality/

The idea that transnational elites based in the West would be any less willing to exert such tyrannical totalitarian power over those they rule than transnational elites based in the East is simply nonsensical, especially given that, geography notwithstanding, their goals and methods of achieving, increasing and maintaining power are identical.

This perverse, dystopian Neo-Feudalism *is* the Endgame of the Left.

ZeSmith and ZherJones are not characters in a future fantasy; to a certain extent, elements of their lives are already here.

Unless we act… unless Big Tech is subjected to Anti-Trust legislation that will bring down its monopolistic squelching of competition, its power to censor speech and thought in order to socially dominate society, *they will be us…* or our children or our grandchildren.

We must not let it happen.

- The Gen-X / Millennial / Gen-Z generational cohorts who will face the Seventh Crisis have been undercut in their ability to overcome it.
- They have been deliberately deprived of the traditional foundations society has depended on during such times by Transnational Progressives who wish to use the Crisis as a pretext to grab even more power and governmental control than they already have.
- Since the main battlegrounds of this struggle will be fought out in the cultural institutions, if political Victory is achieved, a cultural counter-revolution must be launched in order to root out and extirpate the Transnational Progressive poison that permeates the Culture's major institutions including Academia, the Enemedia, the Social Media and the so-called "Entertainment" Industry.
- Congress must be made to call these institutions to account for their actions and their financial ties to the government must be strictly reviewed to ascertain whether they are in violation of their licenses and or agreements and are thus judged unworthy of taxpayer funds.
- The Left must be peacefully but vigorously pursued and overcome in the wake of any major victory in the political struggle and their supporters must be forced to confront the enormity of their defeat via the emasculation of their institutional support systems.
- The Boomers have inflated a debt bubble to continue an unsustainable standard of living at the expense of the succeeding generations. The "solution" to both the Crisis of '08 and the Pandemic's economic crisis was to continue the financial deceit.
- These irresponsible actions will permanently impair any raising of living standards anticipated by Millennials from their economic productivity.
- All the individuals in power responsible for these deceits remain *protected* by the decaying establishment, as will those perpetrating the fraudulent economic scheme post-Pandemic. If the Millennials seek an end to their plundering, they will need to recognize it as a generation and restore the economic pillars of Liberty.
- Another impact of the Boomers' financial deceit has been to deprive the GI and Silent generations of safe, interest-bearing savings in their retirement years with near-zero interest rates. They plan to deprive Millennials of the same in their productive working years.

– 8 –

The Way Forward

Despite the credibility of the "Fourth Turning" concept of four distinct generations facing an existential crisis that shapes their lives and determines the shape of their future, it is still uncertain in which arena the building tensions will boil over, igniting that existential national Crisis. Currently, the national tremors are stressing the debt-ridden economic sphere, the pandemic-driven public health sphere, our upended cultural norms, urban civil unrest, and the Middle East and Chinese challenges facing our foreign policy. Further, the "Fourth Turning" outlines the roles that are likely to be played by those whose lives pass through the Crisis at some point. But it cannot predict with exactitude or certainty when the Crisis will erupt or how much overlap there will be regarding which generations will influence its direction, which ones will directly take part in it, or which ones will be most affected by its results. That is, while the aging Boomer generation may play the role of prophets, they may not last long enough to see the outcome; Gen-Xers will pass through it but Millennials are sure to fight it directly; Gen Z will likely also be drawn into the fight. In any event, Gen-Z will feel the effects of its outcome most directly and thereby be shaped by either the victory achieved or face the consequences of failure.

The generation that fought WWI was blasted by the experience of fighting a brutal war with no real winner; the result was that their younger siblings became part of a "Lost Generation" that partied through the Roaring 20s and fell into such despair in the 1930s that many turned to the totalitarian anti-solutions offered by those who sought to use their generational crisis as an excuse to expand their own power. Generations near or at the front lines may be very well facing the same threat during the Seventh Crisis period.

As the writer G. Michael Hopf has written in his novel "Those Who Remain":

> "Hard times create strong men. Strong men create good times. Good times create weak men. And, weak men create hard times... We don't defeat our enemy by giving him a platform to spread the very propaganda they hope will defeat you... You can only have freedom and liberty when others want that for you. When the other side only uses freedom with the hopes of destroying it later once they're in charge, it's time to shut them down... They will use our Constitution as long as they need to until they get the power, then watch them trash it."

We have suggested that the way to fight and win the Seventh Crisis is to champion a society that centers on the concept of Ordered Liberty as its Animating Spirit. But what is it that this spirit is animating them to do?

How can that spirit counter the false media narratives, failed economic solutions, dangerous expansion of government, debased coarsening of the culture and fanatic advocacy of a pagan "religion" derived from ideologically driven eschatological Climate Change pseudo-science? What can Gen-Xers, Millennials and their younger Gen-Z siblings do to overcome the Seventh Crisis, while not allowing the forces of the Transnational Progressive Left to turn their plight into a vehicle for that group to use in order to dominate their lives? What can they do to avoid falling under the lie that they require expanded government power to "resolve" the Crisis by *destroying* Liberty.

For a start, the Gen-X / Millennial / Gen-Z cohort must take action *to establish their own power* against those who seek to dominate them and turn them into useful idiot pawns. The simple answer is that they should organize... but how?

Power is a far more complex and mysterious quality than any of the simple manifestations of it appear, including the speeches, the elections, the campaigns, the policy plans and papers etc. Rather, much of it is ephemeral and often non-distinct; it is collective celebration and mourning; it is theater; it is one's impression of the credibility of those who enunciate its politics, especially regarding the images surrounding those impressions. It is concepts of authority and persuasion that speak deeply to both human psychology as well as human aspirations and spirit. It is all these things that are put into place so that those who have been targeted (viz. the Gen-X-Mill-Gen-Z cohorts) can be made to collude with those elites who represent the objects of power, in order to strengthen that elite's position of control. The generations on the front lines of the Seventh Crisis must learn this lesson quickly and understand how to implement its teachings to be able to act in its own favor and thus turn it against those Transnational Progressives who wish to dominate them.

Unfortunately, as we indicate when exploring the subversive doctrines of Gramsci, Carlyle and the Progressive Left, much of the groundwork for a Transnational victory has already been put into place throughout the culture… and nothing less than a Cultural Counter-Revolution will resolve the problems that groundwork has already caused and will make worse in the future if left to fester further.

The Gen-X / Millennial / Gen-Z cohort has been placed by the cultural institutions that shape them in a situation where, in the complex and somewhat mysterious manner alluded to above, they are now in an apparent state of contradiction between the life-goals they indicate they desire and the means that they indicate they want to use to bring them about, *which are directly contrary to the fulfillment of what they want.*

Let us examine some of the views of Millennials, which no doubt overlap with those Gen-X and Gen-Z generations that proceed and follow them chronologically. Some of these views may be out of step with those in the other two groups or even in contradiction to them, but since the majority of the responsibility for fighting the Seventh Crisis falls on their shoulders, it is they who are at the center of the conflict and it is they who will suffer most if they fail to meet the threat.

That is, the economic and political solutions they are currently inclined to want to enact are totally incompatible with, and absolutely counter-productive to, the desires they hope to fulfill.

For example, marketing experts tell us that their surveys reveal that Mills express a strong element of practicality; they apply the same "what works" mentality to making political evaluations as they do when doing software assessment.

Yet 69% of Americans between 18—29 would be willing to work for a Socialist, despite the fact that Socialism never has, does not now and never will "work" to accomplish anything other than the most negative of outcomes. Moreover, if one asks a Millennial to define "Socialism" few can do so in anything except the most shallow and naïve manner; that is, it is a system that "helps the poor," "cares about people," "shares the wealth," "provides a clean environment" and "builds a more peaceful world." Of course, exactly the opposite is true. Historically, Socialism results in the polar opposite of anything even remotely resembling a free, prosperous, safe, clean and secure society: rather, it produces societies that lack freedom, wallow in grinding poverty, are dangerously environmentally polluted and are utterly insecure against the ever-increasing power of the Leviathan State.

In line with the thinking of the Left dominated Academia that poorly educates them, the Enemedia / Social Media that mis-informs them and an Entertainment Industry that numbs their senses and coarsens their morals, more than 50% believe more government is the solution, despite the fact that it is government that is largely responsible for student loan programs that have drowned them in 1.2 *trillion* dollars of debt.

Despite this wretched performance, 58% of Millennials "prefer bigger government with more services" despite the fact that the "services" the government "provides" are inferior to those supplied by the private sector at the same time that they are massively more expensive.

Seventy three percent of Millennials desire children, but only 66% desire marriage; 52% say being a good parent is a most important, but only 30% say the same about marriage. However, *all* data indicates that a traditional two-parent family is the best situation in which to raise children to have success in life and that single parent families far more often produce situations where child development is stifled and result in poverty and social pathology. Therefore, Millennials favor a lifestyle that wants children but that rejects the very thing (a two-parent family) that is most conducive to their well-being.

While the Millennials have access to a vast panoply of information sources, they have far less knowledge of current events than prior generations. They spend 46 minutes per day following the news, which is half the time of their close generational predecessors. Reflecting their impatience with traditional media outlets, more than a third (38%) rank "social sharing" as the main way they find out about news. This indicates that rather than being able to compare and contrast different views of the events of the day, they lock themselves into their own tribal subculture where they can feel secure that "everybody agrees with them" regarding this or that particular view of any given news event. This is a recipe for a self-enforcing myopia which can only lead to ignorance… and such ignorance can only lead to manipulation by those elites in the Enemedia and Social-Media that create the easily digestible and specifically targeted memes and images that are designed to advance their Big Government agenda.

And it works.

The general anti-patriotism, anti-American, pro-transnational view of the elites has become imbedded in Millennial thinking. Only 58% of Millennials believe that the USA is the greatest country in the world. They place more faith in the "international community" with 52% saying they want America to "stay out of world affairs"—presumably because they have bought the Transnational Progressive line that America is a force for evil in the world.

Here again we find a peculiar rational disconnect: if America is a force for evil in the world and is not a great country, why would Millennials want to increase the power of its government? This would seem contrary to their express desire that America "stay out of world affairs" since a weak government would be far more constrained at "interfering" in world affairs than a powerful one.

We are left with an entire generation, perhaps more, who have been made to live in what can be described as a social version of the Ptolemaic Universe. This archaic view of the universe is one where the Earth is flat, where the Sun revolves around the Earth and where the stars are merely fixed points of fire only a few thousand miles away that burn through the heavenly "firmament." Further, when certain facts, such as the apparently "wandering" orbits of the planets threaten its basis, the Ptolemaic Universe resolves the problem by adapting the fact to the observation rather than the observation to the facts. That is, it conjectured an "epicyclic model", in which each planet revolves uniformly along a circular path (epicycle), the center of which revolves around the Earth along a larger circular path (deferent). While this view is totally incorrect, it held sway for centuries because although it is completely wrong it *is* internally consistent. Like the view of reality that has been sold to the Gen-X,

Millennial and Gen-Z cohorts, it is wrong but is, at the same time, internally consistent with the false premises and narratives taught to them by the Elites.

These various disconnects from reality have been deliberately created to serve an agenda of centralized power; they must be *un*-created in order to serve a counter-agenda of de-centralized power. It must be exposed and rooted out as the deliberately concocted Gramscian plot to seize power and control that it is.

There is still time to rectify the situation, but very little.

The Seventh Crisis comes, whether those who must face it are ready or not; the only question is, will they be able to overcome it or be crushed by it.

BACKDROP - THE 2020 ELECTION

As the Wuhan Virus Pandemic overshadowed or affected everything in 2020, the presidential election was not to escape, nor the crisis be "wasted" in the infamous words of Rahm Emanuel. At first the Democrats downplayed the danger of the virus, but once they realized its multifaceted usefulness to them, they naturally exploited the crisis, the lockdowns and devastating financial impact to the fullest extent of their subversive imaginations. As the months passed by and they realized the societal disruption could be extended into November, they devised a plan by which they could leverage the pandemic to their electoral advantage.

One tried and true election stealing technique for close and critical elections on the state level is ballot padding through the use of absentee and/or mail-in ballots. The chain of cast-ballot custody in too many locales in the country during the counting process provides ample opportunity for fraudulent ballots to be streamed into, or removed from the count. In addition, where voter rolls are not cleaned and purged of ineligibles after each election, ballots mailed to old addresses in the community can be intercepted, completed and mailed in to be counted, with no secure verification of who completed the ballot. In close statewide elections the margin is often as thin as fewer than one thousand votes.

Beginning in late spring in Democrat dominated states, with the social contact problems of the pandemic as the backdrop, the strategy to push for statewide mail-in balloting began to be popularized. Many states enacted regulations requiring everyone in the state to receive either a mail-in ballot or an application for an absentee ballot. So, with safety from the virus as the "unassailable" justification, the drumbeat accelerated from the leftist media organs calling for mail-in balloting as the safe voting option. With sizable mail-in votes in too many states in the offing, the prospects of an election morning-after looking like Florida's Bush v Gore fiasco in multiple states was sure to seriously forestall the determination of the election winner well beyond election day. Such a scenario would play into the hands of the Left, as they consistently use crisis, chaos and confusion to their advantage.

To that end they jumped into action in June 2020 and convened "The Transition Integrity Project," an election crisis-scenario planning exercise with some one hundred government, campaign and other "expert" participants. The founder was Rosa Brooks, a George Soros confidant and former Special Counsel and board member of his notorious Open Society https://www.law. georgetown.edu/faculty/rosa-brooks/#. The participants were largely leftist luminaries, with the only "Republican" tokens, William Kristol and Michael Steele, functionaries who had long ago abandoned any fealty to conservative principles, or to the truth. Another key player was John Podesta, confidant of Hillary Clinton—what could go wrong? In fact, the leftist confab was convened not to explore ways to assure the integrity of the election and any transition of power, but to illuminate likely morning-after outcomes and game-plan scenarios which the Left could leverage to sway the election to Joe Biden.

The four outcomes envisioned by the Project included: A large Biden victory; a narrow Biden election day win that Trump contested in the courts in several states in the weeks following; a narrow election day Electoral College win for Trump, with a significant popular vote win for Biden; an ambiguous and undetermined outcome where both campaigns call for recounts and file suits in several states for weeks and potentially months thereafter. https:// assets.documentcloud.org/documents/7013152/Preventing-a-Disrupted-Presidential-Election-and.pdf Endless variations and machinations were discussed and played out to determine productive lines of pursuit, all to the benefit of the goals of the Left. Reportedly, the only outcome not resulting in the street violence which played a significant factor in each of the other scenarios was the large Biden victory. Other than a Biden landslide, the obvious mindset of the participants was that street violence would be employed to encourage a determination favorable to the cause of the Left.

The project's 22 page summary is permeated with the devious and inverted presumption that Trump intended to use the mail-in ballot chaos, to steal an election he expected to lose. No matter that Trump had been discouraging mail-in balloting and warning of its propensity to invite fraud since it was first widely advanced in the spring. Then, as a brilliant and instrumental propaganda piece, the summary proceeded to outline every permutation of ballot recounting, lawsuit lodging, state elector selecting, Electoral College tampering and ultimate House of Representative voting that will be initiated by the deep state organs of the Left—and attribute Trump's response to them, all as evidence he intends to remain in office illegally. Once the existence of this entire subversive exercise was leaked into the media in August, every Leftist media organ began blaring that Trump was warning of the problems of unsolicited mail-in balloting so that he could use every manner of these machinations to steal the election. This was a tour de force of the preferred Marxist/Alinsky technique of "projection," whereby you project onto your opponent those subversions which you are currently employing.

Just as a large segment of the public was realizing that mail-in balloting did indeed invite fraud, the media sprinkled in mid-summer stories that Trump was closing Post Office resources to foul the balloting, and used pictures of regular mail box collection and replacement as proof Trump was stealing the mailboxes. Then the leaked Transition Integrity Project Summary was used in an attempt to shift the public's mindset to viewing Trump as the authoritarian, fanning doubt in the electoral process, and willing to employ federal agents to restore order in the streets and steal the election. Though the Left arrogantly never thought their plan would be exposed and publicized so widely months prior to the election, by late September they concocted this rationale which provided perfect cover for them to glide toward the election, their plan intact and continually holding it up as evidence of Donald Trump's subterfuge!

At this point the Enemedia clicked into high gear with Facebook announcing there would be no campaign ads in the last week before the election and that it would cancel any announcements of a winner on FB from either political camp. In addition, it's ongoing censorship of conservative viewpoints, as well as Twitter's, only intensified as the election approached. There was however concern that with Trump motivating his supporters to vote in person, there could appear to be a big Trump victory on election night, and that he would then mount a massive legal assault to stop the counting. So, on August 11th The New York Times published an extensive article positioning Trump as the subversive. Then in an August 20th recorded podcast among NYT columnists Jamelle Bouie, Frank Bruni, Michelle Cottle and Michelle Goldberg it was suggested that "we have to think of the task of getting Trump out as less of a traditional democratic transition and more of something akin to pushing an authoritarian out." https://www.nytimes.com/2020/08/20/opinion/the-argument-democratic-convention-biden.html> We've known the organized Left has no qualms about employing violence in the streets to achieve its ends. At this point its leading print propaganda organ chose to begin "conditioning" the public to accept the idea of removing a sitting president by some manner of force. Indeed, there are weeks when decades happen.

There is one more diabolical link within the Transition Integrity Project, and his name is Norm Eisen. Mr. Eisen appears on the list of participants in the Project. https://www.bostonglobe.com/2020/07/25/nation/bipartisan-group-secretly-gathered-game-out-contested-trump-biden-election-it-wasnt-pretty/ It seems Mr. Eisen is the lead author of "The Playbook" which has been used by the U.S. government in its covert and overt actions in support of the various "color revolutions" in Eastern Europe and the Middle East, where the U.S. attempts to take down authoritarian regimes by means other than utilizing military force. https://www.brookings.edu/wp-content/uploads/2019/11/The-Democracy-Playbook_Preventing-and-Reversing-Democratic-Backsliding.pdf The Orange Revolution in Ukraine is a prominent and illustrative example of Eisen's playbook put into action along the following lines:

- Continually attack the electoral integrity of the sitting leader
- Challenge leadership through the contesting of elections
- Opposition leaders should pursue extreme institutional measures, e.g. impeachment, votes of no confidence, recall referenda
- Employ extra-institutional tools, e.g. strikes, boycotts, street protests including violence
- Be prepared to use electoral abuse evidence as the basis for reform advocacy

If these measures sound familiar, they should. The entire package of strategies and tactics which have been employed in the color revolutions bear a distinct resemblance to the tactics being employed against the Trump Administration during his entire tenure as president. A very concerning picture began to take shape. Operatives within the broader deep state apparatus were coordinating to deploy a CIA styled foreign regime change strategy against the President of the United States to remove him from office under cover of a chaotic national election. Elements of the same cabal which worked to undermine Trump during his entire presidency were now endeavoring to throw an election they perceived to be unwinnable into chaos, recounting and litigation… and blame Trump. It was a bold attempt to shift the selection of a president from the voting booth to the courts and the streets. In the larger strategic picture it was an attempt to shift U.S. "democracy" from the *persuasion* model to the *coercion* model.

Even Defense Department artificial intelligence technology was redeployed and aimed at the Trump campaign and his supporters. The Washington Post, as well as independent outlets, reported the existence of Defeat Disinfo PAC, formed by former DARPA contractor Curtis Hougland. Hougland was redeploying Pentagon funded AI technology, originally developed to combat oversees extremism, to map discussion networks following President Trump's tweets on social media. https://www.latimes.com/politics/story/2020-05-26/democrats-mull-disinformation-counteroffensive The technology would identify the pro-Trump networks, determine the best counter-narratives, and pay users with large followings to launch the counter-narratives against the pro-Trump networks, ostensibly to combat COVID "disinformation." So technology developed for the defense of the country may have been redeployed to work to defeat the President of the United States in his reelection bid.

Add to that the questionable activities of Big Tech. Google's Project Jigsaw, run by a former Hillary Clinton State Dept. official Jared Cohen, utilizes AI technology to seek out and censor "hate speech" on the net. https://www.revolver.news/2020/10/biden-loving-general-is-deploying-military-grade-information-warfare-against-trump-supporters/ As evidenced by numerous incidents and apologies by Big Tech CEOs, the technology Oligarchs reserve to themselves the definition of hate speech. In too many cases during the election season, the subject of their censuring was information and commentary favorable to President Trump's campaign.

Then the worldwide media spotlight was thrown on Big Tech's partisan censuring on behalf of the Biden campaign when Facebook and Twitter blocked circulation of the blockbuster NY Post story on Hunter Biden's entire laptop surfacing with evidence of Joe Biden's corrupt pay-to-play schemes in Ukraine and China. The oligarchs' protection of Deep State interests and one of its consummate players drew congressional subpoenas yet again for the tech moguls, but the impact of a potentially campaign-ending story was blunted.

At this point Joe Biden had every reason to remain in his basement. He had remained there most of the campaign, surely with the reassurance that the fix was in.

As Election Day arrived, turnout was the largest in about a hundred years. A decade ago, the former laughing stock, Florida, had developed and instituted a very solid system for tabulating and reporting the vote. Once proven in several election cycles they had offered it up to the other states. The states in the upper Midwest did not take them up on the offer. Florida and Ohio, very important swing states, completed the count and reported in solid victories for Donald Trump around ten o'clock. But when the numbers started racking up for Trump in Wisconsin, Michigan and Pennsylvania before midnight, counting was simultaneously halted in the big cities across these three states plus Nevada and Fulton County, Georgia.

The country awakened the next morning to reports of 4am Biden-only ballot dumps and a cascade of impossible statistical anomalies across those three states. https://nationalfile.com/suspicious-biden-got-100-of-votes-in-wisconsin-michigan-during-late-night-vote-counting/ https://conservativedailypost.com/every-midnight-ballot-dump-favored-biden-not-just-in-contested-states/

By the end of the first week reports of "irregularities," observed ballot fraud, first hand accounts of illegality, and reports that a computer "glitch" could be part of a multi-state operation. Lawsuits were filed in five states and the Trump team had 234 pages of sworn affidavits reporting questionable and illegal activity. Not one mainstream "reporter" deemed any of it worthy of investigation.

Though not surprising, the turn of events was depressing and frustrating for the Trump supporters. The Left had been telling the country that because Democrat voters were deciding to vote by mail for pandemic-driven reasons, and that Trump voters would be voting on Election Day, there would be a "red mirage" where Trump would have sizable leads on election night that would dwindle over the following days as all the mail-in ballots were counted. That scenario implicitly handed a significant advantage to Trump, placing Biden in a precarious game of catch-up with eyes watching the tabulation of mail-in votes of dubious veracity for what could be a couple weeks. In fact, some leftist mouthpieces were warning on TV that counting could go on for weeks. But after this scenario marinated for a time in public, the leftist agenda-setters decided it was now too risky and inverted the process. They would have to steal the lead overnight and put Trump on the defensive to fight back over the subsequent days and weeks. Hence the simultaneous halting of ballot counting in the key Democrat cities across these five states.

It soon became clear that there were multiple fronts along which there was evidence of a range of fraudulent activity: state election "laws" illegally enacted before the election in Pennsylvania and Georgia; fraudulent ballots entered into the tabulation system; and most explosively, it was alleged that the Dominion tabulation software was programed to flip Trump votes to Biden. For an election the Left told us could take weeks to resolve, there was a month of incessant calls from all leftist mouthpieces for Trump to concede the election.

But the evidence of fraud was mounting daily: Republican poll watchers being denied the opportunity to observe the count; in excess of a thousand sworn depositions claiming observations of, or instructions to commit fraud; the destruction of Trump ballots; massive dumps of Biden-only ballots; the illegal "completion" of incomplete ballots; boxes of completed ballots sent by mail truck from New York to Pennsylvania; suitcases and boxes of ballots being wheeled into the counting areas after counting halted for the night; voter turnout exceeding registration in many counties across the swing states; and finally, one month after the election a "smoking gun" video surfaced showing Georgia poll workers stuffing mysterious ballots from a covered rolling table into scanners when the counting center was closed and vacated of observers.

Then there were the judicial and law enforcement breakdowns: after Republican observers were locked out of a Philadelphia counting center they returned with a court order, but the sheriff refused to enforce it, telling them not to come back https://nbcmontana.com/news/nation-world/trump-campaign-allowed-to-observe-ballot-counting-in-pennsylvania-legal-victory; when Republican plaintiffs in Michigan told a judge they were prevented from observing the count, the judge denied them, indicating that to intervene could be viewed as "judicial activism" https://www.theepochtimes.com/mkt_app/michigan-judge-denies-request-for-audit-in-election-fraud-lawsuit_3577887.html; a Clark County Nevada registrar locked the municipal building so he could not be served a subpoena https://www.thegatewaypundit.com/2020/11/nevada-trump-campaign-says-clark-county-registrar-joe-gloria-hiding-subpoena-service/; a sham recount and "audit" was conducted in Georgia where Republican observers had to impossibly watch 10 teams counting ballots simultaneously https://redstate.com/streiff/2020/11/13/georgia-gop-protests-fake-hand-recount-n279413.

As of this work's publication date, the best compilation of the details and dimensions of the irregularities, fraud and illegalities across the six states is the three volume Navarro Report. The series was published from December 17, 2020 to January 15, 2021. In total, it comprises 82 pages with 322 footnotes citing the source documents, or "evidence" which the Enemedia and politicos claimed did not exist. "Coincidentally" Trump's legal team was shut out from obtaining an official judicial or legislative forum in which to present their case before the electoral votes were ratified in congress. The Navarro Report can be downloaded and read in its entirety at www.peternavarro.com.

As the evidence built and the president's legal team made compelling, outside of official session, presentations to groups of state assemblymen and state senators in the six states in question, formidable clusters of Republican state representatives opposed to their state's respective electoral slates were beginning to grow in each state. However, in no state were they able to prevent the Democrat slate of electors from being sent to the Electoral College on December 14th. Though Biden had advanced to "President Elect" the evidence of ballot tampering and vote fraud continued to mount and briefings of state representatives continued through year-end. The next date of consequence looming on the calendar was January 6th, the day when the electoral votes were to be presented to a joint session of congress for ratification. As the date drew near, over 100 House Republicans and 13 senators indicated they would "object" to the slates of electors from at least six states, setting up a momentous confrontation on the floor of the congress.

There will be books written about the breach of security at the Capitol on January 6, 2021, and the subsequent ransacking of congressional offices. It quickly became clear that those who initially breached the lightly secured Capitol perimeter never attended the rally on the Ellipse, but instead took up positions around the Capitol starting in the morning. The violent breach commenced at 12:45 pm while the president was still addressing the gathering, a half hour's walk away at the Ellipse. The president said nothing to incite violence, which is the reason the Enemedia never replayed his speech. Instead he told the gathering, "I know that everyone here will soon be marching over to the Capitol building to peacefully and patriotically make your voices heard." https://youtu.be/k9nL6BowGJs

Eyewitness accounts of the first to arrive at 2 pm from the speech at the Capitol, indicate that smoke and loud popping noises were already emanating from within the building. The breach was well underway before any of the half million peaceful participants from the rally ever approached the Capitol grounds.

Video of the initial breaches showed both violent clashes plus at least one set of doors methodically opened by Capitol police, who immediately stepped aside and lined the inside hallway allowing the crowd to stream past them - the impression was given that they were being admitted to the Capitol. The groups instigating the initial breaches appeared to be cells of experienced operatives imbedded in the crowds of Trump supporters. Michael Yon, a U.S. Special Forces vet, reviewed enormous amounts of Capitol videos with an experienced and trained eye for analyzing such confrontations, noted familiar actions of the operatives imbedded within the otherwise unaware Trump supporters milling about and entering the Capitol. https://youtu.be/4bIeK-j7fZ8U He has personally observed Antifa in Hong Kong learning the tactics from the local resistance. He then witnessed Antifa employing the same tactics in Seattle and Portland. At the Capitol he observed Antifa "agent provocateurs" blend into the already agitated crowd and take tactical violent actions to accelerate the overall violence of the crowd.

To be sure, there were "Proud Boys" and "Oathkeepers", ostensibly from the right within the breaching crowd as well and were arrested. However, the breach seemed to be an assured success because of the skill and coordination demonstrated by a significant contingent of Antifa operatives who wielded bullhorns calling for equipment to be sent to the front of the crowd. Unfortunately, because of the dynamics of crowds, many Trump supporters followed into the Capitol building, providing the Enemedia pictorial evidence that the intruders were exclusively Trump supporters. Many of their identities were being circulated in the days immediately following the breach. Only a couple Antifas were identified in the immediate aftermath. Curiously the identities of those instigating violence, faces clearly visible, were slow to be identified. As of press time for this book those in coordinated military gear, apparently in cells, were yet to be publicly identified.

The Enemedia played its expected role throughout the weeks following the Capitol breach, showing miles of breach videotape with incessant narration demonizing those marauding in the Capitol, and quickly conflating them with the half million on the mall and eventually by implication, all 74 million who voted for President Trump. This infuriated half the voting population and others who were availing themselves of a consistently developing stream of independently-sourced information which was filling out a picture that this was partly a false flag event.

Now that the Leftist Democrat party was on the doorstep of regaining complete federal political power, it is instructive to refer back to the color revolution "Playbook." The DC government, which had resisted National Guard presence in the summer of 2020 as the city was burned and looted for days by BLM and Antifa agitators, quickly called for the deployment of some 25,000 troops in advance of the Biden "Installation." The Enemedia repeatedly told us this had to be done to protect officialdom from "domestic terrorists" of the Right... namely Trump supporters. On Joe Biden's Installation day the national mall and streets were empty of both spectators and protestors. The entire military drill was a psy-op run on the American people to advance the meme that the country faced a grave danger from violent right wing extremists.

Since the dawn of the Tea Party in 2009, the Left craved for a violent event from somewhere on the Right. They finally got one afternoon of Capitol office ransacking, of Left and Right extremist origins. Two weeks later, the Right returns to form—not a protest or even a terse word in DC nor any of the 50 state capitals put on alert. But not so in Portland, OR—Antifa was out on Biden's first night, attacking the police and burning the city in a reprise of their summer of riots.

The overwhelming military "occupation of Washington, DC", combined with the rampant and blanket cancelling of conservative voices on social media, served to drive an irreconcilable wedge through American society, effectively demonizing half the country. The color Playbook called for power consolidation in victory—there would be no place for reconciliation, or an extension of a unifying hand. Instead we were told Trump supporters had a "virus" which would have to be addressed, possibly through "deprograming."

The plot called for a concession by Trump in November through incessant intimidation, and then a seamless sweeping under the rug of all the subterfuge pursued in furtherance of the scheme. Instead, a mighty pushback from Trump, his lawyers, investigators and Republican officials in six states, and brave citizens willing to swear witness to the fraud, exposed Deep State corruption in state legislatures, election officials and state courts. A ferocious public battle ensued between the Trump forces, the RINOs, the statehouses, the courts, the Enemedia, and Democrat officials and operatives at all levels.

By January 20, 2021 the Deep State had prevailed, but at a cost to them that has yet to be evaluated. Democrats had re-taken the Executive and

Legislative branches, but their usually secretive machinations exposed to the wider public, left their every pronouncement dripping with hypocrisy. More Americans than ever before saw them as a corrupt and fraudulent ruling elite. And more of them than ever were finally ready to join the political struggle against the organized American Left.

FIGHTING BACK

The predicate to any attempt that prepares to face the Seventh Crisis assumes political victory for the forces of those who advocate Ordered Liberty and Limited Government. It is beyond the scope of this work to examine the myriad variegated and complex aspects of the current political struggle between Right and Left that are currently tearing the country apart in a fashion not seen since the 1850—1861 period.

However, it seems obvious that a certain political situation must be in place if the forces of Ordered Liberty and Limited Government are to be able to marshal a resistance to the Crisis.

That is, there must be a conclusion to the Right / Left struggle that has been waged in this country since at least 1965. The multiple attempts at compromise have all ended in failure and we must face the reality that one side must be defeated and one side must win so that American society is not eternally mired in internal dissention and discord. Therefore, let us engage, not in political prediction but rather informed speculation regarding the current political situation.

As of this writing, the Democrat Party controls the Presidency, the House of Representatives and the U.S. Senate; however, the 2020 presidential election has become mired in controversy, with huge, record breaking numbers of voters turning out for both the winning and the losing side. Further, many on the losing side see the election as "stolen" and therefore, illegitimate.

The Democrat majority in the House is very slim and the Senate is evenly split, which requires a vote by the current Democrat Vice President to act as a tie-breaker.

While this is a dire situation for the Republicans, it also represents a situation which may prove perilous to the Democrats as well if they over-extend themselves and seek to pass legislative measures that do not have true majority support across the country.

Moreover, there is a clear Republican majority among the members of the Supreme Court, which will further complicate the implementation of the Democrats' Leftwing programs.

Therefore, while the victory for the Left is clear, it is not by any means overwhelming.

For the Right / Left struggle to be resolved, one side or the other must have a clear ruling majority hold on all three branches of the government.

For those who support Ordered Liberty, such a political victory would look something like this:

(a) The White House must be controlled by a Republican who can maintain and expand the Alliance between the Constitutional Conservatives and the Trump Populist Base. He must be dedicated to the Cause of Limited Government in both word and deed; he must continue to ensure conservative control of the Supreme Court by only nominating justices who favor a strict, originalist interpretation of the Constitution. In such a situation, the Alliance will get to shoot down Progressive Liberal legislation and programs from the SCOTUS just as Progressive Liberal judges have done to conservative legislation and policies *for decades.*

(b) The Senate (ridden as it is with RINOs) must have a Republican majority, which should, all things being equal, be maintained for several election cycles. This seems to be achievable given that, should a Republican majority be gained, the slow-change nature of the institution favors the re-election of the pseudo-aristocratic frauds that populate both parties and who all have 6 years to buy every favor they need to get re-elected.

(c) Most important, Conservatives must do whatever it takes to put the Republicans in control of the House of Representatives.

(d) Should Conservatives, in alliance with the Nationalist Populists that swept Donald Trump into power in 2016, win the House, the Senate and the Presidency for the Republican Party, it will mean Conservatives will *dominate* the Supreme Court for a generation... to say nothing of how it will change the courts that comprise the lower Federal Bench.

This would be a sweeping, historic political victory and its power would open the road for the great cultural counter-Revolution, to be carried out against those institutions that have most deformed and debased our culture, weakened our moral fiber and left the Gen-X / Millennial / Gen-Z cohorts naked and powerless before those who wish to impose their control over them… and who will use the Seventh Crisis as the means to do it.

If it can attain such a victory, the Right must recognize that achieving power that is not clearly and immediately tied to the objectives and goals for which it was fought will tend to paralyze the will, divert attention to that which is contingent rather than central, bog down in the irrelevant, and allow the enemy on the Left to re-group and counter-attack.

While this may seem to be a statement of the obvious, past history indicates several times when a fierce struggle resulted in a victory that was squandered on minutia or wasted entirely. After WWII, victory was not pursued against the Soviets thus resulting in a 40-year Cold War; after the Cold War was won under Reagan, his Establishment successors, both RINO and Democrat, were too limp, tentative and cautious to capitalize on American international dominance to follow through on military victories in the Gulf, Afghanistan and Iraq Wars in order to eradicate a terrorist menace that was allowed to fester and dangerously expand in power.

Further, Reagan's successors failed to follow-through on the strong economic revival he engendered; President G.H.W. Bush was too weak to pursue further and lock in the Reaganite economic agenda and President Clinton, even while falsely posing as a "moderate" was openly hostile to it. The post-Reagan Right was so poorly led that it utterly failed to follow the Principle of Continuity (i.e., to the kind of complete political victory that the Duopoly once achieved during the period from 1933 - 1980) that would have allowed an exploitation of the political victory achieved by the Reagan Revolution. Instead, it stopped well short of the proper point at which to embrace the Termination Principle (viz. the point at which further struggle against the enemy becomes counter-productive and consolidation of victory a higher priority than continued offensive action.)

During the immediate 2020 post-election period, the Democrats have zealously pursued the Principle of Continuity, but demonstrate that they either totally lack any understanding of the Termination Principle or dismiss it as irrelevant to the achievement of their agenda.

There is no point in achieving a political victory and then not translating it into a strategy for achieving longstanding political goals by using the weapons that were won *by that victory* (viz. control of the 3 branches of government) in the continuing political / electoral struggle that the victory has delivered to it… and use them to advance policy goals that serve the Cause of Ordered Liberty; there is also no value in not knowing when to stop and thus creating a situation that is counter-productive to one's goals.

The German military analyst and philosopher of war, Karl Von Clausewitz, was well aware of the danger of *not pursing* a defeated enemy to utter powerlessness; he was also aware of the danger of *not stopping* at the appropriate point and consolidating one's position. Von Clausewitz states:

> "Once a major victory is achieved there must be no talk of rest, of a breathing space, or reviewing the position or consolidating and so forth, but only of the pursuit, going for the enemy again if necessary… attacking his reserves and anything else that might give his forces aid and comfort… Every pause between one success and the next gives the enemy new opportunities… Once victory has been won, one must ensure that it touches off a series of calamities which, in accordance with the law of falling bodies, will keep gathering momentum." Our belief then is that any kind of interruption, pause, or suspension of activity is inconsistent with the nature of offensive war" (Clausewitz, On War p 469—478, 598—600, 626).

Once the struggle is done and the opposition powerless and dispersed, the proper culminating point is reached, beyond which any continuing attack counterproductively diminishes the strength of the attacker and may put him back on defense. Clausewitz considers such unnecessary over-reach to be "a useless effort which could not add to success. It would in fact be a damaging one…" (Clausewitz, On War, p 570).

Thus Victory is found first in the success of the political / electoral struggle and continues its pursuit of the defeated opposition until it loses its cohesion, becomes demoralized and is no longer capable of resisting the implementation of the victor's policy goals… it is then that the struggle reaches the point where fighting ends and the objectives of victory are consolidated.

If the Right can establish such a predicate of political / electoral victory and then follow its subsequent continuity of struggle to the proper termination point, it can ensure accomplishing the objectives for which the victorious struggle was fought. It can accomplish this by continuing to confront the Left with contingencies that it never considered its political opponents had the *will* to attempt. The Left must continue to be confronted *after* the political victory at the polls make any possible counter-attack against the Right infeasible

Prematurely halting the pursuit and reverting to a defensive posture before this is done erodes the ability to achieve those goals for which the Victory was fought. Victory in terms of political / electoral success must never be seen as an end in itself. If the Right keeps in mind that the proper termination point must be correctly determined so as not to overshoot the boundaries of ambition, it will not risk a different kind of diminution of the power; that is, by ignoring or giving short shrift to desired policy goals in favor of piling on more un-needed political / electoral gains in pursuit of some utopian "total solution."

The Right must put aside its often-naïve concept of the Left as simply a "political opposition" that will accept political defeat and deal with the consequences as a "loyal opposition" until such time as they can convince the electorate to give them another chance to enact its programs. This is not and indeed cannot be the nature of a movement that sees life, as the Left does, in brutally zero sum, Manichean terms. For the Right, peace is all too often seen as its own end *and by interpreting it as an absence of conflict, prematurely ends the struggle before its objectives have been accomplished*; to the Left, "peace" is simply *another form* of conflict on the way to the always-just-out-of-reach Socialist Millennium. To the Right, with its Enlightenment concepts of Liberty and Individualism, Man's happiness is an end in itself; to the Left, the individual ceases to exist and Man is forced to find satisfaction by becoming a machine-like cog in the economic and social experience of the collectivist mass.

This is why a political / electoral victory without an immediate pursuit to implement policy objectives is futile. The Left will use any cessation of the struggle prior to its dismemberment and demoralization to use "peace" as simply a pause to revitalize itself for the next round in the struggle. This must not be allowed to happen again.

If Victory over the old politics is accomplished, *the Left should be defeated and pursued so that Ordered Liberty can create the solutions required to solve social problems rather than have them be exacerbated by the dead hand of Big Government.*

This pursuit must be on economic, political, psychological and information persuasion levels so that the Left is prevented from effectively using any element among them to retain even the slightest amount of power. The Right must be adept and skillful in its comprehension of the psychological factors involved in the Left's defeat as well as be as brutally consistent in the application of its principles as it is ruthlessly aware of its own self-interest and policy direction in these areas. It must not be deterred from its path in order to prevent any vestige of power to remain available to the Left which may allow it to extricate itself from its defeat by utilizing any of such economic, political, psychological or propagandistic means to rescue their situation.

Their power must be extirpated if they are to remain a vanquished party.

Should the Right get its chance to attain policy objectives won by their political victory, it should use the opportunity to correct several ongoing, severe problems that have festered and grown under the pre-Trump Transnational Progressive regimes of both parties. Two areas that harbor such underlying, toxic problems created by the Left are found in the Economy and the Culture. The struggle should be continued until specific large-scale policy goals regarding these cultural and economic tectonic plates are enacted and before the power of the political victory dissipates.

That is, the Right should:

(a) tackle one of the major underlying, structural economic problems that constantly threaten to emerge and cause massive economic and social dislocation.

(b) institute a Cultural Counter-Revolution against 50 years of propaganda and educational blight.

What follows is an indication of what types of policy objectives should be *immediately* addressed in the wake of any political / electoral victory of the Right, which can be used to dissolve some important predicates of power on the Left, confuse their strategy, divide and demoralize their followers into impotence and thus disrupt the threat of their political danger for an extended period of time.

REFORM THE FEDERAL RESERVE

Credit the late great Oklahoma Senator Tom Coburn for coining the phrase "The Debt Bomb" as the title of his revealing and prescient 2012 book. It is a most lucid account of how the actions taken in the wake of the 2008 crisis would lead the United States into a debt *implosion* and liquidity crisis. The near complete shutdown of the economy during the Pandemic served to ignite a cascade of financial events which had been building over the decade in which the senator's book was published. It is the lasting damage and dislocation to our economy and financial system which is sure to have the most devastating and far-reaching impact on the lives of every American for years after the defeat of the virus. The causes bringing about the debt bomb implosion go back to the financial crisis of '08 and earlier. The sub-prime mortgage rush, accelerated by collateralized debt obligations and "insured" by credit default swaps precipitated a credit freeze in the national financial markets, a cascading stock market crash, liquidity crisis, and unemployment spike rendering the country in the "Great Recession" in the fall of 2008. These events petrified the financial elite both on wall street and in government, most of whom saw their personal fortunes evaporating before their eyes.

Rather than go through the financial pain of letting the economy find its rightful, economically justified footing through true "price discovery and creative destruction", our leadership's response was to borrow unprecedented sums of money into existence, aka debt, and inject a massive financial narcotic into the U.S. economy. And the narcotic of near-zero interest rate fiat currency continued to be administered to the system monthly over the ensuing decade - and as with any narcotic, the user becomes dependent. The result was an unprecedented bubble in government, corporate, consumer, and education debt—just waiting for a pin, in the form of a "black swan" event, to burst it all. The Fed's intervention in the overnight repo market revealed the addiction. To prevent interest rate spikes the Fed, after QE was ostensibly wound down, began purchases of banks' overnight repos in quantities exceeding $100 billion per night. During the Pandemic the Fed Chair stated publicly these repo purchases could grow to as high as $1 trillion in some instances.

Rather than have to bear public responsibility and criticism for having created the financial disaster, the Federal Reserve had the cover of the Pandemic to take all the controversial actions it deemed necessary to prolong its illusion of a functioning healthy economy. But this time they would not be able to reassemble the pieces. Before the first month of the Pandemic was over the Fed was injecting an additional $4 trillion into the financial system and economy, and Congress was adding an additional $2 trillion of relief and fiscal "stimulus." Sober observers noted that as with any narcotic, this would need to be followed with more, and Congress has been ready to oblige.

The Fed had been suppressing interest rates through both public QE programs, and reputedly, through under-the-radar purchases of bonds and even stocks for over a decade. The Fed didn't do most of the buying directly, although it does have a "trading desk." Most of the buying was carried out by the member banks who were regularly made flush with reserves appearing overnight on their reserve accounts with the Fed. In so doing they had "managed" the yield curve and inflated stock prices. But at the Pandemic's ignition point, the Treasury and Federal Reserve were working in concert publicly to enable the Fed to take equity stakes, purchasing stock, in companies to which it was providing funds—the President and his economic spokesmen presaged the equity program in numerous public statements. President Trump actually said "we have to get *something* for the American people for their investment."

It all sounded so compassionate and helpful, but with the federal government taking ownership stakes in American businesses, specifically the airlines and other strategic industries, the government would be emplacing the apparatus to *control* these markets should it choose to flex its power. When the government either owns stock in corporations, or inordinately controls them through regulation or raw intimidation, that public-private corporate arrangement is historically known as economic *fascism*. The distinguishing factor is that the majority of ownership remains ostensibly in "private" hands, but is ultimately under public, i.e., government, control. This was an ominous turn of events, and if not reversed at some post-crisis point, it could be said the country crossed a *fascist Rubicon* during the Pandemic of 2020. We recognize this could be taken as a charged term, but a growing number of major corporations have been increasingly currying favor with, and doing the bidding of government, for decades. But taking an equity ownership position does indeed codify and formalize a relationship which is dangerous to a free republic, and could well deteriorate to one oppressive to the American people.

Regardless, the nation's financial picture and its health would look vastly different on the other side of the Pandemic. People of good faith could theoretically justify such an unprecedented action, but if not reversed, people utterly lacking such good faith most assuredly will eventually follow in their footsteps. It is the mindset of trusting in the ostensibly good intentions of those in power that the Millennials must overcome. They have been subtly taught in university to focus more on the asserted goals and visions of politicos rather than on their *deeds*. This has placed them in the vulnerable position to accept destructive policies provided they are packaged in a wrapper of *good intentions*. President Reagan's policy of "trust but verify" toward the Soviets, unfortunately must now apply on the domestic front as well.

As the financial effects of the national shutdown manifested, we saw unemployment levels hit 15%. What the Federal Reserve was willing to do made its actions in the '08 Crisis look like mere *coming attractions*.

Back in the '08 Crisis the Fed pointed to enabling legislation as it injected some $800 billion into the banking system. Although it was apparent to all who were watching closely that the Fed used additional facilities, e.g., overnight interbank REPOs, to inject much more cash into the system. Utilizing REPOs, the Fed would inject cash into the banks for overnight needs, holding securities as collateral, thus serving to suppress the banks' borrowing costs. In '08 the Fed's main "money printing" effort was the purchasing of almost all the bad debt on the books of the banks, which amounted to some $2 trillion of "QE". It was magic—the banks' balance sheets were instantly healthy, but they each were required to place much of the money as reserves to shore up their accounts with the Fed. Such money largely stayed static as entries on the Fed's books. Predictions of inflation, not illogical when you print $2T, never came to fruition because the money was locked up in the banking system and hardly circulated. This inordinately low velocity of money was evidenced by the banks' stinginess with commercial loans. Another aspect of the Fed's QE gambit was the direct purchasing of Treasury Bonds. The purpose was to keep interest rates suppressed so that the debt could continue to be financed within the federal budget. The historically low interest rates also served to funnel money into the stock market as there were virtually no other investment alternatives. The upshot was low inflation, low interest rates, and a steadily rising stock market appeared to be a "successful" policy for the balance of the decade.

However, in order to maintain a facade of credibility, the Fed knew it had to "normalize" rates over time and finally began raising rates in 2015, but the Fed "surrendered" in late '18 when the stock market tanked because rates were raised to a mere 2.5%, a prior historic low. This was a huge "tell" as to what was really driving the stock market. There's nothing in the Fed charter enumerating any responsibilities with regard to the stock market. Its charter is to protect the value of the currency and maintain high employment—actually laughable in light of its actions in recent decades. In recent years it's become quite apparent that stock market levels have become dependent on the Fed's interest rate posture. In fact, the case has been made by many unbiased, respected observers that the entire post-2008 decade long stock market boom was simply a result of inordinately cheap money. Both because it was inexpensive to borrow the money to invest, plus there was no alternative to place money for a measurable return. In early '19 the Fed failed to normalize rates and proceeded to quickly reduce them in order to support stock prices. Therefore, when the Pandemic hit a year later, financial markets were stuck in the economists' dreaded "liquidity trap" where reducing rates failed to spur economic activity.

As Congress and the Fed reacted to the Pandemic with authorization to expand the Fed's balance sheet from $4.2 trillion to over $9 trillion it was apparent to anyone with even a casual passing interest that the Fed was simply fabricating those Federal Reserve Notes. To quote Neel Kashkari, the Minneapolis Fed president, at the height of the Pandemic, "the Fed has endless capacity" to support the financial system. If capacity is indeed "endless", the Fed is simply printing money, was publicly stating as much, and Mr. Kashkari was merely the more elaborative among high Fed officials in revealing it.

Though cheap money had kept many marginal businesses on life support throughout the decade between the crashes, it could not substitute for real customers and revenue as the economy emerged from the Pandemic. The lockdown was a nightmare for small and medium businesses. Over 150,000 businesses decided to shutter permanently. Those that reopened were gasping for oxygen, aka cash, in a marketplace where consumers were cash-strapped and understandably hesitant to make consequential purchases. Retailing, restaurants and the hospitality industry were idled completely, putting enormous financial pressure on the real estate investors, mortgage holders, mall owners and banks. These industries required costly permanent restructuring when they emerged post pandemic.

Corporations would find that more staff could work effectively from home and fewer returned to their offices. Less corporate office space was needed, pressuring the entire commercial real estate sector and its bankers. By June 2020 the country was emerging from the Pandemic lockdown into a very different economic, and in many urban locations, depressing physical reality. Desperate economic conditions forced many retail outlets to remain closed, while the riots instituted under cover of the anti-racism protests that followed several police killings involving criminal suspects, left thousands of establishments boarded up indefinitely in cities across the country. If seeing the great New York City avenues empty for three months wasn't enough of a dystopian look, to emerge onto a plywood clad Fifth Avenue in June really was a heartbreaker. Even the most iconic retail stores couldn't re-join the great American reopening.

To stave off collapse, the Fed through its member banks provided the capacity and incentive for a massive expansion of loans to these industries. But this liquidity injection had the effect of ballooning the money supply, with M-1 expanding 20% and M-2 expanding some 30%, doubling the excess reserves of the banking system and further increasing inflationary pressures. The risk is that private businesses will become permanently dependent on Federal Reserve largesse. The national debt bubble continues to expand, with the Fed on the brink, testing fate, as it creates a virtually unlimited supply of credit.

The Federal Reserve has become the most powerful and impactful entity on the planet. Although its chairmen speak in measured tones, it roars through global financial markets with the force of an economic cyclone, and can extend its reach to destabilize political gyroscopes within the United States and beyond. Its roar is heard, and draws reaction, from American corporate boardrooms to foreign financial capitals around the world. Remember, the Fed is a cartel of private banks with ostensible Executive and Congressional oversight. But it has become entirely too powerful and unaccountable—at least, unaccountable to the people of the United States.

At this point there will have to be a reckoning for the damage to the economy and the debasement of the U.S. dollar which has been wrought by the Fed over the past several decades. Though the Fed must be made to protect the money stock, it is already too late for us to escape without a price. The Millennials must master and reform "The Creature From Jekyll Island" and get it under control, or it is sure to devour more than one generation.

They should do so by demanding that, at the least, the Federal Reserve be audited by Congress.

BRING ON THE CULTURAL COUNTER-REVOLUTION

It should be understood that a debased cultural "standard" has been put in place that serves the needs of the Duopoly as well as those not-so-crypto Transnational Progressive forces that control it from behind the political curtain. There are four cultural institutions that are now central to mis-educating, mis-informing, mis-directing and morally corrupting those generations who must fight on the front lines of the Seventh Crisis:

Academia, which prepares the young to accept politically progressive, collectivist, pagan narratives as unquestioningly true;

The Enemedia, which regularly feeds them the news of the day framed as verification of what they have been mis-taught;

The Social Media, which focuses their attention on false narratives and memes the progressive establishment wants to promote while squelching any counter-narrative that opposes them in the name of "fact-checking" or condemned and rejected without appeal as "hate-speech";

The so-called "Entertainment Industry," which normalizes a coarsening of society through a rejection of traditional family values and Judeo-Christian morality by preparing youth to accept a perspective that represents a materialistic, hedonistic, self-obsessed pagan mindset. Such a mindset is essential if the young are to easily accept condemning, "cancelling," ostracizing or even taking violent action against any who the Transnational Progressive Establishment (and their tethered creature politicians in the Duopoly) smears as "racist," "sexist," "religiously fanatic," "greedy," "anti-environment," "militaristic," "oppressive," "anti-immigrant" or "nationalistic." All movies, television programs, video games, music and fads that constitute popular entertainment culture are to be in sync with a depraved progressive mentality that the "Entertainment Industry" seeks to hypnotize the young into believing is "normal."

To oppose these Four Horsemen of the Cultural Apocalypse, the following actions should be taken to undercut the growing authority and poisonous social control they have over young minds.

A) Academia: Pick the top 10 most Leftwing, politicly correct colleges that get grants from the Federal Government.

Start with expensive, non-Ivy League colleges that are utterly dependent on government financial aid to survive.

Bring their officials before the proper Congressional oversight committee and question the college presidents about the heavy load of college debt they have saddled students with in exchange for expensive, yet in far too many cases, worthless degrees.

Ask why the Federal Government should subsidize anti-American, anti-Capitalist, anti-Religious, anti-Traditionalist colleges in their promotion of ideas and attitudes that are undermining the cultural values that solidify us as a country?

Ask why there is such a lack of intellectual diversity on campus, why the overwhelming number of college professors are Progressive Liberals and why the few conservative professors who remain are bullied and pummeled into silence lest they risk losing the ability to get tenure?

Present to the American people a case that indicates that they are not only being robbed by Academia, but that they are often paying for an expensive item that may not be, despite the Social Justice flim-flam, *of any use at all* to their children when they go out into the real world. Ask why the American people should be satisfied with the idea of subsidizing a group that propagandizes and radicalizes their children to reject their religion, their nation, their heritage and, of course, the very capitalist system that is the proven engine of prosperity and success?

Many college presidents must be confronted by the withholding of government funds to the *business end of college* that provides for their lavish salaries and lifestyles until the campuses that have been turned into Leftwing indoctrination centers are reformed. The case that parents and students are being bankrupted to obtain degrees with no worthwhile connection to becoming a productive member of society, and who are turned out into the world without learning a marketable skill, needs to be placed front and center before the American people before any meaningful reforms can take place in Academia. Taxpayers should not be forced to finance academic failure and ideologically driven Social Justice propaganda that sees *them* as a target.

B) Social Media: Hold congressional hearings to confront Social Media owners with scientific evidence of social media addiction.

Use the words of Facebook investor Sean Parker to indicate they are essentially *drug dealers* pushing Dopamine to sell their product:

> "Are Facebook and other social media companies intentionally exploiting people's psychological vulnerabilities to keep them addicted? You bet, says Sean Parker, who made a fortune as an early Facebook investor and its first president. In an interview with Axios Mike Allen this week, Parker said that he has become

something of a "conscientious objector" to social media. And he reflected with some regret on his own role in helping to mold the sort of company that Facebook would become."

The thought process was all about, 'How do we consume as much of your time and conscious attention as possible?'," he said. "And that means that we need to sort of give you a little dopamine hit every once in a while, because someone liked or commented on a photo or a post or whatever, and that's going to get you to contribute more content, and that's going to get you more likes and comments. It's a social validation feedback loop. ... You're exploiting a vulnerability in human psychology... It's useful to know that Facebook was focused almost from its inception on hooking users and getting them to spend lots of time on it—and that there are lots of other companies today employing similar techniques, sometimes with the aid of neuro-psychological research. We should all be more aware that companies are using our own psychological vulnerabilities against us because it helps us to be on our guard against overuse. But it's unrealistic, in our current capitalist environment, to expect Internet companies not to be working hard to insinuate their products into our lives in one way or another. That, for better or worse, is simply the prevailing business model for online media. And with free services that sell us to advertisers as their real product, it is part of the bargain we have so far accepted."

Social Media institutions that sell potentially dangerous *mental addictions,* often to the young and even very young, should be questioned as to why they shouldn't be held to the same standard of others who sell *physically addictive products* to young and old alike. Why should they escape scrutiny and not be made to take responsibility for the problems - be they social, academic, cognitive, relational or psychological - that the distribution of their products causes the society at large?

Is it not a responsibility of government oversight to understand the nature of potentially dangerous products before they are unleashed on our population?

Do not voters, through their elected representatives, deserve to have social media companies explain why they are using addictive algorithms for a profit that could have detrimental effects for which others often have to pay the price?

Again, if such a truth were exposed and focused on, it is likely that at first parents.... and as time went on, others who are negatively affected... would demand reforms that will bring the need for profit more in balance with traditional values and common sense as well as the mental and physical health of their children?

C) **Broadcast Enemedia (CBS, NBC, ABC): Hold Congressional hearings into whether or not Broadcast media companies are in violation of FCC rules and question *whether or not they are actually news organizations under the FCC rules...* or if they are opinion outlets masquerading as straight news organizations?**

Bring in the Media Research Center and other Conservative Media Watchdog Groups to list chapter and verse the extreme Leftwing bias of the Broadcast Media.

Bring in a horde of communications lawyers that are expert in FCC law to search out Broadcast Media actions or non-actions that may be in violation of some FCC rule, no matter how obscure.

Threaten to revoke network licenses unless they come into compliance with FCC licensing rules and end their dangerously biased reporting as well as their politically motivated agenda, which they badly disguise as "straight reporting" and "unbiased news."

Given the rapacious cupidity of the corporate vultures that run these "communications" institutions, it is likely that the mere threat of interrupting already contracted for advertising airtime would send commercial ad-buyers fleeing to the other competitor networks, who can promise more stable platforms than ones that are under investigation as well as the threat of being suspended and thrown off the air for a period of time. The pirates that run competitor networks will certainly be happy to assure ad-buyers that *they* are in compliance with the new attitude and *they* are not in danger of losing *their* license as are their competitors who, under the FCC regulation gun, may be. Surely, their corporate profit motive will outweigh any faux-professional "journalistic" sympathy they may profess for their competitor and they will be happy to comply with FCC rules that require a much *less* biased broadcast media.

D) Entertainment Industry: Hold Congressional hearings into violent, misogynist, pornographic and anti-patriotic movies / video games.

Bring in experts who will discuss how such content is having a detrimental effect on child development and acts of mass violence. Ask why, when guns were far more prevalent and laws were far less strict, we never had as much random or especially school gun crime as we do now, during the era of "gun free zones." Could it be due to the glorification of cruelty and ultra-violence that we see in "games" where players get points for the virtual victims they murder and rape? Could it be the dearth of any connection to spirituality and traditional Judeo-Christian values that were once commonplace in American schools and that now have been totally divorced from it?

Compare how "Old Hollywood" used to re-enforce social cohesion by artistic portrayals favoring the police over the criminals, the decent over the indecent, the family over the hedonistic, the hero over the villain, America over her critics and enemies, patriotism over transnationalism, order over anarchy, art over dreck, religion over non-belief, traditional morality over moral relativism, legitimacy over illegitimacy and a moral attitude that respected the Right to Life of the born... *and the unborn.*

All those things that were formerly long held as essential to social stability are now opposed by today's transnational progressive zeitgeist, which considers such values as archaic, reactionary, greedy, individualistic, intolerant, superstitious and, of course, racist. Instead, we are inundated by the contents of a constantly open sewer that is piped directly into our homes via cable tv and the internet, which makes a fetish out of all that is ugly, shallow, rebellious, anarchic, violent and debased.

Let us put this information before the American people and, as the Left is so fond of saying, "*start a discussion*" about *what the Entertainment Industry's responsibility is* regarding the potentially destructive nature of the vile sludge they pollute the general entertainment culture with... and see if the public wants to perhaps stop patronizing some of their venues if they fail to take such responsibility.

That is, the only thing that will make Hollyweird change its tune is the threat from the public to reject the cultural sludge it is offering and thus crater its TV ratings and box office receipts.

POPULARIZING THE COUNTER-REVOLUTION

The question of how to "popularize" the concept of a cultural counter-Revolution may seem difficult but it has, in the recent past, been successfully accomplished by the Progressive Left.

The WWII generation was traumatized by the constant insecurities of a Great Depression that was immediately followed by a catastrophic World War and a subsequent nerve-wracking Cold War. Constantly under the threat of descending into an apocalyptic nuclear conflict, they sought solace in the creation of stability in their domestic lives through conformity with what they thought represented a traditional standard of American success: hard work, individual responsibility, a nuclear family, their own home, a stay at home mom, children that were more healthy and better educated than their parents, a religious-based morality, a patriotic community, a morally edifying concept of entertainment, a press which, if not totally "unbiased" was at least not propagandistic. They ceaselessly attempted to build a society that increased equal opportunity to succeed for all by overcoming, no matter how imperfectly or slowly, past prejudices, inequalities and racism. This generation created a successful community based on GOD, Liberty and Capitalism and in doing so created a period that produced unprecedented peace and security in America even in a world that sometimes tottered on the brink of nuclear Armageddon. Further, they were able to protect their achievement by enveloping it in cultural conditions that kept destabilizing political and economic ideas as well as divisive and anarchic social messages under control. They achieved freedom tempered by responsibility, attributes which are the foundations of Ordered Liberty. They did this through the strong sense of community fostered by the World War as well as by confidence in the underlying traditions... religious, economic, moral, cultural... that maintained the stability that the WWII generation desired most as an antidote to the recurrence of the crushing poverty and devastating warfare they wanted to get as far away from as possible.

Made acutely aware of the existential danger totalitarian ideologies by their bitter and cruel experience in WWII, they quickly awoke to the threat of Communism, both foreign and domestic, after 1945. The saw how the old, hard-core Stalinist Left, posing as well-meaning Liberals, Progressives or simply "confused," or "harmless fellow travelers," had infiltrated into high positions of influence in many parts of the Government as well as into many aspects of the culture, especially the popular culture. However, by the mid-

1950s, these subversive Leftwing elements had been so reviled and shunned that for all intents and purposes, they vanished from the public scene and retreated into the shadows… into Academia, inside large corporate establishments, on major law firms and all the other labyrinthine corridors that make up the bureaucracy of the permanent "Deep State."

There they wallowed in frustration, waiting to be set free by the Red Diaper Babies they nurtured in the educational system, where they labored on behalf of the ideology they served by enslaving the minds of the young to Socialism. It didn't take long…

Enter their children in the 1960s generation who, in an act of selfish, self-righteous cultural vandalism not only blasted to bits the outer framework of the secure, stable and prosperous state of affairs their parents created, but went on to undermine its long-established religious, economic, moral and cultural foundations.

In the name of an ever-expanding system of "rights" they created an ever-expanding rouges gallery of villains out of those who disagreed with the utopian socialist nostrums they were indoctrinated to believe by their well-off teachers in Academia: greedy capitalists, hate-filled racists, toxic male chauvinist, unfair sexists, cruel homophobes, dangerous militarists, Western cultural imperialists and basically anything else associated with the Enlightenment and Judeo-Christian values that was the creation of "Dead White Males" whose worst sin was that they "clung to their guns and bibles." Worse still, they interwove all these grievances into the concept of "intersectionality" which claimed that the "threat" was so vast as to impact on various "disadvantaged groups" across racial, religious, gender and class lines.

This meant that the opposition was to be considered so guilty of moral opprobrium that extreme governmental action had to be taken to rectify the situation. Further, that situation was to be considered so threatening that the regular democratic and constitutional processes (which allowed for considered, incremental change) was rejected in favor of "experts" who changed long-standing social conventions via bureaucratic fiat and judicial diktat. Finally, while gathering all so-called victims under its umbrella as an indication of its egalitarianism it nonetheless created a demonic "other" out of that which was to be considered the ultimate enemy: white male heterosexuals (as well as the women who were "brainwashed" and "subservient" to them) who supported Capitalism, Judeo-Christian morality, an ethic of self-help individualism and Ordered Liberty.

This resulted in a wholesale rejection on the part of a large section of the Baby Boom generation of the previous, highly successful conservative social / political / economic and moral status quo. Further, it turned its Liberal opponents into a party of Leftwing totalitarians who were utterly intolerant of opinions expressed by an "enemy" that their propaganda built into the epitome of hateful evil, greed, bigotry and aggressive militarism.

It is questionable that the country will ever fully recover from the ravages so many in this wretched generation have inflicted on those who came after it, but perhaps something positive can be learned and salvaged from their example, horrible as that example has been. That is, can the Gen-X / Millennial / Gen-Z cohorts channel the natural inclination of the young to "revolution" against the *current* Leftwing status quo and leverage it against the politically correct, multi-cultural, transnational progressive ideas it consists of, and under which these generations suffer?

What would be the nature of their protest and their rebellion? What actions would they take against their centers of power? What would constitute the underlying spiritual, metaphysical mentality required for their struggle against the forces that threaten to leave them morally weak, intellectually naked and spiritually helpless against the Seventh Crisis?

Struggle is uniquely suited to the young as it requires idealism, strength, perseverance and, most importantly, enough life remaining to devote to accomplishing its aims. It is not something for the cynical, the weak, the tentative and the old. It requires that those who undertake it understand that much of what they have been taught is a fabrication of those forces seeking to expand and entrench their power over them and conclude that it will lead to nothing less than the decay and decomposition that pro-socialist, anti-Liberty, atheist / pagan "progressive" societies inevitably always create.

What is required is for these generations to separate the essential from the contingent and the spirit of the law from the letter of it so that they can attain an inner fortification and a strengthened certainty regarding the need to win the struggle and overcome the Crisis.

In the final analysis, what is required, from both men and women alike, is for them to engender within themselves the ability to create and carry a sense of "Heroic Experience" that transcends mere fighting over politics and instead raises the struggle to a spiritual level, one which has the capacity to transfigure those individuals capable of experiencing it. In this manner, identification of the struggle with one's inner spirit… that is, to understand it as being at one with the path of GOD… allows those fighting the struggle to find the divine manifestation of the heroic in themselves.

For only a people who achieve peace *through victory over themselves* can adapt their inner spiritual strength and energy to the external, material world and thus manifest the character of power and irresistibility that are needed to triumph over the forces of socialism, poverty, weakness, spiritual ennui, cultural rot and all other aspects of human limitation that result from the metastasis of antinomianism. One who conceives of them self as a fighter in such a struggle is the one who recognizes their own inner nobilty, which is measured by the extent of their resistance, to accomplish against the odds that which must be done. Without doubt nor hesitation, one must act out that which their inner spiritual power drives them to defend against… as well as fight for those positive things their spiritual power drives them to create.

It will allow those who struggle against the forces that currently constitute the transnational progressive status quo to tap into their higher spiritual consciousness and use it against those who, existing purely on a material level devoid of spiritual underpinnings, will not be able to resist.

This inner spirit must find Unity in GOD. It must find Diversity of thought in the independent and critical thinking demanded by Ordered Liberty. It must find Harmony and community in Nation. These spiritual values must be chiseled on the hearts of those who would save themselves and others from the Seventh Crisis by *Squaring the Circle between Freedom and Order.*

We have tried to express this precarious balance through a mathematical symbol, seen on the back cover of this book, which depicts the Square Root of Pi. Just as Pi is a number that can never be expressed as a fraction and therefore results in a decimal representation that never ends, so it is with the endless desire for more and more Freedom, regardless of the danger that such a reckless desire must ultimately result in chaos and anarchy. Because of its very nature, Freedom must be protected from such a result by forever nurturing and preserving it within the boundaries of Ordered Liberty. Hence the problems of chaos and anarchy produced by the endless demand of ever-expanding Freedom (which is the circle represented by Pi) is just as perpetually protected by the equally endless solution of Ordered Liberty represented by the Square Root symbol.

For only in GOD can Humanity discover that which extends beyond the sterile anti-values of empty materialism and thus be able to find the strength to overcome the danger of the coming Crisis. Only in Ordered Liberty can there be true Diversity of thought regarding political opinion, economic models, religious faith, choice of diversions and attachments to various sub-cultures that encompass the Civil Society... all of which must be put to the test of moral scrutiny, democratic debate, open discussion and honest appraisal so that society can best decide how and in what manner they should proceed in dealing with the issues they face in life and still be able to govern themselves in as non-coercive a manner as possible. Only in Nation can all the various races, religions, ethnic groups, political factions and philosophical schools find a home where they all intermix and voluntarily contribute their various inputs to the national whole from the bottom up *rather than being coerced and directed from the top down.*

There must be GOD; there must be love of Nacio; there must be Ordered Liberty... or there can be no America.

The young must struggle against those who seek to poison their minds, pollute their morals, impoverish their economy, debase their culture and kill their spirit.

Where the status quo demands a bigger government and more Socialism, they must fight back with a strong advocacy for Limited Government and Capitalism; where the status quo advocates Gaia Worship, they must advocate traditional Judeo-Christianity; where the status quo pushes multiculturalism, they must be opposed by a stout defense of American Exceptionalism; where the status quo demands political correctness they must be met with a vigorous counter-attack of freedom of thought; where the status quo extolls the joys of hedonism as an end in itself, they must extoll the joy of the ascetic experience in the service of higher values such as GOD, Family and Nacio; where the status quo pushes gender fluidity, they must push back with notions of womanhood and manhood in their *natural* / biological... *not concocted / sociocultural...* terms; where the status quo endlessly pushes all that coarsens and debases social norms, they must proudly and boldly extoll that which embraces traditional values that uplift and edify.

When radical feminists representing the status quo attack masculinity as toxic, women must defend men; where male "experts" representing the status quo attack femininity by advocating *sex* and *gender eliminationism,* men must defend women; where militant feminism demeans and disparages marriage and family and where the status quo seeks to eliminate any differences between the sexes, they must stand up against it *as men and women together in defense of their children's future.*

Of course, it is perfectly logical that there is a coherent way to combine characteristics and behaviors that are acquired through preference and choice along with those which are unalterably genetic and hormonal. Accepting the differences between the sexes should not be used to exclude or discriminate against or to oppress those who exist outside the sociocultural / sexual boundaries and norms of what is considered traditionally male and female.

But those who consider themselves outside the majority tradition should not allow the State to use preference and choice as a political cudgel to destroy what constitutes maleness and femaleness and do it in the service of a politically correct agenda designed to debilitate many of the traditional norms which undergird society.

Sympathy for and protection of "the other," even if it is misplaced, *should* be practiced in the name of Justice, but it must not be allowed to castrate the ability to restore and uphold a stable society by securing its cornerstone: viz. the traditional nuclear family.

The Heroic Experience formulates the morals, habits, dress, language, music, art and political culture of its rebellion as being the opposite of those forms that are popular among those who are activists and political soldiers on the Left.

Men must connect with their inner warrior, their inner Kyshatria, their inner masculine rationality and drive to protect their family, their Nacio, their way of life. Where their opposites on the Left in the Antifa present themselves as thuggish, wild and unkempt street rebels, they should present an appearance that resembles a subdued military look and a pronounced sense of inner confidence and self-control. Where the Left extolls excess and anarchy, they should represent asceticism and order. They should indicate a masculine concern for the safety of women and children and treat women with the propriety and respect equals deserve. They must be ready to fight and sacrifice for their inner spiritual values that connect them at a metaphysical level to the political, economic and social conflict that they face in the material world.

Women must connect with their inner Amazon, their inner Matriarch, their inner chthonic-creative power and join Men as fully equal political warriors in this struggle. They should reject the anti-male venom of the feminist Red Guard *Eumenides*, who think that they will find freedom in a rejection of their own sexuality and find joy in some tortured "genderless" twilight zone that does not and indeed, *cannot*, exist and still keep humanity human. They must embrace the defense of innocent life and reject the siren call to become one more barren serf on some corporate version of a feudal manor, condemned to the sterile pleasures of serving, in an almost prima noctum style rape on their youth and fertility, the financial bottom line of business elites, all while their biological clock ticks away the time they have left to find lasting value and true happiness in motherhood.

Men and Women must unite against the false promises of ever-bigger government, which is in all cases blind to their miseries; they must not put their trust in false, utopian hopes that inevitably fade away to reveal the wretched realities of Socialism, Paganism and a divisive, multicultural agenda that seeks the destruction of Ordered Liberty, Traditional Values and Nacio as its ultimate goal.

But in a society that is increasingly militarizing politics as it careens towards its rendezvous with the Seventh Crisis, the Gen-X / Millennial / Gen-Z will need to find those among them who have the capability to control their inner, spiritual struggle, which seeks to overcome the negative, debased, weak and defeatist elements within themselves... and then mobilize them to externalize that self-control in order to prevail in the outer, material, political struggle. This inner struggle must precede the outer struggle *in order for the political warrior to develop the Will to take control of the direction of society, win the Struggle and bring us out of the Seventh Crisis into a state of Ordered Liberty.*

To succeed in this, those who are able (through inner struggle) must make an "Heroic Experience" out of the outer struggle so that the debased, negative elements that are now manifest in society can be overcome and sublimated to positive effect.

Once those elements have been overcome and sublimated into the positive and spiritually edifying ethos of Ordered Liberty, the struggle will itself be transfigured into myriad positive qualities including Justice, Prosperity, Security, Stability and greater scope for Individual Achievement.

The Heroic Experience is capable of committing itself to aligning one's spiritual core not with the empty, ideologies of the Left, but with the ultimate authority within oneself: GOD... as well as His absolute and sweeping force of Ordered Liberty, in the struggle against the de-spiritualized, totalitarian, materialists on the atheistic Left.

Although many are not capable of achieving the Heroic Experience, their commitment to Ordered Liberty is nonetheless widespread. Since the Heroic Experience seeks to overcome all that is tame, conformist, collectivist, group-thinking, pseudo-intellectual and idealistically empty, it sets a standard for behaviors that are successful, edifying and worthy to be emulated. Faults may be rampant among those who lack interior spiritual strength but they can still be motivated to support those embodying the Heroic Experience because they realize its value to their own lives. Unfortunately, those faults and that specific lack of inner strength makes them loathe to get involved in the struggle because of their lack of... *heroism.*

Therefore, the Heroic Experience is not a bourgeoise, nor a bureaucratic, nor a corporate experience.

It is at heart, *a warrior experience.*

It is not for the many who follow but for the few who seek to lead the fight.

It is for those who, having overcome the negative and fearful within themselves, are capable of mastering their inner weakness and of externalizing that strength to overcome the struggle in the outer, material world where the Crisis will manifest itself.

This is the task of the warrior, the Knight, the Valkyrie, the Kshatriya, the Amazon.

This is the political warrior standing fast in midst of the struggle.

This is the Heroic Experience that produces Victory... *and there is nothing to compare with it or prevail against it on the materialist Left* beyond their futile anti-qualities of hate, bitter resentment, fanatic egalitarianism and empty devotion to a sterile political faith.

It is the hammer and the anvil on which Ordered Liberty will be forged and then carried into political battle.

It is the key to victory over the Left, prevailing in the Seventh Crisis and conquering the negative within ourselves.

– 9 –

The Battle Terrain Ahead

T he organized American Left is relentless in pursuing its cultural, economic and political transformation of the United States. With the watershed elections of 2020 receding, we can expect transformational proposals from congress, onerous regulations from the bureaucracy, subversive gambits from social agitators, demands from grievance merchants, coercion of employees and cancellation of customers in the corporate world, all while the Enemedia and Big-Tech mislead and censor anything that counters their progressive dogma. Millennials and Gen-Xers throughout the West are certain to have their lives affected by the actions being readied by a Transnational Progressive movement which believes it is advancing with historical momentum.

The COVID-19 Pandemic has been grasped and exploited by the Transnationalists to accelerate their Globalist agenda. Like the American Left, the international "Plutocrat Party" is practicing the international version of "not letting a crisis go to waste." A brief perusal of the website of the World Economic Forum (WEF), which famously meets annually in Davos Switzerland, reveals the current centerpiece of its global agenda, "The Great

Reset." The WEF is probably the most influential NGO on the world stage today. In the words of Klaus Schwab, the founder and chair of the WEF, "the pandemic represents a rare but narrow window of opportunity to reflect, reimagine and reset our world." The Great Reset is the inescapable international force which will drive its tentacles of change into virtually every critical aspect of modern life. And the unassailable crisis, the unquestionable justification for it all, is the specter of "global climate change" and its orthodoxy of "sustainability."

To usher in this Reset, they tell us sacrifices will be necessary. In order to prepare the youth of the world for the role the WEF has assigned to them, it posted a video targeted toward Gen-Xers, Millennials and Gen-Z on its website. This video told them: "You'll own nothing and you'll be happy; whatever you want you'll rent, and it will be delivered by drone; you'll eat much less meat…for the good of your health and the environment; a billion people will be displaced by climate change and we'll all need to do a better job of welcoming refugees; the United States will no longer be the leading superpower…in its place a group of countries will dominate." Indeed, the video represents an ominous litany of diktats from the WEF, which also states "in short, we need a great reset of capitalism."

Though the term The Great Reset was coined a decade ago, it has acquired new relevance and momentum by Schwab's linking its agenda with the global economic recovery from the pandemic. The WEF agenda also states that, "we must build entirely new foundations for our economic and social systems," which is simply another ominous sounding goal for which they offer no further elaboration. It has become clear that the target is free-market capitalism. The entire, in-the-open Davos agenda dovetails with globalist objectives reanimated at the close of the Cold War. Many WEF goals had been cast as more intermediate or long-term, but the pandemic has provided the cover to advance them to the near term and renewed vigilance is warranted.

In the past decade it has also become clear that the high-tech "Oligarchs" have engaged with the agenda, and have been doing their part to increase its acceptance through social media "conditioning" and outright censorship. These Tech Oligarchs comprise another powerful force which will be shaping events throughout this decade and beyond. Their absolute willingness to do the bidding of the one-party government in the aftermath of the January 6th, 2021 Capitol breach, provided a glimpse into their power to lay waste to the careers, incomes and reputations of anyone who falls out of favor of with them or the officials who regulate them.

The Tech Oligarchs have amassed power comparable to the industrial Robber Barons of the 19th century. While the Robber Barons' objective was to maximize profits, the Tech Oligarchs' objective is the shutdown and denial of Conservative speech to curry favor with the Democrat political power structure. Technically, illegal "collusion" requires evidence of a meeting or verbal coordination. To avoid that technicality, in the days following the Capitol breach it appears the Tech companies merely signaled their intent in public by their actions to de-platform President Trump and other important conservative voices. Big Tech simply took the type of censorship actions which are prohibited for the government under the Constitution. The big three, Twitter, Facebook, and Google acted in unison on Friday, January 8th 2021 in what may be remembered as "The Night of the Long Tech Knives".

Twitter controlling national instant messaging, and Facebook controlling the social network, acted in unison to shut down President Trump's accounts. Google, controlling internet search, announced its intent to de-platform Parler, Twitter's competitor, so that Trump could not use that platform as an alternative. In addition, Amazon and Apple announced they were blocking the downloading of the Parler app. In one night, some 88 million Americans following Trump on Twitter were cut off from the president. Big Government effectuating its will via control over big business through threats and intimidation, is a cornerstone of classic fascism. Expect to see similar gambits in other industries.

Big Tech, heavily involved in business arrangements with the Chinese Communist Party (CCP), had also been carefully studying the CCP's sophisticated tech-driven censorship of the Chinese people. Largely staffed by left leaning executives and technicians, the tech companies readily sought to curry favor with a national Democrat party on the cusp of complete political power in the United States. They were only too happy to do their part to silence the critics of the Biden Administration waiting to assume power.

The incalculable value of Big Tech capabilities and tools in the service of the state was recognized back in the Obama years. Once out of office in 2017, many Obama officials from the State Dept. and National Security team made their way into the Tech companies, influencing their mindset and direction during critical years of the industry's development. These linkages between the corporate and tech structure, as well as the national security departments could result in the domestic re-purposing of that apparatus for the purpose of crushing the conservative/populist movement.

The Leftist sabers were also rattling with threats to advance a Domestic Terrorism bill in the wake of the Capitol breach. Rather than focus on defined, largely fringe groups, the end result of such legislation could be the labeling of any of the 75 million Americans and more who voted for, or voiced support on social media for President Trump as "domestic terrorists." If successful, the corrupt politico-techno regime could drop a fatal hammer on the Liberty movement in the United States.

Such actions indicate that Big Tech is more and more openly enforcing the new cultural values and norms preferred by the transnational elite and is thus adopting the role once played by the Medieval Church, albeit with an infinitely greater reach and a far greater ability to exercise its control over speech, actions and even thought.

That is, if one is kept from the information that is required to make critical judgements, people will never know what types of judgements should be made or when to make them. People will only know the elitist approved orthodoxies that support the continuance of their servitude to it; they will embrace them automatically because there will be no competing conceptual model for them to reference.

These rapidly developing events will make clear in the coming months and years that the struggle we face is not capitalism vs. socialism, but a free people vs. a corporatist regime designed to relegate us to be serfs to a transnational elite.

Joel Kotkin's book, "The Coming of Neo-Feudalism" is an effort to fill in and illuminate the cryptic vision of these elites. Extrapolating on the undefined aspirations of the globalists and Tech Oligarchs, Mr. Kotkin contends that the middle class of the capitalist West may be sleep-walking its way into a modern feudalist era. From the technocrat's perch, there's no longer upward mobility for the middle and working classes—that is a privilege to be reserved for themselves. "While the Oligarchs might speak of a commitment to building what Mark Zuckerberg calls 'meaningful community,' they rarely mention upward mobility. Having interviewed 147 digital company founders, Gregory Ferenstein notes that they generally don't expect their workers or consumers to achieve more independence by starting their own companies or even owning houses. Most, Ferenstein adds, believe that an 'increasingly greater share of economic wealth will be generated by a smaller slice of very talented or original people.

"Yet unlike the 'Penthouse Bolsheviks' of the 1930s, they have no intention of allowing their fortunes to be squeezed. Instead, the middle class would likely foot the bill for guaranteed wages, health care, free college, and housing assistance, along with subsidies for gig workers, who do not receive benefits from their employers. This model could best be described as oligarchical socialism" (Kotkin, 2020, p 34—35).

If Mr. Kotkin's view is at a minimum *directionally correct*, and we would assert that it is, the Millennials, Gen-Zers and their successor generations will need to marshal themselves with the goal of maintaining and expanding their private property and their own self-reliant career paths, networks and lifestyles.

For 70 years the agenda of strengthening the leverage and influence of international governing and regulatory bodies, has been inhibited by the absolute need to reduce the global power and influence of the primary player on the world stage, the United States. America is the historical bulwark standing in opposition to the forces represented by The Great Reset, and as such it is the target of an array of developing multi-layered and multi-pronged attacks. The attacks originate from both foreign actors and domestic threats; the confrontation will be engaged on political, economic, social, religious, financial, and cultural levels.

It will be a sustained, across the board attack—its totality will climax the Seventh Crisis.

Crisis is the perennial cover, under which the Left advances its agenda. The greater the instability caused by the Crisis, the more frustrated the population becomes, and the more susceptible it will be to the dangerously false but easy answers provided by those driving the Crisis. Then when the "solutions" predictably fail, they engender demands for more radical solutions from the Democrat Party Base and the storm trooper elements (Antifa and BLM) they control, as a way to "fix" problems the Transnationalist policies and actions created in the first place.

Until 2020, secrecy was the most valuable asset of the Left in advancing its agenda. But the collective cultural, political and illegal efforts expended in wresting power from Donald Trump exposed those machinations of the Deep State in real time for all to see—the mask was removed. Post-election Rasmussen polling showed 75% of Republicans, 30% of Democrats and 47% of all voters "think Democrats either stole votes or destroyed Trump ballots in several states to ensure Biden would win." The people's eyes were opened, and the permanent government would now be forced to make its self-interested moves in the plain light of day.

Beyond taking retribution against President Trump following the Capitol breach, the results of the stolen 2020 election will open the doors for a series of demands for "solutions," which will be deliberately designed to exacerbate the problem, and thus result in the call for even more radical policies and more governmental power to resolve issues that will be proclaimed to be *worse* than originally thought.

One cannon to be rolled out will likely be a massive spending, aka "Porkulous" bill to "stimulate" the economy and pay for "social programs" that have historically had an overall negative impact on those they were purporting to help. Money will be lavished on pork-ridden projects supposedly designed to "create jobs," but which in actuality are created, as was the Obama "Stimulus Plan," to provide taxpayer-funded financial aid to political allies, bureaucratic sycophants, Big Labor, Big Tech and special interest identity politics groups… as well as paying for mega-expensive bail-outs for corrupt and insolvent state and city governments long run by the Democrat Party.

Another cannon to be rolled out will likely be tax hikes, initially via repeal of Trump's 2017 tax cut law. Such tax increases are supposedly designed to make the rich "pay their fair share," despite the fact that, according to the Tax Foundation "The top 1 percent of taxpayers paid roughly $616 billion, or 38.5 percent of all income taxes, while the bottom 90 percent paid about $479 billion, or only 29.9 percent of all income taxes." https://taxfoundation.org/summary-of-the-latest-federal-income-tax-data-2020-update/

And even this will not be enough. The Leftwing Base of the Democrat Party will seek to displace the aged, sclerotic "leadership" of the party's current Corporate Wing and re-form it as a New Socialist Democrat Antisemite Partei. This N.S.D.A.P will condemn the radical policies enumerated above as too anemic and weak and will seek to… *re-imagine* it along authoritarian lines that will permanently lock them into power.

A caretaker Biden presidency will only open the way for his much younger, far more vibrant successor who, once Biden succumbs to the effects of his growing senility, will seek to accelerate the Seventh Crisis on all fronts. The "soft tyranny" will turn hard and street violence described by the Enemedia as "peaceful protest" can always be deployed to enforce compliance.

Looking over the horizon, we see the following issues, gambits and actions which must be engaged on the political, economic and cultural battlefield, if we are to emerge from the Seventh Crisis with our Constitutional Republic intact. Avoidance is not an option - the action will find you, for in the words of Erick Erickson, "you will be made to care."

The following is the battle terrain on which the Left expects to reap its whirlwind of "fundamental transformation," through the Seventh Crisis and implement a global Great Reset that is designed to destroy the United States, which is the only power capable of stopping them from achieving their evil goal.

Expansion of Big Tech's De-Platforming of Conservative voices

In the immediate wake of the Capitol breach the Tech Oligarchs did the bidding of the incoming Democrat regime by de-platforming President Trump and other highly visible conservative voices. Those not immediately de-platformed saw their online followers dropped or winnowed to a shadow of their former numbers. Expect to see these techniques and more, refined and distributed across virtually every current social media platform in the United States. Eventually anyone indicating their fealty to conservative or populist ideals will be throttled down by the tech overlords. This portends a dark future for Millennials and Gen-Zers who expect to employ their Constitutional rights of free speech and assembly to combat the ominous blanket of censorship descending upon them.

These Big Tech Robber Barons have restricted competition through deceptive conduct and have achieved monopoly-like power in the marketplace. They need to be combatted in similar fashion to their industrial predecessors. Anti-trust legislation mandating a level playing field would be an opening gambit. Expect to see unfair-trade actions by state attorneys general. Also, removing the immunity from liability suits granted in section 230 of the Communications Decency Act and treating Twitter, Facebook et al as publishers, subject to suit, would represent a sea change for their respective business models. But nothing less than pursuing the trust-busting legislative efforts of the Gilded Age will be as effective. Watch for any of these legislative efforts to surface and vigorously support the legislators advancing them.

Expect a coordinated effort to legalize up to 15 million illegal aliens currently living in the United States

The legalization of illegal aliens already in the country, aka amnesty, has been a political football for the past 20 years. It is about to become a battering ram to be driven through both the body politic and the culture. It is no secret that the Democrat party hungers to legalize those illegals who have violated federal law by either sneaking into the country or overstaying their legitimate visas. Once "legalized" they expect to propagandize most of them to register with the Democrat party and vote for Democrat candidates. Obviously, such a turn of events would foreclose on any possibility of a Republican candidate winning a national election.

In the first two years of Obama's presidency they had the power but lacked the fortitude. Their radical base is providing the nerve and energy this time in the form of bayonets in the backs of the party leadership. Expect an Immigration Bill more onerous than the prior "gang of eight" version of 2013. Although this version will affect 11 to 15 million illegals already here, it is likely to include provisions to facilitate the "chain migration" of family members remaining back in the countries of origin. All in, such legislation could open the door to some 50 million or more new "citizens."

The Specter of a "Truth and Reconciliation Commission"

Truth and Reconciliation Commissions have already been trial-ballooned by the likes of Elizabeth Warren and Robert Reich; in their hubris these leftist apparatchiks may actually attempt to roll out a South African styled Truth and Reconciliation Commission. Such commissions have been enacted in over forty Second and Third World nations following the reigns of notoriously terroristic and violent regimes, for the purpose of setting the history straight and administering "justice." Historically, restorative commissions aim to reconcile divided societies following conflict. But the "retributive" or "reparative" types tend to live up to their descriptors doling out fines, incarcerations or worse. "Reparations" are also levied to compensate aggrieved groups and victims of all manner of injustice, real or imagined. Discussion of reparations is currently reverberating in the halls of state capitals, and legislators in Pennsylvania, California, New York, Vermont, Texas and Florida have proposed legislation to provide monetary compensation to descendants of former slaves. The ACLU is also championing such an effort.

There will be lists… long lists of deplorables who will face a reckoning. The Trump family will be on the list. If you served in the Trump Administration, openly supported it or worked on the campaign, you will be on the list. If you are a visible Conservative on campus, you will be on a list. If you are a small business owner who was crushed by arbitrary, unscientific, politically motivated Covid-19 lockdowns and supported Trump's resistance to them, you will be on a list. If you are a policeman, a soldier or person of religious faith, you will be on a list. If you were ever accused of engaging in politically incorrect speech or actions, you will be on a list. If you spoke out effectively for individual liberty at a rally, you will be on a list. If you were interviewed on cable news supporting Trump, you will be on a list… and if you wrote an effective article or op-ed or appeared in an online video counter to the corporate, transnational progressive view, you too will be on a list.

No one will be safe because the only way to remain off the lists will be to submit to the commands of the authoritarians who are compiling them.

Acceleration of the enhancement & enforcement of hate-speech codes

While this attack on the First Amendment is part of an overall attack on the entire Bill of Rights, it is a key contributing element to the success of the overall anti-Constitutional agenda. In order to dominate, one must control the narrative; to control the narrative, one must control the language. When the Left, using its friends in the Culture dictate what is and is not within the permissible parameters of public parlance, it becomes impossible to voice or even formulate opposition to the Left because they will have deprived their opponents the language that is required to do so. The point of the spear of this attack on Free Speech is the so-called "Anti-Hate Speech Movement."

The First Amendment was designed not simply to protect non-offensive speech, but to defend all speech, regardless of its decency or offensive or even hateful nature. It is true that for Free Speech to conform to the structure of Ordered Liberty, there were some boundaries that could not be crossed including incitement, speech that creates a *clear and present* danger or speech that engages in physical threats. However, by identifying anything it disagrees with as "Hate-Speech," as well as expanding the definition of such speech so that it can be manipulated to cover almost any speech one wishes to censor, the Left has created a situation where all oppositional language can be accused of engaging in language that is proscribed as being dangerous to the public. Without being able to use certain speech to express thought, thought itself atrophies and becomes difficult to express; barring the types of exceptions mentioned, *there is no speech that is so "hateful" that it cannot be uttered.* Hate Speech laws and regulations emanate from the statehouses. Organized push-back will be needed at the first mention of this insidious form of censorship.

State Attorneys General, and any future Democrat U.S. AG, will increase the practice of suing conservative 501(c) 3&4 groups into bankruptcy

In August 2020 the NY AG's office grabbed the headlines by filing a civil lawsuit against the NRA, charging misspending of funds, engaging in self-dealing and making false and misleading disclosures to the AG and IRS. The purpose, of course, is to force such groups into outlays for legal defense expenses, which will drive many of the groups into bankruptcy. The NRA did in fact file for bankruptcy and re-domiciled in Texas. Similar lawsuits have been pursued against conservative organizations in California and Oregon. In addition, the IRS joined the practice with its infamous withholding of approval of Tea Party 501(c) 3&4 filings, which resulted in a massive scandal in 2013.

Expect more of this abuse from a perverted legal system that seeks to "weaponize" both federal and state regulations in an effort to distract, intimidate, financially bleed and bankrupt conservative-oriented organizations. Expect it to be ratcheted up and enabled in all Democrat led states which are home to conservative groups. Such groups should consider moving their domicile to solid Red states.

Joe Biden will institute "Critical Race Theory" training for Federal Employees

Joe Biden has indicated his willingness to issue his own Executive Order reversing President Trump's Executive Order, which prohibited Critical Race Theory from being taught to federal employees. Biden's order will instead make the controversial race theory indoctrination mandatory for all federal employees. Trump characterized the training as "rooted in the pernicious and false belief that America is an irredeemably racist and sexist country; that some people, simply on account of their race or sex, are oppressors; and that racial and sexual identities are more important than our common status as human beings and Americans." Such "training" under the guise of employee racial sensitivity sessions, requires white participants to proclaim that they benefit from racism. This indoctrination, is corrosive rather than redemptive, and will leave the participants either despising the history of the United States, or resentful of the bureaucrats requiring them to make such proclamations. Since it can all be accomplished by Executive Order of the president, it cannot be prevented, but its profound and devastating impact must be recognized and understood. And this is only the start.

Much of this is reminiscent of so-called "Struggle Sessions" and "Line Rectification" meetings held in the former Soviet Union and in Maoist China; they are likely still being held in one form or another in brutal Communist regimes such as North Korea. Such forced meetings required attendees to denounce themselves by "confessing" their failures to live strictly accord-ing to Communist Party dogma and to denounce others who did the same. Attendees were made to swear to take action to rectify their mistakes, inform on others and happily agree that whatever punishment, including capital punishment, that the Party meted out to offenders was justified as defending Socialism. Such sessions were heavy on ritual humiliations, including demean-ing confessions, the wearing of placards indicating their treacherous "crimes" or dunce-caps indicating their criminally stupid inability to act in sync with the continually shifting Party Line.

Similar ritualistic "Struggle Sessions" are now running rampant and increasing in intensity on Campus, in "Diversity Training Sessions" run by Corporate Human Resource departments and, of course, within the Federal Government. At such sessions, attendees are made to personally denounce their "privilege" and accept responsibility for all racism or sexism or classism, past and present. They are pressured to denounce or deny any traditionalist or religious social views they may hold as being reactionary, intolerant, "rac-ist" or "_____-phobic." Any objection is considered to be ipso facto proof of such "anti-social" tendencies. Further, any resistance to such self-denunciation regarding Identity Politics "solutions" designed to "eliminate" discrimination against the policies promoted by Leftwing sociological dogma is considered proof of guilt and therefore subject to employer sanction. Critical Race theory is merely the initial step; full-fledged Struggle Sessions, designed to enforce increasingly authoritarian government ideology and destroy freedom of thought and speech is the goal.

Continue and expand the reckless "defund the police" movement into a reordering of the entire criminal justice system

The current campaign to "defund the police" springs from the Transnational Progressive agenda's call for the "reordering" of society, by transforming people's traditional modes of thinking across a broad range of social issues. This Socialist defunding vision has emanated from the fringes, but is now being pushed into, and being adopted by, an increasing number of town councils and other local governing bodies across the country. Such ideas… as well as the various semantic dodges used to cover it up with deliberately vague though less ridiculous-sounding proposals (such as "redirecting funds" or "re-imagining the police") can lead nowhere except to an anarchic situation of increasing crime, riot, theft, rape and murder. Of course, this is precisely the plan; create such a crisis in maintaining law and order, that is supposedly due to systemic racism, that international organizations such as the U.N. will be asked to intercede. This brings us back to the U.N. Agenda 21 scheme, which was relentlessly pushed at us during the Obama years. Under it our system can only be "redeemed" by international "experts" who have not been "poisoned and soiled" by retrograde American attitudes.

Should the Left prevail we will lose control of our own law enforcement system. We will face an increasing "moral inversion" where activity that was previously considered "criminal" will now deemed to be true retributive justice, designed to redress past and present "systemic racism." Reordering law enforcement will be followed by a push to replace our "traditional" justice system with a system of progressive "Social Justice," which will be defined as anything that favors those who support and enforce the policies of the Elites. And, once the moral base of society is inverted, prohibited speech, prohibited gun ownership, "racist" attitudes, protection of private property and even self-protection against government favored groups will all become severely punishable "crimes." In such a perverted and twisted society, it will be Traditional America that will be administered a stern dose of "fundamental transformation."

Acceleration of the "De-carceration" of both State and Federal prisoners

While we have spoken of the incessant attempts by the Left *to seize* a Crisis and use it as a means to increase their power, it is also true that they seek *to create* crisis where there is none and then use that crisis in the same manner. Thus, was created the issue of "De-carceration" of criminals; that is, the curtailment of imprisoning criminals and the unilateral release of those already there. As insane as this idea appears on its face, the Left doesn't shrink from the creation of a moral inversion; in fact, they go further and claim that the rights of violent criminals take precedence over the rights of law-abiding citizens. This is justified by saying that law-abiding citizens are part of an oppressive, racist, class structure that has created criminals out of individuals who are said to be simply reacting to their oppression in the only way open to them. The special interest groups that align with the Left are encouraged by Progressives to fight back against what is alleged to be a systemically racist, White power structure whose laws are, by the very fact the White power structure created them, oppressive and unjust.

The size of America's prison population isn't created by systemic racism or legalized social injustice; it is created by the need to lock up violent felons to prevent them from preying on the innocent, where most of them are serving time for violent offenses. If prison sentences were unilaterally reduced or even eliminated by legal "reforms," it would expose law-abiding citizens to far larger numbers of recidivist criminals who will repeat criminal acts against them. Chaos and mayhem are the tools that the Left uses to create the crises they seek to exploit and nothing creates crisis like mass instability and insecurity. Legislation and regulation on this front have been driven from both State and Federal legislative and budgeting processes. All who fight as political warriors must oppose the Left giving a "get out of jail free" card to violent felons so as to use them as a catspaw to drive a frightened population into the false protection of the far greater prison they wish to make of society.

Corporations can expect increased extortion by Leftist grievance groups, while they curry favor with federal regulators to avoid financial and market scrutiny

The practice of "shaking-down" corporations by adroitly threatening them should they fail to donate to the proscribed cause, has been perfected over the past several decades by the likes of "race hustlers" such as Jessie Jackson and Al Sharpton. The Black Lives Matter movement is currently perfecting this technique while capitalizing on recent events and has raked in pledges of hundreds of millions from corporate America both for its cause and its affiliated groups. Given its success, we can unfortunately expect this "protection racket" to be deployed by more Leftwing grievance groups. The past decade has also seen a steady increase in the practice of penalizing and firing employees who speak out or issue social media posts standing up for traditional values or calling out the subterfuge of the Left. They are putting our jobs on the line through intimidation and American workers can expect to face their own moment of truth in their workplace. In addition, because corporations are caving into Leftwing Progressive pressure to inject the Marxist cultural agenda into employee training, product designs and ad campaigns—expect this nauseating practice to increase.

More corporations are kowtowing to their respective federal regulators with the purpose of avoiding scrutiny. They are vocal about promoting the "green" economy, "sustainability" and social justice in hiring. Many of the CEOs are seen in TV ads and interviews proclaiming their allegiance to the Leftist "Social Justice" agenda. Bill Gates and Warren Buffet are infamous for very timely public calls for higher taxes on the wealthy during the Obama Administration. Their very clear virtue-signals were appreciated by Obama. The Deep State apparatus showed its appreciation by sparing Microsoft and Berkshire Hathaway the relentless IRS harassment so many companies, led by vocal Obama critics or defenders of conservative values, had to withstand during Obama's reign. Expect more of this, as the incestuous relationship between federal regulators and the corporations they regulate continues—all to the detriment of the American people.

Expect Antifa and BLM members to disperse to form local advocacy groups in heavily Democrat areas, where they will function as local militias

These "local advocacy groups" will serve as the intimidating street-enforcers for radical leftist city and town councils. They will emerge in parallel to local police as enforcement arms for the more extreme mandates of the town councils, which the police may shrink from enforcing in the field. Sympathetic local leftist representatives could be expected to push for "qualified immunity" to cover these basically paramilitary groups. With such legal cover they would be fully equipped to function as the vanguard enforcers of Leftwing dogma among the town's abject citizens.

Our darkest imaginings are the limits to what nefarious actions we could anticipate from such empowered groups, e.g., guarding access to polling places, enforcement of pandemic-driven public assembly restrictions, forced compliance with any number of "green" regulations, or even home searches for firearms or other items the Left deems inappropriate for personal possession such as flags, hats with forbidden slogans and/or refusal to kneel in favor of some ideological cause. Successfully implanting ideological muscle on the ground would represent a keystone advance in overturning our democratic society. Any talk of this in our locales will need to be vociferously opposed at first mention.

Expect an effort of some configuration, under some contrived pretense, to confiscate private firearms

With recent statements made by candidates running in the 2020 Democrat Party primaries, the idea that they would confiscate privately owned guns and rescind the Second Amendment can no longer be seen as paranoid. When asked if he supported a mandate that forced Americans to sell their firearms, presidential candidate Beto O'Rourke responded "Hell yes, we're going to take your AR-15, your AK-47." While he later equivocated and said he wasn't talking about "confiscation" but rather a "mandatory buyback," it was obviously a distinction without a difference if there ever was one. The Left's agenda knows no limits in its jihad against the Second Amendment. They want to limit access to guns and ammunition by passing onerous taxes on firearm and ammunition sales; they want to pass legislation requiring all gun owners to carry expensive liability insurance, again increasing the costs of firearm ownership… and they want to bypass state laws by passing such legislation at the Federal level.

Given the extent to which modern technology can marry electronic monitoring to efforts at social control, will Bank and Credit Card companies be pressed into "patriotic" service to deny credit to gun owners or gun dealers? Will they be denied mortgages or have their travel restricted because they own, once owned or hold "dangerous" views on guns? All this makes it clear that the Democrat desire to eviscerate the Second Amendment remains as inflexible and extreme as ever. They want your guns and if given the power, they will try very hard to take them from you. They know full well that an armed citizenry is one of the greatest threats to their ability to control our lives. Nothing would make them happier than the destruction of individual gun ownership, which serves as the armory of Ordered Liberty. The latest euphemism for gun control is "gun safety" and various congressional members are continually testing the waters to try to put this hoax over on the American people. Any federal action would commence in either the House or Senate, but heavily blue states will continue to see similar stirrings in their own statehouses.

The Left's war on traditional religious values can be expected to intensify

Just as it can countenance no alternative to its political or economic beliefs, neither can the Left allow any spiritual or religious belief that conflicts with, or worse, condemns its moral relativism or its replacement of religion with the ecological paganism of "Gaia Worship." The Left seeks to usurp the place traditional religious morality has in our culture, and replace it with a politicized pseudo-religion and an ersatz, ad hoc "morality" that consists of whatever serves its purpose.

Their virulent antipathy to traditional religion can be seen in their reaction to the Covid-19 Virus state lockdowns of 2020 in areas they control. Houses of Worship were ordered closed to comply with "social distancing" and "mask wearing" rules, imposed in the name of not only good health, but also in the name of "patriotism." However, favored businesses—such as liquor stores, abortion clinics, gambling casinos and others—were deemed "essential" and therefore allowed to stay open. Worse, far-Left political groups, who gathered in large numbers to take part in both violent and non-violent demonstrations, were exempted from such rules in the name of "the right to peaceably assemble." It doesn't matter which traditional religious group you belong to; to the Left, all traditional religion is *The Enemy*. Attacks on religious practice are always well-masked, coming within legislation aimed elsewhere; such as the attack on the Little Sisters of the Poor. The indirect attack on this harmless and charitable religious group was buried within ponderous legislation that created Obamacare, which mandated that all groups provide birth control as part of its insurance coverage. This action sought to coerce groups like the

Little Sisters of the Poor to violate its deeply held religious convictions or go out of business. These insidious attacks will intensify. Watch for them both in Washington and your state capitals.

Completely eliminate the senate filibuster

Senate rules provide for seemingly endless debate. The actual practice of running an endless debate is referred to as a filibuster. It provides the minority in the senate to block legislation by preventing a vote on a bill. In order to end debate and open the way to a vote, a "cloture" motion needs to pass with a super-majority of at least 60 votes. Its historical justification is that it enables the minority to prevent the passage of legislation it deems to be particularly onerous to the interests of the minority or country at large. Although it has been diluted over the decades, it still applies to most legislation—most importantly appropriations.

The majority could take a rules vote to simply eliminate the filibuster. This has been threatened in the past and is referred to as the "nuclear option." A credible threat to do just that is currently emanating from the Democrats, who are just aching to regain the majority. Should they succeed and end the filibuster, the country would be subject to the most onerous bills on spending, green energy, health care, gun control, immigration, and whatever else they could imagine. Eliminating the filibuster will subject the country to the tyranny of the majority and pave the way to fiscal, political, and cultural ruin.

A serious effort will be made to "Pack" the Supreme Court

The idea of "packing" the Supreme Court in order to ensure that its decisions will always be congruent with the political group that controls who it is "packed" with, is not new. Outraged that important New Deal legislation he passed through a receptive Democrat Congress was being overturned by the Supreme Court as unconstitutional, President Franklin Roosevelt tried to go around it by the "Court Packing" method in order to get more rulings that were favorable to his statist agenda. He withdrew the legislation in the face of both public and several SCOTUS justices' opposition. While he failed, the idea remains alive and has recently received a fresh look by Liberals and Progressives in the wake of the passing of liberal icon Ruth Bader Ginsburg and the confirmation of originalist Amy Coney Barrett. And the Progressive nightmare of younger, more Conservative replacements derailing their Big Government agenda for a generation looms larger than ever before. All that is required is a president willing to nominate additional judges and a senate majority willing to vote to confirm them.

Any attempt to "pack" the Court… which is constitutional if only because the Constitution doesn't specify how many judges there can be on the Supreme Court… is a recipe for tyranny in the hands of a Transnational Progressive elite that will use it to "fundamentally transform" the United States by legalizing policy through judicial fiat rather than through the elected representatives of the people in their legislatures. This will allow the Courts to utterly override the Congress and make "legislating from the bench," by an unelected branch of government that is created and controlled by the Elite; the possibility of the Elites creating such an Imperial Judiciary is a terrifying reality. Given the nature of the Seventh Crisis, where all radical change is used as a stepping stone to ever more power for an ever-smaller Elite, such radical change cannot be tolerated. Court Packing can too easily be turned into a super-highway to bypass Congress and place far too much power in the hands of yet another unelected elite group under the control of the Left.

Congress will attempt to legislate "Medicare For All"

During a monumental struggle to enact ObamaCare in the winter of 2010 the Tea Party warned that it would not improve access or the expense of health care but instead massively increase its costs. After 10 years, healthcare costs have gone up by multiples and Democrats are still complaining. They fervently assert that healthcare is an "unalienable right," though our foundational rights are rights to *action*—not rights to another person's labor. Of course, we know that their decades long goal is to finally push into place, the cornerstone of Socialism—single payer state-run healthcare.

Its latest formulation is "Medicare for All." It's a catchy phrase to which they believe most everyone will have a positive response. With state-run medicine they think they have costs managed but they account for neither quality nor availability. It's a guarantee that we will follow the experience of the UK and Canada, where the care is rationed and wait times for basic procedures stretch into many months and longer. We will need to face the specter of this nightmare once again, and this time we must prevail. For the underlying objective of state-run healthcare is the broad opening it provides to control

THE BATTLE TERRAIN AHEAD

so many of the activities of our daily lives by withholding care if we do not behave as the government proscribes.

Regular trial-balloons will be floated to make Washington DC the 51st State

The Far Left's plan to overwhelm the rules by which our Constitutional Republic is run includes using an insincere desire to "expand our Democracy" by seeking to permanently control the Senate and the House by creating "Democrat only" new states. Per the Constitution's Admission Clause, "New States may be admitted by the Congress into this Union," and Article I, Section 8 of the Constitution allows Congress to create a "District" (not exceeding ten miles square)" to become the seat of government. Should the Left succeed in creating a state out of the Federal District, it will gain two Senators and at least one Congressman who will almost certainly be Democrats serving for life.

Given the electoral dynamics of certain other areas where Democrat voters are heavily concentrated, what is to prevent the Left from not only making a State out of Washington DC, but also out of New York City; or out of Puerto Rico or some other reliably Democrat area? Such a policy would drown the United States in artificially created pseudo-states that serve only to perpetually keep Democrats in power. We should not scoff that such things are "implausible" or "alarmist" when there are daily calls for other previously unthinkable proposals such as the defunding of police forces and spending 50-*trillion* dollars over 10 years on utterly impossible, pseudo-scientific policies to halt "climate change." Ideas that were once thought to be too ridiculous to consider, now often have a way of becoming "mainstream." Once such ludicrous ideas are placed in the capable hands of the pseudo-intellectuals in Academia and the Enemedia, they are twisted into any grotesque shape their clients on the Left demand of them so that they can be justified as "normal" to the public. Any proposed legislation calling for the politically created pseudo-states to be created as a means to ensure permanent majority status for the Left must be opposed the moment it surfaces.

The National Popular Vote Compact (NPV) project will receive renewed visibility and pressure in the state houses where it has yet to pass

The National Popular Vote (NPV) is an effort to abolish the Electoral College without passing an amendment to the Constitution. Our government is not a "Democracy"—it is a Constitutional Republic that elects its representatives under democratic processes such as elections. Indeed, the Founders were extremely frightened of the idea of a majoritarian "Democracy," where individual rights and free elections could be overwhelmed by a potentially dangerous implementation of a Democracy where gross majority rule could simply over-ride or destroy the Constitutional protections of the individual and/or the minority view.

The NPV plan is to get enough states to agree to allocate their respective electoral votes to the winner of the national popular vote. The legislation is moving through most of the nation's statehouses and will go into effect when enough states totaling 270 electoral votes pass the legislation. All the states do not need to pass it—just enough so that the winner of the national popular vote triggers those 270 electoral votes necessary to elect the president.

In most states the measure has to pass both legislative houses and be signed by the governor. As of late 2020 it has been enacted into law in 16 states and DC representing 196 electoral votes—that's 72% of the 270-vote threshold. California, New York and Illinois are the biggest states to pass it. And it has passed at least one legislative chamber in 9 states possessing 88 additional electoral votes. This is a dangerous end-run around the Constitution, intended to effectively neuter the representation of the minority or smaller states. Make no mistake, the NPV is not a friend of "democracy"; it is a tool of would-be tyrants who want to ensure their victory through a grotesque manipulation of the national vote. It has passed in California, New York, Illinois, New Jersey, Massachusetts, Connecticut, Colorado, Maryland, New Mexico, Oregon, Washington, Delaware, Hawaii, Rhode Island, Vermont and the District of Columbia. If it hasn't yet been enacted in your state, check the status with your legislature, for it most likely will have an "active" status.

Unbridled wealth transfers to accelerate via the laundering of tax dollars, to benefit Democrat Campaigns and charitable organization management personnel

As Obama demonstrated in the 2009 economic "stimulus" legislation, when in control of all levers of federal power, Democrats can move hundreds of billions to public service union rank and file workers through government to government transfers. Also clearly demonstrated at that time was a considerable transfer to public and private agencies purportedly in business to serve the economic underclass. All the government's anti-poverty agencies are tied to the Democrat party, while most of the private agencies have strong ties to the Democrat fundraising machine.

The incestuous ties have spawned countless scandals whereby the agency management have raked in obscene amounts of cash for their personal accounts, and have laundered plenty of their largesse back into Democrat campaign coffers. Many Community Action organizations and Needy Family programs have been caught up in corruption scandals. In recent years, the most infamous of these was ACORN, which was compelled to shut down operations as a result. With Democrats in full federal control of congress and the presidency in 2021, we can expect to see these offline campaign arsenals to be overstocked, and their managers flush with taxpayer sourced lucre. Administrators of these agencies will again be feathering their nests as they channel and launder funds through the neediest communities, leaving only a pittance in the hands of those who truly need our help.

Beware the federally sponsored "Guaranteed Retirement Account"; the gateway drug to government confiscation of your 401Ks

The Guaranteed Retirement Account (GRA) was conceived as an "option" to traditional 401Ks and IRAs, for businesses to offer should they not sponsor a 401K for their employees. But congressmen Jim Himes and John Larson of CT have co-sponsored "Automatic IRA Act" legislation, which would force businesses not offering a 401K to automatically enroll employees in a GRA… with only an opt-out provision. Employees would incur automatic monthly payroll deductions to be invested in an investment portfolio of the government's choosing, including U.S. Treasury bonds and bills. The bill, like so many other nefarious measures, waits in the DC wings for a favorable political wind to propel it to the House floor.

The strategy is to incrementally move closer to federal authority over our savings, which remains one of the last deep pots of money the government seeks to access in the event of another financial crisis. When we face the inevitable implosion in the financial markets, with the GRA or Automatic IRA in operation throughout the country, our rulers will be perfectly positioned to walk to the microphones as they did in October 2008, and offer their solution. We would be advised the crisis is so great that the federal government will need to access our GRAs and 401Ks to rebalance the federal budget. They would propose taking 10% of our savings or more to save the financial system. Should public pushback be vociferous, they might offer to deposit a special-purpose federal IOU in our accounts to quell the commotion. Once this insidious siphon has been inserted into our savings accounts, they will have no hesitation returning to this ample well when inevitable future crises arise. An emergence of any permutation of this legislation needs to be smothered at first sight.

The rise of a Federal Reserve crypto-currency is on the horizon, poised to usher in an insidious and oppressive era of government monitoring and control

According to Federal Reserve Board transcripts, the Boston Fed has been working for years with MIT to develop a Central Bank Digital Currency (CBDC). Supposedly, China is readying the launch of its own CBDC, so naturally the Fed seeks to compete with a digital-dollar codebase. It will be sold to us under the guise of "security and convenience" and sadly too many Americans seem disposed to go along with this deceptive gambit. From universal healthcare, to workplace PC rules, to pandemic restrictions, there are none that pose a more ominous government threat to control our lives than moving the American consumer economy onto a digital currency platform. The government will know what we own, what we spend, and what we spend it on—daily!

The COVID Pandemic era has seen the crippling and dissolution of millions of small businesses. These businesses represent the largest portion of America's independent middle-class private wealth. Many are enduring desperate circumstances and instead of reopening opportunity, Leftist/Democrat politicians are calling for Universal Income payments. But, as soon as it's feasible, the government would make any such relief payments digitally with CBDC units. Other economic systems e.g., airlines, hotels, banking and real estate transactions, and even access to driver's licenses could quickly follow suit. And in the entire amalgamation, our individual economic lives, and hence our freedom, would gradually become tethered to the approval of the Federal Government. We could become a mirror image of China's "social scoring" system, whereby the government digitally "scores" your behavior and dispenses approval and "currency" to travel, or to buy/sell your property, or what schools you may attend; all to be based on its scoring of your behavior over the past period of time.

Watch when Leftist mouthpieces invoke Modern Monetary Theory (MMT) - a clear sign that a consequential financial deceit is to be played upon the American public

As illuminated in The Economic Deceits above, MMT is the magic elixir economic theory increasingly being sprinkled on the Left's most audacious spending proposals. Since the dawn of the Obama years, Democrat officials have pushed forward several outsized-spending proposals which were truly unprecedented in terms of both absolute dollars (trillions) and percentage of either the federal budget or the GDP itself e.g. the '09 "Stimulus" bill, ObamaCare, Infrastructure and the Green New Deal. Even LBJ's Great Society programs didn't hold a candle, proportionately, to the economic impact these whoppers would have upon the nation's finances. When pressed into the corner on these, the Democrats have impudently cited MMT as economic justification, in an effort to soothe the fiscal concerns of the incredulous. The Left views MMT as the big cannon to be used to silence all rational concerns and budgetary criticism of their trillion-dollar pipedreams.

We've already seen smoke signals for additional spending fantasies now parked in the wings e.g., Medicare for All, Universal Income, Infrastructure II, and when the Democrats think they have the juice to push these swindles onto the legislative calendar they will. Expect the coordinated Left, i.e., the politicians, academicians and the Enemedia to provide air cover for the legislative ground troops by citing MMT as intellectual accreditation. They will with straight faces, attempt to rationalize and pass otherwise non-passable, budget decimating legislation into law. Watch for citations of MMT as the signal that a massive swindle is on the runway. Any of these proposals would be economically devastating to the nation's already debilitated finances and will need to be opposed at first sighting. The nation would not be able to withstand the enactment and economic ravaging of any such proposals.

Expect severe restrictions on taking U.S. currency out of the country and opening a foreign bank account

The U.S. Customs and Border Protection (CBP) department requires any citizen transferring or carrying more than $10,000 out of the U.S. to report the transfer to CBP. Moving more than $10,000 in cash at a customs checkpoint will place you under suspicion; if such activity is not declared and it's found, your cash will be confiscated. Currently, an American citizen can legally wire transfer most any amount out of the country…it's just that the government is aware of the transaction and its destination. Americans can open bank accounts in many foreign countries, but those countries set the local rules on foreign-owned accounts.

To get the foreign banks to report such activity back to the United States, the Foreign Account Tax Compliance Act (FACTA) requires that any foreign bank seeking to participate in the U.S. financial system, must report to the U.S. Treasury department activity in all such accounts held by U.S. citizens. Naturally, to remain in compliance, U.S. citizens must declare these accounts and their earnings annually on their IRS 1040 filings. Both CBP and FACTA are administered in the Executive branch. Any president seeking to restrict or stop the flow of U.S. currency from the country can do so by Executive Order. Americans seeking such offshore protection for a portion of their personal wealth need to be aware just how swiftly this particular door could be closed under a presidency hostile to the private property rights of its citizens.

Efforts will intensify to weaken and destroy Private and Charter schools in favor of anti-American, transnational, centralized education, further empowering teacher unions

With the centralization of Education standards increasingly under the control of the inept Federal Education bureaucracy and the corrupt Teacher Unions, what is taught in public schools has become a weapon in the hands of those who serve a political agenda that is anti-American, multicultural, politically correct, culturally transnational and progressive. Through false, politically biased and racially incendiary curriculums, such as "Common Core" and "The 1619 Project", the Left seeks to promulgate hatred for traditional American values, history, heroes, accomplishments and myths as well as instill a sense of guilt and self-loathing among non-minority students. Conversely, minority students are denied the right to self-achieve by impressing on them the idea that concepts of merit, hard work and pride in educational accomplishment are "racist" values based in "White Supremacy" that must be ended, even if by violent means, to serve "Social Justice."

Charter and Private schools are harassed and attacked by teacher unions and their tethered creatures in the Public School Administrative System because of their proven ability to succeed with poor and minority students where public schools have presided over cratering performance scores and high dropout rates. Public schools, like everything else, must be forced to perform far better via the competition provided by Charter and Private schools. Further, local decisions about curriculum should be made at local, not national levels, so that parents will have more control over what is taught and know that their values will be respected rather than undermined. Most important, decentralizing education will better ensure that their children's ability to think critically will not be deliberately destroyed by those who want to use them as brainwashed pawns… or even street fighting cannon-fodder… to advance their Transnational agenda.

Gradually and methodically end the "Meritocracy" system in both the public and private spheres, and replace it with a "quota" system

Meritocracy is an idea that is co-existent with modernity; in premodern societies, merit was trumped by those with access to class privilege, aristocratic/elitist connections or family wealth. The current concept on the Left that a Meritocracy is "unfair" and indeed even "impossible" is based on the politically correct, radically egalitarian idea that posits the advantages an individual starts out with in life in terms of inherited class, wealth and resources is inherently unequal in a non-Socialist society. That is, other individuals without such "born with" advantages cannot have an equal opportunity to succeed based on "merit" as those that do. Therefore, according to this view, a meritocracy is impossible in a society where everyone does not start out with *socially equal* advantages because unequal outcomes among individuals will result from inherited opportunities rather than be based solely on individual merit. However, the essence of Modernity is the creation of new ideas and improved processes, and such ideas are not limited to the Elite; in fact, denying ideas that "merit" inclusion into society because they come from outside a restricted elite would be deadly to the very concept of modern progress. Of course, some are born with more privilege than others; however, if a person can, through his own merit, create a multi-billion dollar enterprise and thus become a multi-billionaire himself in the process, then it matters little that such a person was born with relatively less privileged status than another who, despite the advantages, created nothing. Simply put, Meritocracy works.

However, such pragmatism is at odds with Social Justice ideology and therefore must be made to conform to it. Quota systems supposedly must be erected to make up for past oppression of groups that have been historically considered socially "inferior." To rectify such past injustice… and indeed, to punish those whose ancestors perpetuated it… the concept of "Merit" is dropped in favor of "Identity Politics"—that is, *who you are* and *how much you or your identity group have suffered in the past* becomes far more important than the meritocratic idea of *what you can do* and *what you are capable of accomplishing in the future.* Such thinking seeks to create a different "elite" where one's individual "merit" is cancelled in favor of one's identity. According to such thinking, your race, your gender, your sexual orientation, your religion (or lack of it) are all given far more weight than your individual ability to produce and contribute. Millennials will soon learn that it is the former that is rewarded and the latter that is ignored.

The Quota system looms large on the horizon concerning Millennials' hiring, career opportunity, and promotion landscape, and is a growing impediment to success. When they guide their children toward placement in good schools and colleges they will have to grapple with a vast web of quota-driven bureaucracy that was unknown just a decade ago, when Merit was still the prime criteria for admission. Millennials will long for the days when society chose Merit as the neutral, objective standard based on the success of a better idea or better job or academic performance; if society chooses Identity as the standard, it will be based on the biased and subjective views of ideologically driven judges who will determine which socially favored Identity group most deserves a chance regardless of the worth of their ideas or the value of their performance. Millennials will have a formidable challenge dealing with this hideous societal inversion. But it must be challenged, halted and reversed if they are to avoid becoming second-class citizens.

Nationwide Redistricting will tilt the political playing field to the Left

The 2020 census will serve as the benchmark for congressional redistricting during the next term. Redistricting power generally lies with the state legislatures and governors. Partisan Gerrymandering is not new, but due to recent infusions of technology, district map drawing has become very effective at producing the desired results. State capitals dominated by Democrats can be expected to press every available redistricting advantage. The model is the New England states where all 21 congressional seats east of the Hudson River are held by Democrats.

Once the New England "straight flush" was completed in 2008 it has been impossible for the Republicans to regain even a toehold in the region. Fierce redistricting battles can be expected to be waged in Democrat-leaning states where party leaders see the possibility of carving Republican representation completely out of the picture. Democrat success in redistricting can prove ominous for the chances of Republicans regaining any House majority. Some states have independent "non-partisan" commissions which redraw the maps. State legislators in increasing blue states should be lobbied to move to the independent commission model.

Expect a gambit to reduce the national voting age to 16

What better way to engorge your voter base with blind supporters than to give the vote to those children the Democrat-controlled teacher unions have been propagandizing for the last 10 years? How else can Democrats ensure that the new voters, without experience of war, peace. life, how business works or anything other than the most juvenile conceptions of what such issues entail be expected to only cast their votes for Progressives? By limiting, with the ultimate goal of *destroying,* any alternative that might offer a conservative perspective, the Left is virulently opposed to private, charter or home schooling. They want no alternative to schools that opposes their pro-Socialist, multicultural, politically correct Globalist curriculums which are forced on parents by Democrat cronies in the teacher unions and the Department of Education in

Washington DC. They are guilty of birthing a modern Hitler-Jugend whose minds they rape in K-12 before feeding them into the paramilitary arms of the on-campus Antifa.

By giving 16-year old's the vote, the Left seeks to lock-down their minds at as early an age as possible and then exploit their innocence, idealism and youthful enthusiasm to do whatever "social justice work" that Democrat teacher unions have convinced them are vitally needed "to make the world a fairer place." It is as devious and cynical a political exploitation of the young as can be imagined and should be opposed at all costs. Though it took an arduous process, the 26th Amendment to the Constitution lowered the voting age to 18; do not discount the potential for another Democrat-led strategic end-run around basic common sense to lower it further.

– 10 –

A Signal Call to Millennials

To this point we have provided insights as to how the ruling political class has squandered our trust, betrayed the principles on which this great republic was founded and with its actions, brought the country into our current crisis. We have tried to illuminate and expose the methodology of the Left, which extends its tentacles of power like a virus throughout our political system and American society. Guided by experience and informed by History, we have provided the contours of the endgame of the American Left. We have identified the idea that can serve as the animating spirit for a free, secure, prosperous and mutually respectful society: Ordered Liberty. And with the 2020 election behind us we have provided a look at the terrain on which the political and cultural battles will unfold in the coming months and years.

We must recognize that government will not take actions beneficial to the citizenry if those actions materially impair government interests. Government action is always in furtherance of increasing its power.

We did not want to leave our Millennial brethren with only an analysis or polemic, but also provide a tactical guide so every reader can go forward, take action, and get traction in the great effort to return our Republic to the foundational principles which served it so well, as it grew into arguably the most prosperous and influential society and culture in recorded history. As part of the Baby Boom generation, we owe it to those who come after us to warn them not to be seduced by the siren call of the Left, as so many Boomers were, much to the detriment of our Nation and Culture.

Ordered Liberty is peaceful, but it is not Peace. It is not a utopia of unrestricted freedom, but a system of self-control that makes freedom possible. It is the spirit which gives each generation the strength and ability to fight whatever enemy of freedom History puts in its path. It is that which will save the Millennial and Gen-Z generations from the catastrophic consequences of the Seventh Crisis.

But recognize that the restoration of our founding principles cannot be achieved through pressing for government actions on liberty's behalf alone. Each of us must put our shoulders to the wheel in our social networks, in our places of employment and our own towns to bring about the restoration of a free republic. It is a heavy lift, but if we are each actively engaged we will prevail.

So we close out with a list of suggestions... or, if one prefers, "marching orders" to use in this mighty effort to preserve America through the Seventh Crisis and lead to a rebirth of American Liberty.

Criticize no one on the Right—save all criticism for the Enemy; the time for internal debate on the Right will occur after Victory is achieved.

Do not associate with any group which advocates race hatred, racial or ethnic supremacy, religious intolerance, cult behavior or violence not taken in self-defense that purports to be on the Right; they seek to co-opt your agenda and use it as a cover to push their own. Spurn, scorn and banish any racist, supremacist, neo-Nazi, religiously intolerant, violence advocating group that opposes the principles of Ordered Liberty or tries to use those who support Ordered Liberty to subvert their own Cause by falsely attaching it to fringe, extremist ideas in search of a large audience that they can't garner for themselves.

Avoid pointless debate with friends and family; concentrate on learning the facts and forcing those with whom you discuss the issues to accept the reality those facts present.

Seek out, network with and organize other like-minded people in your area; always push to expand this Base of Activists.

Expose the Leftists wherever you uncover them.

Never trust the words of a RINO Republican; oppose them whenever possible and pressure them by forcing them into primary races with conservatives committed to Ordered Liberty. RINOs are not worth defending and they must be ideologically purged before the political victory of Ordered Liberty can be assured; let them go join the other party that they have helped so much and served so well for decades with their weakness, appeasement and subversion of Conservative principles.

Always support the Rule of Law and assert it against those who seek to overthrow it.

Continually pressure local government officials to fully prosecute those who break the law in open Town Council Meetings, through Letters to the Editor and in-person meetings with your local representatives; let them know that unless they enforce a non-tolerance policy against rioters, looters and law-breakers of all types they will be voted out of office.

When you see corrupt or illegal activity by officials in your town e.g. illegal activities regarding vote harvesting or mail-in irregularities, immediately amass a peaceful group at the town registrar's door, demanding investigation and rectification. Make the Left and the corrupt feel our pushback everywhere they turn.

It is clear that Big Tech has become the 21st Century version of the manufacturing trusts and other predatory monopolies that existed in the late 19th Century. As a functioning Cartel that seeks to buy candidates, rig elections and crush competition, legislators must be pressured by Millennials and Gen-Z voters to take action against Big Tech. They must do this not only by demanding that Anti-Trust laws that are already on the books be enforced against Big Tech, but also by creating new legislation that is directly attuned to this new industry and its technically complex arrangements. Voters must insist that their representatives create new Anti-trust legislation, designed to prevent such new digital monopolies from illegally curtailing commerce and eviscerating privacy at the same time they are squelching free speech, critical thinking and economic liberty.

In the wake of Big Tech's de-platforming and silencing of conservative voices on social media, Millennials in the technology industry need to endeavor to establish independent platforms and apps, beyond the reach of the Tech Oligarchs. Then seek out and use the new platforms to keep your voices in the national debate and defy those who wish to silence you.

Express zero tolerance for and be vocal against all forms of divisive Identity Politics.

Reject dangerous Leftist fantasies regarding immigration, race, gender, ethnicity and false history; do not allow such dangerous fantasies to infect your school system and vote any school board member who supports such ideas out of office.

Fight the push to normalize Transgenderism to children; such an attempt at normalization is not tolerance of the different...it is child abuse of the innocent.

Fight the exacerbation of gender conflict; oppose the demonization of Men as well as discrimination against Women; the sexes are equal under the Law and should be treated as such *in all circumstances*.

Counter the false narrative that the Black Community is hated by and targeted by the police; use statistics and polls that prove the Black Community wants more, not less, effective and fair policing.

Counter the false propaganda that America is in the grip of "systemic racism"; legal racism has been outlawed in the United States for decades and the idea that society still maintains a "Jim Crow" mindset is belied by the observable facts of modern life.

Confront, expose and oppose Black Lives Matter as the subversive, racist, Marxist organization it is in letters to the editor, in candidate forums, in campus lecture rooms and in the streets.

Oppose unscientific and politically arbitrary "lockdowns" that are "justified" for dubious and contradictory reasons regarding "public health"; encourage the small business community to demand clear and rational scientific justifications before ever again agreeing to "lockdown" their businesses only to find it is, as is much of the hysteria regarding "Climate Change," really just a political ploy to shackle free enterprise and remove access to wealth by the middle class.

Use the power of Alumni Organizations to fight campus radicalism; withhold your and fellow alumni's funding from universities that support or appease Leftwing organizations that attack our Constitution, our culture, our history, our heroes, our myths, our religious values and our Capitalist economic system.

Be public about your views to deprive any university that attacks traditional American culture of taxpayer funding.

Expose false charges regarding campus sex abuse and demand the facts before false judgements are made in Campus Kangaroo Courts run by the Left and the radical professors who enable them to ruin lives for political purposes.

Challenge the power of campus radicals and the University Administrators that support them; hold them accountable for any violence or property damage perpetrated by those they have brainwashed to hate their own country and culture to the point of wanting to destroy it.

Fight politically correct speech codes on campus, in business offices and in the public square by demanding that all speech that is within legal bounds be free regardless of who finds it offensive, degrading, disparaging or "hate-full"; organize a racially, religiously and ethnically diverse group to deliberately use "proscribed" words to demonstrate that the Constitution protects all such speech, not just that which is anodyne and blandly inoffensive.

Form counter-Antifa groups on campus; counter not just their ideology but reject everything about them in all manner, form, dress and attitude that immediately identifies you as an opponent of Antifa and all for which it stands.

Fight the anti-American cultural narratives pushed by rich, arrogant elitists in the gated communities of Hollywood and the rest of the so-called Entertainment Industry by refusing to buy their film, TV, internet or music products; demonstrate that the "cancel culture" is a two-way street.

Those Millennials in the trucking industry whose hard work keeps our country alive and thriving should organize a ready response to those cities and localities that aid and abet the lawless actions of rioting anarchists and leftwing subversives; they should refuse to enter and make deliveries to lawless areas until order is restored.

Those "blue collar" workers who are the backbone of this country should do the same; electricians, plumbers, carpenters, construction workers and others should refuse to work in any area where the local officials fail in their duty to uphold law and order against rioting mobs.

If Leftwing cities can nullify Federal Immigration Law and declare themselves "sanctuaries" for illegal immigrants, the Right should declare certain cities "sanctuaries" for the unborn; like cancel culture, "nullification" is also a two-way street and the Left should get to know what it feels like to travel upon it.

Do not allow the Left to be the only side that is permitted to pressure and frighten Corporations into prioritizing their agenda; use the same tactics to intimidate Corporations that the Left uses and force them to realize that caving into the Left's demands carries the price of angering those on the Right.

Use your contacts and make new ones inside mainstream media companies and large corporations which do the Left's bidding—build a network of insiders. Use them to provide intelligence on media methods and planning. Also, motivate them to blunt and sidetrack the Leftist messages emanating from these powerful mouthpieces whenever possible.

If you find an NGO or 501(c)(3) Tax Exempt Organization performing any kind of electioneering for a candidate on the Left, report it to the IRS on IRS form 13909. Tax exempt organizations cannot be used to influence an election.

If male, make a point of being respectful of women and a supporter of their fight for equal rights; if a woman, make a point of standing against the demonization of men.

Vocally, visibly and loudly disagree with Leftwing professors in classrooms and lead demonstrations against the most onerous anti-Americans among them.

Reject ALL multi-cultural, politically correct dogma out of hand; openly ridicule Gaia Worship and so-called "Gender Studies."

Be openly politically incorrect and, when sanctioned for it, use that sanction to target the policies that support politically correct censorship, which is designed to subjugate you and control your thoughts.

The hour is late, but the horrible catastrophe that the Seventh Crisis portends is still avoidable. The man who stood in the breach, at the great historical gate of the 20th century, British Prime Minister Winston Churchill, speaks inspirationally to us with an insight for this very moment.

"If you will not fight for the right when you can easily win without bloodshed; if you will not fight when your victory will be sure and not too costly; you may come to the moment when you will have to fight with all the odds against you and only a precarious chance of survival. There may even be a worse case. You may have to fight when there is no hope of victory, because it is better to perish than to live as slaves."

Never abandon your principles.

Never stop fighting and always stay on the Offensive until total victory is won.

Never surrender on ANY issue to the Left or their allies.

Never treat the Left with anything but the same disdain and contempt that they have for you.

Never be concerned with being liked if you stand up for American values; nice guys don't last in this game...

...and always, always, always rebel against the Leftwing status quo!

YOU ARE THE REBELLION!!

ABOUT THE AUTHORS

Bob and Tony are both in their late 60s and first met in *the* late "60s."

They attended Queens College in NYC in the early '70s, and at that time the city university system was already heavily populated with leftist professors and administrators. They attended many history classes taught by newly minted "red diaper" professors. They cut their teeth challenging the Leftist version of American history by aggressively pushing back in those classrooms against the budding indoctrination now prevalent across the nation's university systems. An aggressive prosecution of the facts put those young Marxist professors in their place then, and can do the same today. The authors have closely studied history and followed the nation's political developments ever since. Most of their premises regarding the American political parties and system they developed then, still maintain today. Those premises have served as a reliable political compass, guiding their understanding over the past 50 years.

Bob MacGuffie was a financial executive over a 40-year corporate career. He gained brief national notoriety in August 2009 when his Tea Party rallying memo, "Rocking the Town Halls," was cited by the national press as the inspiration for the raucous eruptions in town halls across the country. Several TV news and talk radio appearances followed. He co-led the Connecticut Tea Party movement and was tapped as a thought-leader within the national movement. He addressed the massive Tea Party rally at the nation's capital in September 2010. He was a member of the national Tea Party Debt Commission in 2011, which presented its recommendations to the Senate and House Republican leadership. Bob also served as head of Senator Ted Cruz's presidential primary campaign in Connecticut in 2016. He has penned dozens of Op-Eds and LTEs, and has been guest speaker at many Conservative gatherings and dinners across Connecticut.

Antony Stark has had a long career as a project manager in several large financial institutions and media outlets, including one of the three major broadcast television networks. He and Bob formed the Tea Party Group Right Principles in late 2008, and in 2010 Tony wrote the "Tea Party Declaration of Independence" which was adopted and publicized by over 60 Tea Parties across the country. It received significant electronic and print media coverage and was generally perceived by many in the Tea Party Movement as their Mission Statement. His work has been published under various pseudonyms in *American Thinker* and other internet publications. Tony campaigned for Senator Ted Cruz in 2016 and worked with the campaigns of many successful conservative candidates for office. He is a prolific speech writer for conservative candidates and conservative causes.

Made in the USA
Las Vegas, NV
10 April 2021